CENTRAL ASIA

Also from *M. E. Sharpe*

THE RUSSIAN FAR EAST
An Economic Handbook
Pavel A. Minakir, Editor

CENTRAL ASIA IN TRANSITION
Dilemmas of Political and Economic Development
Boris Rumer, Editor

CENTRAL ASIA

The Challenges of Independence

Edited by

Boris Rumer
Stanislav Zhukov

M.E. Sharpe
Armonk, New York
London, England

Library of Congress Cataloging-in-Publication Data

Central Asia : the challenges of independence / edited by
Boris Rumer and Stanislav Zhukov : translated by Gregory Freeze.
p. cm,
Includes bibliographical references and index.
ISBN 0-7656-0254-7 (hardcover : alk. paper)
1. Asia, Central—Economic conditions—Congresses.
2. Asia, Central—Economic policy—Congresses.
3. Asia, Central—Foreign economic relations—Congresses.
I. Rumer, Boris Z.   II. Zhukov, S. V. (Stanislav Viacheslavovich)
HC420.3.C465   1998
338.958—dc21   98-15194
CIP

Printed in the United States of America

The paper used in this publication meets the minimum requirements of
American National Standard for Information Sciences—
Permanence of Paper for Printed Library Materials,
ANSI Z 39.48-1984.

∞

BM (c)   10   9   8   7   6   5   4   3   2   1

Contents

List of Tables

Acknowledgments

The preparation of this collection of essays was made possible by the Sasakawa Peace Foundation (SPF). For a number of years, SPF has conducted an ambitious and highly productive program, "Implementing a Market Economy in Central Asia: Implications from the East Asian Experience." That program has supported a broad range of empirical research, training, and education to help the countries of Central Asia to facilitate and maximize opportunities in market transformation. A substantial part of this book was presented in the form of papers at the third Issyk-Kul Forum, which was organized by SPF and held in Tashkent (October 1997). It is a great pleasure to acknowledge the contribution of SPF and, in particular, Mr. Akira Iriyama, Mr. Takashi Shirasu, and Mr. Lau Sim Yee, in making the preparation and publication of this book possible.

In addition, the editors wish to express their gratitude to the National Council for Eurasian and East-European Research (Washington, DC) and the Boston Institute for Developing Economies (Boston), which supported the research upon which Chapter 6 (on economic integration) is based. Thanks too are due to Gregory L. Freeze for his assistance in preparing the manuscript for publication. Finally, the editors also wish to acknowledge the support of their home institutions—the Davis Center for Russian Studies (Harvard University) and the Center of Comparative Research of Russia and the Third World (Institute of World Economy and International Relations, Russian Academy of Sciences).

CENTRAL ASIA

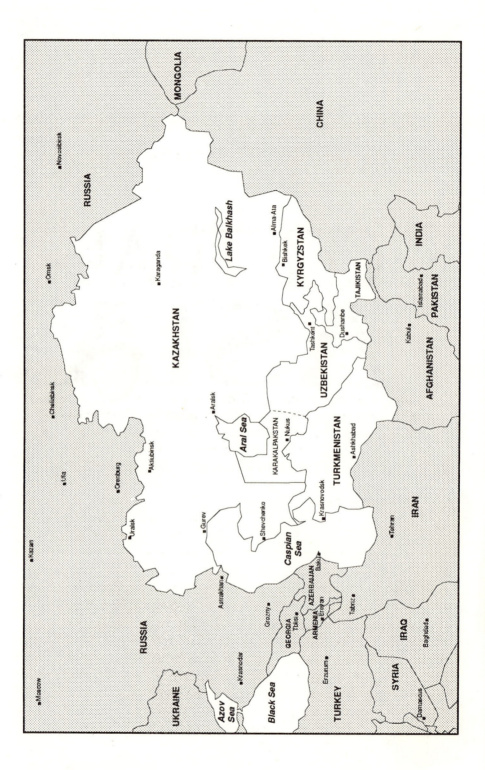

1

Introduction

Boris Rumer and Stanislav Zhukov

The current surge of interest in post-Soviet Central Asia derives largely from the fact that the world recognizes its enormous potential as a source of oil and natural gas. This region is regarded as an energy and fuel reserve for industrially developed countries. Thus, an editorial in the *Washington Post* offers this bald statement on the West's interest in this region: "The broad Western strategy must be to take the political steps necessary to exploit the immense energy resources of the Caspian Sea area. In this way, the West can diminish dependence on the oil and gas of the uncertain states of the Persian Gulf."[1] The question, however, is whether the states of Central Asia are any less "uncertain" than those in the Persian Gulf. Stability in this potential tinderbox depends on many factors, but the most important revolve around economic conditions and the prospects for development. The struggle for the resources of the Caspian Sea and contiguous territories now constitutes an important area of world politics. This struggle has engaged virtually all of the great oil and gas corporations and the leading world powers that support them. The next few years is certain to witness an intensification of global competition for dominance and influence in this region. However, this book is not primarily concerned with the "great game" or the battle for oil and gas resources. Rather, it seeks to explore the economic situation in Central Asia—precisely that factor which strategists of the competing parties must inevitably take into account. For, in the final analysis, the grandiose oil and gas projects will depend on whether these Central Asian countries can overcome their protracted economic crisis and thereby maintain political and social stability, or ineluctably slide toward balkanization and civil war.

Six years have now elapsed since these states acquired independence. That is a sufficient period of time to determine the basic economic problems that face each of these new countries and their prospects for future development. It is important to consider how these countries have used this historic opportunity, whether ruling elites have met the challenges of independence and economic development, how successful they have been in using the economic potential inherited from the former Soviet Union, and whether they have devised and implemented a coherent, national strategy of development.

Not one of the five Central Asian states (Kazakhstan, Kyrgyzstan, Tajikistan, Turkmenistan, and Uzbekistan) existed as a sovereign entity in modern history, and the very acquisition of independence came suddenly and unexpectedly. In any case, they did not undergo a prolonged anticolonial, anti-imperial struggle to prepare them for independence. On the contrary, the party elites *(nomenklatura)* of Central Asia actually resisted, to the very end, the breakup of the USSR.

But the dissolution of the Soviet Union by the Slavic republics (Russia, Belarus, and Ukraine), together with Russia's adoption of the "shock therapy" variant of economic reform, forced the Central Asian countries to proclaim their sovereignty and independence. Russia's decision to issue its own national currency then forced these states to undertake fundamental economic reform.

The disintegration of a unified Soviet economy, the disruption of ties among the former republics, the frequent changes in economic policy, the unprecedented rapid rates of privatization and de-statification—all these things have generated a rapid pace of change. The application of diverging, contradictory policies, which have affected virtually every sphere of the economy and society and which had proceeded at a high pace, makes it difficult to grasp the essence of these changes. The countries of Central Asia have yet to achieve a fundamental breakthrough and restructuring of the old system and, in some branches and spheres, have not yet even begun. However, as the time since the breakup of the USSR increases, it becomes increasingly clear that both the current economic situation and the prospects of economic development in the region are determined—to a significant degree—by a number of objective factors.

These factors include the structural characteristics in each state, including the special features of its economic structure, its geographic situation, the abundance of natural resources, and the particular profile and quality of human resources. As the newly independent states become more established, such factors will become all the more tangible and critical in determining the economic potential of each state.

At the same time, one should not exaggerate the influence of objective factors. To a significant degree, the current economic crisis in Central Asia is justifiably attributed to the inherent features of the Soviet economic system, as well as the natural difficulties associated with the transition to a market economy. However, it must also be acknowledged that these countries have inherited a rather well-developed economic base. For all the structural asymmetry of their economies, in no sense can these states be compared to third world countries in the initial stages of independence and economic transformation. At the point when the five countries of Central Asia acquired independence, all had a relatively complex economic and social infrastructure and a rather well-developed industry and agriculture. Nor can these countries, in terms of educational level and intellectual potential, be compared with the third world or the Muslim East. It is only fair to say that these positive elements are also part of the legacy from the Soviet era.

Since the breakup of the USSR, it has become commonplace to argue that the fundamental impediment to economic stabilization in Central Asia is the set of structural disproportions in their economies—something bequeathed by the Soviet system. Thus, it is frequently asserted that Moscow turned Kazakhstan into a "raw-material colony" and Uzbekistan into a "cotton plantation." And attention is only given to the negative sides of Moscow's role in developing these local economies. Without in any way denying the disproportions and subordination to a centralized economy (with all the negative, including ecological, consequences that this entailed), it is simply unfair to see only the negative side of Kazakhstan's specialization in raw materials and grain, or Uzbekistan's emphasis on cotton production. In fact, the Soviet Union created enormous capacities here—for example, the plants in Kazakhstan to produce iron ore, steel, nonferrous and rare metals (including gold), uranium, and so forth. Moscow also constructed a complete system for the use of atomic energy (from research centers to the production of atomic fuel), the cosmodrome of Baikonur (worth billions of dollars), an agricultural sector that produces a surfeit of grain, large plants to produce mining equipment and agricultural machinery, a construction industry, a network of research centers, and so forth. Thus, thanks to the investments allocated by Moscow, Kazakhstan acquired an industrial-agrarian economy with powerful export potential.

Much has been written as well about the harmful consequences of the hypertrophic development of cotton growing in Uzbekistan.[2] But the time has now come for a more balanced approach. To be sure, ideologically minded economists in Uzbekistan still argue that the Soviet policy aimed to turn Uzbekistan into its cotton plantation, thereby preventing the harmonious development of its economy (especially the agrarian sector), and forcing the republic to bear inordinate costs to maintain this cotton potential. In response, critics argue that, despite all the negative aspects of this cotton monoculture, despite all the excesses and disproportions, one cannot ignore the fact that post-Soviet Uzbekistan has reaped colossal revenues from its cotton exports. It is therefore hardly feasible to argue that the cotton complex is an inordinate burden for the republic; on the contrary, Uzbekistan gained much more than it lost from the targeted development of cotton growing. It won in economic terms, since this contributed to the growth of the gross domestic product (GDP), the development of the infrastructure, and so forth. In fact, some circles in the Uzbek intelligentsia believe that the main achievement of Sharaf Rashidov (the former first secretary of the Central Committee of the Uzbek Communist Party and now a national hero) was to accelerate the development of cotton growing. In other words, all this not only resulted from pressure in Moscow but also corresponded to the interests of the republic itself. However that may be, the point is that today the cotton complex is the very foundation of Uzbekistan; for the moment, cotton is virtually the only Uzbek good (save gold and uranium) that is competitive in foreign markets. And it is also the basic source of financing for the industrialization and development of Uzbekistan.

Foreign factors also exert an enormous influence on the development of the new states and on the trajectory of their economic development. Remnants of the former, unified economic organism find themselves in a maximally favorable external environment. The end of the Cold War and the developed system of international cooperation (e.g., in the United Nations, Conference on Security and Cooperation in Europe, International Monetary Fund, World Bank, and other political and financial-economic organizations) have enabled the world community to take the fragments of the former USSR in tow and, without delay, to propose concrete strategies for economic and political development. Significantly, from the very outset, this assistance included real financial resources, which—by the standards of the Central Asian economies—were quite substantial.

For diverse reasons, the leading world powers have a vested interest in maintaining stability in Central Asia. Even Russia—despite aggressive rhetoric from certain segments of the political elite—conducts a constructive policy toward its partners in the Commonwealth of Independent States (CIS). Foreign assistance, coming through sundry channels, has played an important role in bolstering relative stability in Central Asia and helped avert a catastrophic collapse of the economy and society.

In the first half of the current decade, all the newly independent states, including those in Central Asia, experienced an acute economic crisis. In 1990–95, for example, the GDP fell by 55 percent in Kazakhstan, 49 percent in Kyrgyzstan, and 18 percent in Uzbekistan. Nor did the crisis leave a single branch of the economy untouched. Thus, during these same years, agricultural production decreased by 45 percent in Kazakhstan, 38 percent in Kyrgyzstan, and 16 percent in Uzbekistan. The contraction in industrial production was still greater: 68 percent in Kyrgyzstan and 56 percent in Kazakhstan. The sole exception was Uzbekistan, where, by the mid-1990s, industrial production was still at the same level as it had been five years earlier.

Beginning in 1996, information about the countries of Central Asia became more optimistic. According to official statistics, the crisis—including the decline in production—had apparently bottomed out. In fact, in 1996–97, the volume of GDP and industrial production increased in Kazakhstan, Kyrgyzstan, and Uzbekistan.

Simultaneously, the ideology of stabilization (which had dominated the first half of the decade) began giving way to the idea of economic growth. Indeed, the latter idea has increasingly turned into an official ideology of development. All this raises some important questions: what foundations have been laid in recent years for growth in Central Asia, what factors will support and propel this growth, and which branches are most likely to enjoy this new phase of expansion?

The goal here is to address those questions, to assess the results of the first six years of independent development in Central Asia, and to analyze whatever preconditions have been laid for future economic growth. In contrast to most studies of post-Soviet transformation, which tend to focus on the financial-economic aspects of development in transition countries, this volume lays its main emphasis on the real production sectors. It analyzes, through the prism of economic growth, such special questions as regional cooperation, the politics of attracting foreign investment, and the choice of development strategy.

Chapter 2 ("The Geo-Economic Significance of Central Asia") provides a short economic description of the region and individual countries. It is clearly the rich reserves of hydrocarbons that bestow global significance on Central Asia and especially Turkmenistan and Kazakhstan, followed by Uzbekistan (which has more modest reserves of oil and natural gas). The ruling elites in Kazakhstan and Turkmenistan realize that the economic and political prospects of their countries depend totally on realizing this raw-material potential. As a result, both countries have advanced ambitious programs to expand the extraction and export of oil and natural gas.

The keys to economic growth in the region actually lay beyond its boundaries. That is, a number of objective factors predetermine the extremely severe conditions for bringing these raw material reserves to world markets. The location of the oil and natural gas (the great depths, high pressure, and shelf zone), together with the qualitative characteristics of Central Asian oil, mandate the use of the most advanced technologies and hence large-scale capital investment. And both the technology and the capital are only available from American, West European, and Japanese corporations.

In Chapter 3 ("Post-Soviet Modernization in Central Asia: Realities and Prospects"), the author analyzes the political and economic developments in Central Asia since the collapse of the USSR. In no sense can Central Asian states be regarded as democracies: none has a democratic legal order, efficient state apparatus, system of parties and political organizations, and a free economy based on the rule of law. In essence, the countries here (like the other newly independent states of the former USSR) have not yet acquired a stable state order. Strong authoritarian regimes reign, but that does not mean that a strong state order has emerged. On the contrary: although presidential authority is virtually unlimited, the state order is weak, law observed in the breach, and the bureaucracy powerless to collect taxes. Such a state simply cannot force people to heed and obey its imperious commands and "ukases." Nor have these states created an honest, efficient, law-abiding state apparatus; in the absence of a Weberian bureaucracy and *Rechtsstaat,* measures to create a market economy and to conduct privatization turn into a massive plundering of state property. As Dmitrii Furman has aptly said of the post-Soviet states: "It is possible to concoct whatever plans for privatization and market transformation, but this will come to naught if those who implement these plans are not thinking about transformation, but only about stealing something."[3] This chapter concludes that the emerging political regimes of Central Asia have nothing in common with Western democracies, that, in terms of their authoritarian essence, they are similar to Asian regimes of the Singapore, Malaysian, or Indonesian type, and that essentially a Central Asian variant of the authoritarian Asian regimes is emerging in the region.

The supporters of such regimes in Central Asia justify their existence with two main arguments: (1) they support stability and the status quo within the region; and, (2) that type of governance corresponds to the mentalité and culture of the population. As for the first argument, the present authors would suggest that several factors have also played a role in maintaining stability in the region. One factor is indeed the creation and consolidation of authoritarian regimes that are determined to maintain the existing state borders (i.e., those inherited from the Soviet era) and that take decisive measures to prevent interethnic conflicts. A second factor is economics: although the economies here are beset by crisis (which has degraded what was already a low standard of living), these countries have nonetheless averted a full-blown economic collapse. The intensive export of raw materials and metals, credits from international financial institutions, investments from Western corporations (especially to finance the exploration and extraction of oil and natural gas), the preservation and recent renewal of economic ties with Russia and other republics in the CIS, the upsurge of entrepreneurial activity by the local population (in the wake of a liberalization of economic life)—all this has helped avert a total economic meltdown. A third factor is the sobering effect of the fratricidal carnage in neighboring Tajikistan—a conflict that has wrought so much hardship and suffering on the people there. A fourth factor is the threat of radical Islamic movements, which, despite fears to the contrary, have thus far not become widespread in Central Asia. Last, but not least, is one other factor: the obvious desire of the two most powerful neighbors—Russia and China—to maintain the status quo and avoid destabilization in the region. In sum, an array of internal and external factors are working to preserve stability and order in Central Asia.

As for the second argument (about a backward "mentalité and culture" that mean a low level of political mobilization), one cannot altogether disregard either the enormous role of tradition, popular psychology, and culture, or the powerful significance of previous regimes. Nevertheless, the present authors eschew any kind of cultural determinism, which purports to doom certain societies to have nondemocratic orders. Rather, democracy has become the norm of the modern world, not only in the West but in the East as well. It is simply unacceptable to impute nondemocratic systems as inherent to certain peoples, like some kind of ethnic and cultural *Sonderweg*.

Moreover, economic modernization, in the long run, also presupposes a democratization of the state order and liberalization of civic life. As President Jiang Zemin of China declared during his visit to the United States in November 1997: "We believe that, without democracy, there can be no modernization."[4] The experience of countries in East and Southeast Asia confirm that economics and politics are inextricably intertwined with each other. To be sure, some regimes here have attempted to separate the economic and political systems, in effect, to liberalize the economy but not public life. But that kind of dualism cannot be sustained indefinitely and, indeed, ultimately leads to a profound crisis. That is because a healthy market economy requires a democratic political order; it presupposes transparency, full disclosure, and public control so as to forestall corruption, cronyism, and abuse of power. In assessing the economic crisis that has overtaken Malaysia, Thailand, and Indonesia, an editorial in the *Washington Post* observed: "All three countries got into trouble in large part because their governance did not keep pace with their growing economies. A lack of democracy allowed corrupt, crony capitalism to flower. There was too little accountability and transparency in the regulations of banks and other financial institutions."[5] These words apply as well to the regimes in Central Asia and can serve as a warning to their societies.

Chapter 4 ("Broader Parmeters: Development in the Twentieth Century") examines the regional context over an entire century, from the prerevolutionary Tsarist era to the 1990s. The next three chapters provide a synoptic analysis of the economic structures in Central Asia, consider the potential for regional economic integration, and assess the prospects for economic relations with Russia and China.

These chapters, especially Chapter 5 ("Structural Changes"), make it possible to discern the emerging models of economic development. For all the differences in scale and concrete details, Kazakhstan and Kyrgyzstan have chosen the same model of development: both rely mainly on exogenous factors. In the case of Kyrgyzstan, this means international assistance and credits, but also a possible influx of capital to the mining industry. The model chosen for Kazakhstan counts on direct foreign investment in metallurgy, electric power, and oil production. One distinctive feature of this development model is its "island-like" character: capital-intensive projects involving foreign capital generate a limited demand for labor. As a result, indigenous labor is forced to concentrate on urban services or the agrarian sector, which already suffer from a surfeit of labor. In the next five to six years, the economic growth of these two states will assume features of third world countries: a few spheres of growth will coexist with an intensification of backwardness and poverty.

Uzbekistan chose a different model, deliberately spurning the neoliberal economic ideas that shaped decision making in Kazakhstan and Kyrgyzstan. Instead, it unabashedly favors an active, overt étatisme. This republic also proved to be the only Central Asian state to construct the rudiments of what is usually termed the nation-state. Given the backwardness of other structural components of a nation-state, the key bonding element here is an authoritarian regime. True, from a macroeconomic perspective, these efforts have served to preserve the disequilibria of the late Soviet era. In the coming years, Uzbekistan must demonstrate that it has laid the foundations to overcome these disequilibria and to embark on a trajectory of accelerated economic growth. Otherwise, the preconditions laid for dynamic expansion will simply dissipate as the regime seeks to cope with the demands of demographic growth.

Chapter 6 ("Economic Integration in Central Asia: Problems and Prospects") considers the potential for intraregional economic cooperation. The ideology of integration is favored by the global processes of regional economic integration at work throughout the modern world. Although the post-Soviet realm is unstable (and likely to remain so for a long time to come), the initial centrifugal tendencies of the early 1990s have given way to integrationist tendencies—expressed in a multitude of ideas and theories, which are constantly discussed as proposals for federations, confederations, Eurasian Union, and other forms of association. To this point, however, all these schemes have proven stillborn, as political motives and interests prevailed over economic realities. The process of regionalization in post-Soviet space is only in its gestation, and one must assume that the political map of Eurasia will not acquire a completed form anytime soon.

The first impulse for consolidation by the Central Asian leaders came from the arrogant behavior of the "brother Slavs" (the leaders of Belarus, Russia, and Ukraine), who, unilaterally and without consultation, summarily liquidated the USSR. From the moment that the Soviet empire ceased to exist, the idea of a Central Asian regional union inexorably came to the fore. This notion arose as a counterpoint to the "Slavic union"—that is, as a due response to the three Slavic leaders who had not seen fit to invite the Central Asian leaders to the Belovezh summit and have a voice in dismantling the Soviet Union. The post-Soviet era has thus witnessed a steady deluge of declarations, the signing of countless documents, and the convening of innumerable regional summits. Thus far, however, this has been far more symbolic than practical. This silent spinning of wheels is due to a multitude of causes—some dating back to the Soviet era, others arising during the recent period of independence. And at work are not only economic but also political motives and interests.

The overlap of affiliation is complex. Whereas all the Central Asian states belong to the CIS, only two (Kazakhstan and Kyrgyzstan) joined with Russia and Belarus to form the "Customs Union." Three countries of Central Asia—Kazakhstan, Kyrgyzstan, and Uzbekistan—have joined in the "Central Asian Union" and in the "Economic Cooperation Organization" (together with Iran, Turkey, Pakistan, Afghanistan, and Azerbaijan). Apart from participating in these associations, each country in the region has its own special bilateral relations with Russia and other republics of the former USSR, and each is expanding ties with countries outside the CIS—above all, in the West and in East Asia. What is realistic here? Which of these ties are significant and viable? What are the prime economic interests of the Central Asian countries? In assessing these issues, one should recognize that the flurry of recent developments are more in the realm of intention than implementation, and bear more political than economic substance. But the economic reality—given the growing ties with industrially developed countries as well as the dependency on investment from foreign countries and international financial agencies—is nonetheless gaining in import.

Chapter 7 ("Between Two Gravitational Poles: Russia and China") explores the current relations and potential economic cooperation with two neighboring superpowers. In particular, the analysis here suggests that, in the immediate future at least, one should not expect a significant expansion of economic relations with Russia. That is because Moscow does not possess (nor, for a long time to come, is it likely to possess) the investment resources so urgently needed to restore growth throughout the post-Soviet realm. Moreover, structural changes now unfolding in Central Asia serve to diminish the significance of cooperation with Russia. If this region, in the coming years, shows any kind of substantial growth, it will be limited chiefly to oil and gas.

The final four chapters of this book focus on two "regional superpowers"—Kazakhstan and Uzbekistan. These two countries hold much of the economic potential of Central Asia—approximately 80 percent of the GDP, population, and fixed capital. As Chapters 8 and 9 (on foreign economic activities of these two states) demonstrate, it is impossible to analyze a particular country without giving close attention to the world context. For every post-Soviet republic, without exception, external conditions play a critically important role. Above all, world markets have a major impact on the dynamics and pace of economic development as well as the structure of national economies. The export-oriented economies of Kazakhstan and Uzbekistan are only beginning to gain access to world markets, but this factor will clearly be of waxing importance. Chapters 10 and 11 consider "the critical issues" that now confront these two countries. In the case of Kazakhstan, this is the policy decision to allow foreign companies to control, or directly own, strategically important sectors of industry—the very foundation of the national economy. In Uzbekistan, the key issue is the degradation of agriculture (the key sector of the economy) and the decision to transform this into a donor for industrialization.

A few words should be said about the degree to which the data, even when objectively analyzed, reflects economic realities in the region. The authors have used many different sources; these include official statistics, data compiled by the World Bank, the calculations of regional research centers, information from various publications, and expert estimates by the authors themselves. Nevertheless, it should be obvious that economic life in this region is larger and more complex, and the economic activity of the population is considerably more intense than what is reported in official publications. The reliability of official post-Soviet statistics is substantially inferior even to that of the Soviet era. The scale of the shadow economy on the territory of the former Soviet Union, including Central Asia, is immense. In the case of Russia itself, this sector is estimated at 25 to 40 percent of the GDP. There is every reason to believe that these estimates can be applied to Central Asia as well. If one assumes that the shadow economy in Central Asia is on the order of one-third of the GDP, then one must acknowledge certain limitations in our picture of economic realities in the region. Moreover, one must also take into account all the economic consequences of the drug business, which—as suggested by press reports and much anecdotal testimony—has become very widespread in the region. Given the foregoing, one should bear in mind that the published information on the economic situation tends to exaggerate and overdramatize the situation. The economic decline is apparently not so grave as the official statistics would have us believe. The output in certain sectors of the economy (above all, in those connected to exports and servicing the domestic demand) is actually higher; likewise, the incomes of the population (especially its economically active segments, which have fully adjusted to the new situation) are also underreported. Nevertheless, the authors have made every effort to use raw unpublished data, to obtain information from a variety of sources, to compare these differing sets of data for consistency and accuracy, and to subject all this information to a careful and critical assessment. Above all, the skeptical and rigorous approach to the data employed here make it possible, at least within broad parameters, to determine the macroeconomic tendencies, structural changes, and chief problems that now impede economic development in the countries of post-Soviet Central Asia. Although, in a few instances, individual authors have chosen to rely upon different sources (and hence use slightly different figures), the overall picture does not substantially change.

This volume thus seeks to rethink some favorite shibboleths—regarding the Soviet legacy, the years of so-called transition, and the real prospects for economic recovery, democratization, and integration into the world economy. It is as misleading to demonize the Soviet past as it is to idealize the prospects for political change, social stability, or economic transformation. Even if the economic free-fall has slowed, structural problems remain and will cast a long shadow for many years to come.

Notes

1. *Washington Post,* 14 October 1997.
2. In the late 1980s, one of the present authors gave a dramatic description of the manifold destructive consequences of the extensive, one-sided cultivation of cotton in Uzbekistan. See Boris Rumer, *Central Asia: A Tragic Experiment* (Boston-London: Unwin Hyman, 1989).
3. D. Furman, "Sluchai Rossii," *Svobodnaia mysl',* 1997, no. 9, p. 33.
4. *The New Republic,* 24 November 1997, p. 45.
5. *Washington Post,* 16 October 1997, p. 8.

Part I

Central Asia on the Eve of the Twenty-First Century

2

The Geo-economic Significance of Central Asia

Boris Rumer and Stanislav Zhukov

The breakup of the USSR was followed by the formation of five newly independent Central Asian states: Kazakhstan, Kyrgyzstan, Tajikistan, Turkmenistan, and Uzbekistan. None of them had ever existed in their present form, in which present borders correspond to those of the former Soviet republics.

In 1993–94, all five of these states established new governmental structures, introduced national currencies, created modern financial systems (including central state banks), and created gold and hard currency reserves. In a word, they have acquired the usual economic and political attributes of a modern state. However, what do these new states represent in sheer economic terms?

In the mid-1990s, these five states had an aggregate population of 54.5 million people, a GDP of approximately 32.9 billion U.S. dollars, exports worth 11.7 billion dollars, and imports with a value of 9.4 billion dollars (see Table 2.1). The largest population is found in Uzbekistan (23 million inhabitants), followed by Kazakhstan (16.5 million); Tajikistan, Kyrgyzstan, and Turkmenistan rank as the smaller countries, with populations of less than 10 million people.

Kazakhstan has the largest GDP in the region, with Uzbekistan ranking second. This indicator is much smaller for the other three Central Asian states, where the GDP in 1995 was less than 5 billion

Table 2.1

Basic Characteristics of Central Asian States, 1995

Indicator	Central Asia	Central Asian Union[a]	Kazakhstan	Uzbekistan	Kyrgyzstan	Turkmenistan	Tajikistan
Population (millions)	54.5	44.1	16.5	23.0	4.6	4.5	5.9
GDP (billions of U.S. dollars)[b]	32.9	28.1	16.7	10.0	1.4	4.2	0.6
Exports (billions of U.S. dollars)	11.7	9.1	5.0	3.7	0.4	1.9	0.7
Imports (billions of U.S. dollars)	9.4	7.2	3.6	2.9	0.5	1.4	0.8

Sources: Calculated from the following sources: World Bank, *Statistical Handbook 1996. States of the Former Soviet Union* (Washington, DC, 1997), pp. 10, 216, 256, 527; Goskomstat SNG, *Strany Sodruzhestva nezavisimykh gosudarstv v 1996 godu. Statisticheskii sbornik* (Moscow, 1996), pp. 21–22, 79.

[a]Consisting of Kazakhstan, Uzbekistan, and Kyrgyzstan.
[b]According to the official exchange rate.

dollars. Kazakhstan also ranks as the largest regional exporter. In recent years, the primary economic indicators (GDP, exports, imports, and other macroeconomic indices), as expressed in dollars, have shown a tendency to grow. Thus, in 1995–96, the GDP of Kazakhstan rose from 16.7 billion to more than 20 billion dollars; simultaneously, the GDP of Uzbekistan grew from 10 to 13 billion dollars. Nevertheless, in comparison with the mid-1990s, there is no reason to expect any fundamental changes in the next few years.

Although often lumped together by outsiders as a single entity, the five states of Central Asia are anything but homogeneous. Their boundaries are in fact the product of a drive by the Russian state in the nineteenth century toward the southeast; these were further distorted by arbitrary territorial divisions in the Soviet era. As a result, state borders blindly traverse ethnic enclaves, turning Central Asia into a patchwork quilt rent by complex disputes (ethnic, regional, tribal) over land, water, and natural resources. The veneer of a common religion and, to some extent, Turkic language only conceals the deep fissures below—territorial conflicts, interethnic tensions, clan rivalries, and class antagonisms. Thus the fault lines here are far more prominent than the putative common interests and the purported will to make a united assault on common challenges and problems.

Today this is all the more true, since one can hardly speak of a harmony of interests among the indigenous populations of Central Asia. These peoples are now divided into separate states and, after three generations of Soviet rule, they have come to see themselves as Kazakhs, Uzbeks, Kyrgyz, Tajiks, and Turkmen.

The architects of Kremlin ethnic policy have repeatedly redrawn the administrative map of Central Asia and, in the final analysis, succeeded in sundering ethnic bonds among the five republics. Moscow was, of course, determined to prevent the formation of any autochthonous bloc within its empire and sphere of influence, especially in the case of Muslims.

In economic terms, however, Moscow took a rather different approach toward Central Asia. Thus, in the territorial economic planning for the USSR, Moscow divided the entire territory into eighteen economic regions and combined four Central Asian republics— Uzbekistan, Tajikistan, Turkmenistan, and Kyrgyzstan—into a single economic region. The economic integration of Uzbekistan, Kyrgyzstan, Tajikistan, and Turkmenistan has at times led to the formation of special party and state economic organs to provide overall supervision and control. For example, Moscow created a Central Asian Bureau of the Soviet Communist Party (first established in 1924, then revived in 1962–65), a Central Asian *sovnarkhoz* (regional economic council established during the era of Nikita Khrushchev), the State Committee for Cotton Cultivation, the Ministry of Construction in Central Asia, and a number of others. One of their main functions was to establish an integrated Central Asian economy. These attempts to achieve economic integration in the Central Asian republics show a characteristic Soviet inclination to concentrate production and other forms of economic activity, the transparent purpose being to assert effective control over an immense economy and resources within a vast territory, and to do so from a single center. In accordance with the investment planning in Moscow, Gosplan (the state planning agency) allocated resources to Central Asia as a whole and then, within the parameters of these allocations, examined the needs of individual republics and distributed resources among them. Similarly, investment in the infrastructure (e.g., transportation, energy, and irrigation) was also allocated to the region as a whole. That approach, to a significant degree, led to the creation of an integrated infrastructure in this region.

Kazakhstan, by contrast, represents a special case. First, about half of its population is not ethnically Kazakh, but consists of a motley of non-Muslim peoples—Russians, Ukrainians, Germans, and so forth. Hence, in this important respect, Kazakhstan is quite distinct from Central Asia, where 80 percent of the population consists of indigenous ethnic groups. Second, Kazakhstan is also sharply distinguished from the other states of Central Asia in terms of its natural resources and its economy.

In the midterm and especially in the long-term perspective, some states of Central Asia enjoy—at least in theory—favorable preconditions for dynamic economic growth and for becoming a major supplier of raw materials and fuels on world markets. Specifically, Kazakhstan has already become a rather large exporter of grains and various nonferrous metals; Uzbekistan has become a significant supplier of cotton, gold, and uranium; and Turkmenistan is an important source of natural gas and cotton.

The mineral resources of Kazakhstan contain especially rich reserves of nonferrous and ferrous metals as well as fuel and energy resources. According to data for 1991, the aggregate reserves of anthracite in Kazakhstan were estimated at 32.3 billion tons. The largest natural deposits are concentrated in the Karaganda and Ekibastuz basins, where coal mining is based on open-cut methods. This republic also has immense natural deposits of iron ore, which constitute approximately 10 percent of the world's reserves. The most famous mineral deposits are the so-called iron-ore belts of Turgai (Kustanai Oblast); the iron content of these ores lies in the range of 35 to 43 percent, a very high indicator by world standards.[1]

It is fair to say that Kazakhstan also enjoys a unique position with respect to its supply of nonferrous metals. Its reserves include a large part of the world reserves for lead (19 percent), zinc (13 percent), copper (10 percent), and manganese (25 percent). The proven reserves of barite and tungsten exceed the entire amount of reserves found elsewhere around the world. The deposits of chrome iron ore is estimated at 319.4 million tons, which represents 30 percent of world reserves. Moreover, during the Soviet era, Kazakhstan had already established itself as a major producer of aluminum oxide, asbestos, and phosphates. And, until recently, the republic was a relatively large producer of gold and silver. In 1991, for example, Kazakhstan produced approximately 15 tons of gold.

At the same time, under conditions of economic regression and fundamental change from the conditions that had prevailed under the Soviet system, the prospects for growth—in agriculture, industry (including metal production), and exports—remain uncertain. Hence it is only the rich reserves of hydrocarbon raw materials that endow the economic complex of Central Asia with significance. This concerns, above all, Turkmenistan and Kazakhstan, followed by Uzbekistan, which has more modest reserves of oil and natural gas. Table 2.2 contains the highest estimates known to the present authors, whereas other sources offer more modest indicators. Moreover, official data provided by the states of Central Asia evoke skepticism among specialists. Nevertheless, even if one were to accept the minimal estimates for hydrocarbon reserves, Turkmenistan and Kazakhstan still have the opportunity of joining the top ranks of the world's oil and gas business.

The ruling elites in Kazakhstan and Turkmenistan are perfectly well aware that their country's political and economic prospects—as independent states—depend totally on the exploitation of these raw material reserves. Accordingly, both countries have advanced ambitious programs to expand the extraction and export of oil and natural gas

Table 2.2

The Share of Central Asian States in the World's Oil and Natural Gas Industry

| Country | Share of world production (in percent) | | | | Estimated reserves | | World rank in terms of reserves | |
	Oil		Natural gas		Oil (billions of tons)	Natural gas (trillions of cubic meters)	Oil	Natural gas
	1995	1996[a]	1995	1996[a]				
Turkmenistan	0.1	0.2	1.4	2.0	6.3	15.5	9	3
Kazakhstan	0.6	0.7	0.2	0.2	6.1	5.9	10	5
Uzbekistan	0.2	0.3	2.1	2.3	0.3	2.0	—	13–15

Sources: Compiled from Oksana Reznikova, "Transnational Corporations in Central Asia," in Boris Rumer, ed., *Central Asia in Transition. Dilemmas of Political and Economic Development* (Armonk, NY: M.E. Sharpe, 1996), p. 69; *Biulleten 'inostrannoi kommercheskoi informatsii,* no. 24 (27 February 1997), p. 13.

[a]First half of 1996 only.

[b]Includes gas condensate.

Table 2.3

Plans and Forecasts for the Increase in the Production of Oil and Natural Gas in Kazakhstan, Turkmenistan, and Uzbekistan

Country	Product	1996[a]	2000	2010
Turkmenistan	Oil (millions of tons)	4.0	28.0	80.0
	Natural gas (billions of cubic meters)	35.1	130.0	230.0
Kazakhstan	Oil (millions of tons)[b]	23.0	100.0	170.0[c]
	Natural gas (billions of cubic meters)	6.4	15.4	36.1
Uzbekistan	Oil (millions of tons)	7.5	10.0	—
	Natural gas (billions of cubic meters)	49.0	55.3	—

Sources: B. Kuz'menko, "Kazakhstan mechtaet o svoem 'Gazprome,'" *Delovoi mir,* 30 June 1997; "Pochemu Nazarbaev nedovolen Rossiei," *Novaia gazeta,* no. 21 (26 May–1 June 1997), p. 3; *Delovoi mir (ezhenedel'nik),* 1997, nos. 17–18, p. 2; *Sotsial'no-ekonomicheskoe polozhenie Respubliki Kazakhstan,* p. 8; Umirserik Kasenov, Klara Rakhmetova, and Sholpan Zhaksynbekova, "Toplivo-energeticheskie resursy Tsentral'noi Azii i problemy ikh effektivnogo ispol'zovaniia" (mimeographed paper, Kazakhstanskii institut strategicheskikh issledovanii, 1994), pp. 16, 18; Stanislav Zhukov, "Economic Development in the States of Central Asia," in Boris Rumer, ed., *Central Asia in Transition* (Armonk, NY: M.E. Sharpe, 1996), p. 129.

[a]Actual figure.
[b]Including gas condensate.
[c]Estimate for the year 2012, not 2010.

(see Table 2.3). And, with each passing year, both countries are adjusting these programs toward higher goals. A large part of the hydrocarbons extracted are intended for export. In the longer perspective, the development of these resources can serve to transform both of these Central Asian states into promising markets for the sale of finished goods.

It is not the authors' purpose to evaluate how realistic such plans might be. We wish only to underline some key elements here.

Clearly, the presence of enormously wealthy, untapped reserves of hydrocarbon raw materials and precious metals are key determinants in the fate of these states in the foreseeable future. Unless this raw-resource potential can be realized, not a single country of Central Asia can expect to launch onto a trajectory of sustained economic growth based on the market model. These same raw-material resources create a special configuration of global forces and interests, which have come to interact, and compete, ever more intensely and openly in Central Asia.

The superabundance of oil and gas resources makes this region an epicenter of geopolitical (more precisely, geo-economic) competition.

The point is that, in contrast to the "big game" played here in the late nineteenth and early twentieth centuries (involving mainly spheres of political and military influence), this time the competition centers on an attempt to establish control over natural resources. Another distinctive feature of today's "great game" is the different composition of those seeking to assert their interests: namely, the main players in the struggle for resources are no longer states, but transnational corporations and banks.

These interests of corporations and financial institutions stand behind many of the significant changes in the economy and the politics of Central Asian states. However, since they do not necessarily express these interests openly, one can only draw indirect inferences about their main thrust and import. Even the leading world powers are often used to camouflage the interests of the most influential companies and banks.

A number of objective factors superimpose the exceedingly severe conditions for bringing the natural resources of Central Asia into world markets.[2] One critical factor concerns the unfavorable location and structure of the oil and gas deposits: these are found at great depths, are under high pressure, and located in the shelf zone. Moreover, the elevated corrosiveness, viscosity, and high sulfide content of Central Asian oil require that the region use the most advanced technologies, and that in turn means large-scale capital investment. And the latter are only to be obtained from the American, West European, and Japanese corporations.

A second factor is the long-term dynamic of energy consumption in the main centers of the world economy. In essence, Japan and Western Europe need to diversify the sources of their oil and natural gas supplies. The same is also true of China in the event it maintains its current high rate of economic growth.

A third factor is the geographic structure in the distribution of the world's oil industry. It is reasonable to expect that, for purposes of minimizing production costs, development of Central Asian resources will, as far as possible, adhere to the existing system of pipelines, ports, terminals, and refining complexes.

Finally, competition with the other regions holding rich hydrocarbon resources will of course be a significant factor. The leading transnational corporations and banks follow a global strategy, carefully weighing costs and potential profits. Notwithstanding all the power of the world oil industry and transnational financial institutions, the volume of resources that they can mobilize in a given period of time is nonetheless finite and limited.

The presence of hydrocarbon raw materials bearing global significance, together with the ambitious plans for their development, create the preconditions for the transformation of the Central Asian region into one of the nerve centers of geopolitics and geo-economics in the next decade or two.

Notes

1. The data for these and other natural reserves of Kazakhstan are taken from N. Nazarbaev, "Uroki i perspektiva," *Nezavisimaia gazeta-Stsenarii,* 10 July 1997, p. 4.

2. The following text draws heavily on Oksana Reznikova, "Transnational Corporations in Central Asia," in Boris Rumer, ed., *Central Asia in Transition. Dilemmas of Political and Economic Development* (Armonk, NY: M.E. Sharpe, 1996), pp. 69–71.

3

Post-Soviet Modernization in Central Asia: Realities and Prospects

Umirserik Kasenov

Modernization: Development Under Conditions of Dependency

The Kazakh khanate, along with its subordinate units (the Small, Middle, and Senior Zhuzy) were gradually incorporated into the Russian Empire from the eighteenth century, but the Central Asian khanates and emirates underwent the same process about a century later. Having lost their independence, they were later subjected to the grinding forces of modernization as they made the painful transition from a traditional to an industrial society. However, this path was lengthy, rocky, and uneven, perhaps best divided into three main phases:

- prerevolutionary (as part of the Russian Empire until 1917);
- Soviet (as part of the USSR, 1922–91);
- post-Soviet (1992 to the present).

During the prerevolutionary tsarist era, although the traditional society here did not undergo any substantial transformation, it did experience the palpable impact of Russian colonial administration, the merchant class, and various entrepreneurial activities. This period witnessed not only the establishment of fortresses and forts but also the creation of new cities and settlements, commercial routes, primary and secondary schools, public libraries, a postal system, the telegraph, the telephone, and railroads. New agricultural crops (cotton, potatoes, sugar beets, etc.) were introduced, along with enterprises to process them. Nevertheless, the basic way of life, culture, and beliefs remained intact.

In the ensuing Soviet period, modernization acquired the character of large-scale social experiments—which basically used the peoples of the USSR like laboratory animals. These changes were indeed far-reaching: the forcible collectivization of agriculture and the involuntary conversion of nomadic and seminomadic peoples to a sedentary way of life; industrialization and the development of virgin and fallow lands; influx of an immigrant population, whose arrival brought a fundamental transformation in the ethnic and demographic situation in Central Asia and especially in Kazakhstan; and the degradation of national cultures in the face of Russification and dissemination of atheism. All this took place during the period hailed as "the construction of communism," a process in which the peoples of Central Asia—against their will—were forced to participate.

The Soviet period in the history of Central Asia, however, consisted not only of losses, but also of gains. These include the development of agriculture as well as considerable achievements in the spheres of culture, science, education, and public health. All this distinguishes the former Soviet Asian republics from non-Soviet neighbors like Afghanistan and Pakistan.

Noting the special characteristics of the modernization process in the Turkmenistan region in the period of Tsarist Russia, historian A.I. Iakovlev writes: "The cessation of wars, clashes, and incursions among the Central Asian emirs, the irrigation projects in the Golodnaia steppe, the manifestation of elements of a new agriculture (development of cotton cultivation, silk-raising, and viticulture), and of course integration into the enormous all-Russian market (with the development of a transportation network, Russian industrial and commercial capital, the rapid emergence of cotton-cleaning plants of local owners, and opening of branches of Russian banks)—all this significantly accelerated the pace of economic growth."[1] As for the radical social and economic transformation that the Bolshevik Party superimposed on Central Asia by dint of sheer coercion, Iakovlev notes that—for all their positive dimensions (industrialization, urbanization, and creation of a modern system of public health and education)—"the development of state and economic structures there did not become part of the organic process of social evolution."[2]

The ease with which the peoples and state-party elite *(nomenklatura)* of the former Soviet Asian republics accepted the breakup of the USSR, and renounced any communist ideology, serves to confirm Iakovlev's conclusion.

The economy of the Soviet Asian republics thus became an integral component of the single national economic complex of the USSR. Central subsidies (and other avenues for injecting funds and resources) to Central Asia played a major role in accelerating the process of modernization in this region.

According to S. Zhukov, "by the beginning of the 1990s, the direct centralized subsidies amounted to one-fifth of the gross domestic product (GDP) of Uzbekistan and one-seventh of the GDP of Kazakhstan and Kyrgyzstan."[3] However, he also rightly notes that such calculations of the redistribution of resources "do not consider the fact that the all-union center controlled the acquisition of oil and gas, gold and other precious metals, uranium, etc., for sale on world markets. Obviously, such economic activity is not reflected in the system of republican national accounts. Nevertheless, there is no question that all the Central Asian republics (with the exception of Turkmen SSR) were, to a greater or lesser degree, subsidized."[4]

Industrialization and urbanization in Central Asia became a dominating, powerful phenomenon during the Soviet period. A decisive factor was the sharp acceleration of immigration from the European part of the USSR and, above all, from the Russian Federation. Thus, whereas ethnic Russians amounted to only 500,000 people before the outbreak of World War I, their numbers swelled by another million during the period between 1926 and 1940.

Following the attack by Nazi Germany in 1941, the evacuation of industrial enterprises—and people—from the western parts of the USSR brought a further increase in the number of immigrants to Central Asia, approximately an additional 800,000 inhabitants in the course of the 1940s as a whole. Although postwar reconstruction entailed the return of many evacuees to European Russia, immigration resumed in the 1950s, when approximately 1 million migrants came to Central Asia. According to the calculations of Zh. Zaionchkovskaia, in 1959 the size of the migrant population (including heirs) in Central

Asia amounted to 3.7 million people—slightly more than a quarter of its population. Ethnic Russians represented 60 percent of the migrant population.[5]

The leading agent for modernization of Soviet Central Asia was precisely these migrants from the European part of the USSR, especially Russians. Most important, migrants constituted the backbone of the region's industrial enterprises bearing "all-union" significance; they also supplied the technical personnel in such branches as agriculture, construction, transportation, and communications. A considerable number were also prominent in the spheres of administration, science, culture, education, and public health.

At the same time, it should be emphasized that these accomplishments of the Soviet era—modern industry, agriculture, and transportation infrastructure—served largely to satisfy the general needs of the central state, not the republics of Central Asia. Above all, the economy of the Soviet Asian republics preserved a clear "raw-material" orientation; the processing branches either were poorly developed or altogether wanting. Because the finishing phase in the production cycle was usually situated outside this region, the republics of Central Asia shipped out raw materials and obtained finished goods in return.

The indigenous peoples of Central Asia have been marginally involved in the processes of modernization and in the newer branches of the economy. Rather, they have continued to work in traditional spheres of production, primarily in the agrarian sector.

The Zigzags of Post-Soviet Modernization

With the acquisition of state independence in 1991, the peoples of Central Asia embarked on a new, post-Soviet process of modernization. Catapulted into independence as a result of the unexpected breakup of the USSR, the former Soviet Asian republics have been forced to hastily work out their own strategies of development and to seek a new geopolitical niche. What are the realities and prospects for this "post-Soviet modernization"?

The leaders of the newly independent Central Asian states have acted under the influence of the "demonstrative effect" of events in Russia as well as the far-reaching changes in international relations—above all, the collapse of the socialist system in the USSR in its struggle against the "free world." With the "Cold War" thus coming to an end, these leaders have proclaimed a desire to make the transition from hyper-centralized to a market economy, from a totalitarian state to democracy, and from a condition of powerlessness and subjugation to complete sovereignty in the international arena.

Economic and political reforms conducted under conditions of independent development have wrought fundamental changes in the profile of the former Soviet Asian republics. Independent access to the international arena also brought a basic change in their geopolitical and geo-economic role in the modern world.

However, as five years of independent development have demonstrated, it is impossible—in such a short span of time—to overcome completely the Soviet legacy in economics, politics, ideology, and mentalité. It is thus difficult to sunder the bonds of the former empire, however vitiated these may have become.

The depth, tempo, and vector of market reform have been anything but equal in the newly independent states of Central Asia. Rather, these countries are obviously very different with respect to the radicalism and progress made toward the effective implementation of reform. In any event, state control over the economy and a significant level of state property ownership continue to dominate the economic development of Central Asian countries, especially in Uzbekistan and Turkmenistan. The situation in Tajikistan requires separate consideration.

Despite manifest problems, the first five years of independent development have not passed without positive results. The Central Asian states, albeit with varying degrees of intensity, are transforming their economic systems, creating and developing a market infrastructure, expanding the service sector, and accelerating the rate of integration into the world economy.

For the moment, however, there are not sufficient grounds to say that the newly independent states of Central Asia have taken decisive steps to make the structural transformation of the economy irreversible and to overcome its raw-material orientation. On the contrary, the export of raw materials is actually increasing, even if the geography of trade connections has changed. Hence Central Asia continues to remain a "raw material appendage," no longer within just the post-Soviet space, but for other regions of the world as well.

The exodus of Russians and other nonindigenous peoples from Central Asia actually commenced in the 1960s and accelerated after the dissolution of the USSR. This outmigration has caused a contraction in the size of the most skilled strata of the labor force; in particular, it has weakened the pool of engineering and technical personnel, workers in industrial spheres, specialists in agriculture, and those employed in science, education, and public health. This has inevitably created serious problems for the economic development of the newly independent states of Central Asia.

As earlier, the role of exogenous factors in the modernization of post-Soviet Central Asia is more important than that of domestic factors. Nor could it be otherwise, since the states of this region do not have a surfeit of their own investment capital. During the Soviet era, these republics received subventions from Moscow in exchange for the natural resources of the region. Today, such capital comes from foreign investors, but essentially in exchange for the same natural resources. Only time will tell whether this exchange is more or less equivalent and justified. In any event, the states of Central Asia, which do not have sufficient financial resources of their own, do not have any real alternative to their current policies.

Unfortunately, during the last six years, the countries of Central Asia have lost much of what had been achieved—in social and economic terms—during the preceding Soviet era. This is confirmed by the precipitous decline in industrial production, by the fall in living standards for the majority of the population, and by the degradation that has overtaken education, science, culture, and public health. The basic economic indicators of the Central Asian states during the last years of independent development attest to a large-scale regression in the social and economic spheres. It should be obvious that these negative processes reflect not only the consequences of the breakup of the USSR and the transition period but also miscalculations in the strategies for independent development.

This sharp decline is apparent in the basic economic indicators—using 1996 as a percentage of levels in 1990—for Kazakhstan, Kyrgyzstan, and Uzbekistan. Thus, in Kazakhstan, the GDP decreased to 45.9 percent of the 1990 level, total industrial output to 48.1 percent, gross output of agriculture to 56.1 percent, cargo volume on common carriers (excluding pipelines) to 22.3 percent, and capital investment to 13.0 percent. Similarly, in Kyrgyzstan, by 1996 GDP had decreased to 53.1 percent of the 1990 level, the total volume of industrial output to 38.8 percent, gross agricultural output to 64.5 percent, cargoes on common carriers to 5.1 percent, and capital investment to 43.7 percent.

Uzbekistan proved more stable: its GDP declined to 83.3 percent of the 1990 level, gross agricultural to 76.9 percent, cargoes on common carriers to 69.5 percent, and capital investment to 57.7 percent, while industrial output actually increased slightly (rising to 105.9 percent).[6]

In the opinion of Russian economist, L. Fridman, during the period of 1989–96 the Central Asian states of Kyrgyzstan, Tajikistan, Turkmenistan, and Uzbekistan underwent several main processes. First, this region underwent an "agrarianization" of employment. Fridman's calculations show an increase in agricultural employees in the total labor force in Kyrgyzstan (from 32.0 to 47.3 percent, an increase of 1.46 times), in Turkmenistan (from 32.7 to 43.8 percent, an increase of 1.18 times), and in Uzbekistan (from 35.2 to 40.6 percent, or 1.24 times). The exception was Kazakhstan: despite the fact that the GDP fell by more than half, the proportion of people employed in agriculture remained virtually unchanged (22.4 percent in 1989; 22.2 percent in 1996).[7]

Second, Central Asia also experienced de-industrialization, as measured by a significant decrease in the proportional share of people employed in industry, construction, and transportation. Fridman's data demonstrate that this decrease was substantial in Kazakhstan (from 41.7 to 27.6 percent, or 1.5 times), Kyrgyzstan (33.3 to 18.7 percent, or 1.8 times), and Tajikistan (29.1 to 15.5 percent, or 1.9 times). By contrast, the pace of de-industrialization was less intense in the case of Uzbekistan and Turkmenistan; here the proportion of the industrial labor force decreased from 31.1 to 23.8 percent (1.26 times).[8]

Third, Central Asia underwent another structural change in the branch structure of employment: the proportion of people working in the trade and service sector increased. Fridman offers the following calculations: "The most significant increase in the number of jobs in this sector, according to official data, occurred in Kazakhstan, where this indicator rose from 35.9 to 50.2 percent (a 1.4 times increase)."[9] In other words, to judge from these data, the scale of growth in the service sector fully corresponded to the indicator for de-industrialization.

One should note that the increasing economic involvement of developed countries in Central Asia (along with growing foreign investment and ever greater integration into the world economy) will play a major role in shaping the pattern of development in this region. It is entirely feasible for Central Asia not only to export energy and other natural resources but also to develop an export-oriented industry and agriculture. The creation of new transportation networks—which will link Europe and Asia and pass through Central Asia—can contribute to such a development.[10]

Kazakhstan

The sharpest contraction of production in Kazakhstan occurred between 1991 and 1995. During those years, the country experienced precipitous declines in the chemical and petrochemical industry (71 percent), light industry (84 percent), timber and wood-working industry (76 percent), machine-building and metalworking (64 percent), construction materials (82 percent), electric power (30 percent), ferrous metallurgy (48 percent), nonferrous metallurgy (28 percent), and the fuel and energy branch (40 percent).[11]

There are several basic causes of the massive fall of production in Kazakhstan, including: (1) the disruption of economic ties among the former Soviet republics following the breakup of the USSR; (2) the loss of markets for sales and for suppliers of goods; (3) inflation; (4) the nonpayment phenomenon; (5) budget deficits; and (6) high interest rates.

Faced with the very real threat of a total collapse of the economy (as a result of the massive fall in output), the government of Kazakhstan adopted a policy of transferring enterprises in different branches to trusts under the control of foreign companies. As a result, at the present time the government has forty-one contracts involving 89 enterprises: eighteen contracts (28 enterprises) for the metallurgical complex, 10 contracts (27 enterprises) for processing plants in the agro-industrial complex, and three contracts each for the chemical and petrochemical, transportation, and communication industries.[12]

G. Khuber and Zh. Davil'bekova, after investigating the operation of these enterprises, have come to the following conclusion: "An analysis of the results of the work of enterprises transferred to the control of foreign and domestic firms demonstrates that the majority have restored production and that some have even increased output, retained the number of jobs, and liquidated the wages, electricity, railroad tariffs, payments due to the state budget, and tax arrears. Nevertheless, a number of enterprises (the firms VSV and River International) find themselves in a critical situation: production is declining, unpaid salaries are mounting, and the labor collectives have filed appeals to have the contracts with these firms abrogated."[13]

Kazakhstan's policy of transferring enterprises in such branches as industrial production, energy and fuel, communications, and pipelines to foreign control and ownership is extremely risky. Only the future will tell whether this policy will bring success or a devastating failure—above all, the complete loss of economic independence.

The process of economic reform in Kazakhstan has entailed fundamental changes in the structure of ownership, with a strengthening of private, mixed, joint-stock, and other nonstate forms of property, which now account for over 70 percent of all property—compared to just 7 percent before the onset of the reforms.

On 1 June 1997, the total number of people employed in the small and middle-sized business sphere amounted to 555,000 people. The employees in small enterprises constituted 10 percent of the total labor force in the republic.[14] These substantial changes in the structure of employment reflect the results of a process of massive privatization and a policy aimed at providing support for small and middle-sized business.

On 1 January 1997, a reformed agrarian sector reported that 52,500 producers of agricultural commodities were operating. These included 44,300 peasant farms, 2,900 producer cooperatives, nearly 4,000 associations (of all types), 453 joint-stock companies, 451 state enterprises (of various categories), and some others. The state farms *(sovkhozy)* and collective farms *(kolkhozy)* of the Soviet era no longer exist in Kazakhstan.

The privatization of agriculture was essentially realized in 1994–96. This process accompanied a contraction in state support for agriculture in the form of finances and credits. As a result, Kazakhstan largely lost its former status as a major producer of grain, meat, wool, milk, and other agricultural products.

In the opinion of academician G. Kaliev, the condition of agriculture could hardly be worse: "The current indicators for the agrarian sector of Kazakhstan attest to a dangerous state of decline. Thus, the volume of gross output of agriculture dropped by half between 1900 and 1996. The indicators for labor productivity and the head of livestock are similar. Mineral fertilizers are applied to only 1 percent of the cultivated land area. More than 80 percent of the rural commodity producers of all types are operating at a loss. All this raises doubts about the correctness of the state's economic policy, including that pertinent to the agricultural sector."[15]

The statistical data are indeed alarming. Thus, the gross harvest of grain has fallen from 28.5 million tons in 1990 to 11.2 million tons in 1996; the corresponding data for wheat are 16.2 million tons in 1990 and 7.7 million tons in 1996. The head of livestock (all categories) decreased from 9,757,200 in 1991 to 5,410,400 in 1997; this includes a decline for cattle (from 3,368,000 to 2,535,500) and sheep and goats (from 35,660,500 to 13,741,900). Finally, the production of meat (dead weight) fell from 1,555,600 tons in 1990 to 806,400 tons in 1996. There were corresponding decreases for milk (from 5,601,300 tons to 3,579,400 tons), eggs (from 4,204,000 to 1,276,000), and wool (from 107,800 tons to 40,900 tons).[16]

In assessing the results of privation in agriculture and the agrarian policy of the state as a whole, historian N. Masanov writes: "Collectivization in Kazakhstan at the time caused the death of 1.7 to 1.8 million Kazakhs (nearly 45 percent of the entire Kazakh population), more than a thirteenfold reduction in the head of small livestock and almost a sevenfold reduction in the number of large livestock. The current stage of 'reform' has already greatly reduced the head of livestock in Kazakhstan, caused the migration of hundreds of thousands of rural inhabitants to the city, and in general reduced the country as a whole and in the sphere of agriculture, at the very least, to the level of the 1950s."[17]

Uzbekistan

The strategy of state construction and economic reform here is based on the five principles formulated by President I. Karimov:

- the economy has priority over politics;
- the main agent of reform is the state;
- priority is to be given to law and legal obedience;
- adherence must be given to a strong social policy, which takes into account the demographic structure of the nation;
- transition to a market economy must come through evolutionary means.[18]

In 1993, the fall in production was less than 11 percent. In 1994, this negative indicator decreased to 4 percent. In 1995–96, the country achieved a substantial growth of industrial output in oil and gas production, coal mining, machine building, and the metalworking industry.

Until 1991, Uzbekistan imported approximately 4.5 million tons of oil each year from Russia. After the country achieved independence, Uzbekistan embarked on a policy of developing its domestic oil and gas branches. As a result, the republic gradually began to increase the production of oil. Whereas in 1991 the oil branch produced 2.8 million tons, it had increased its output to 7.5 million tons in 1995 and 7.6 million tons in 1996.

With the assistance of foreign investors, Uzbekistan has opened a petroleum refinery in Bukhara and a natural gas compressor station at Kokdumalak (one of the largest deposits of oil and gas condensates in Uzbekistan). It is also completing the reconstruction of the Fergan refinery. As a result, oil imports from Russia have fallen from 3 million tons in 1994 to 1 million tons in 1995.

In 1996, the Republic of Uzbekistan acquired a new enterprise in the machine-building branch: motor vehicle manufacturing. Constructed jointly with the South Korean company Daewoo, the motor vehicle plant "UzDeuavto" (located in the city of Asak of Andizhan Oblast) has made Uzbekistan one of the world's largest producer of motor vehicles. This plant produces the large-engine vehicle Nexia, the small-engine vehicle Tico, and minivans that are fully capable of driving the Russian vehicles (Moskvich, Zhiguli, and Volga) from the Central Asian market. The annual projected capacity of the UzDeuavto plant is 200,000 cars and vans that are comfortable, efficient, and relatively cheap.

When the Uzbek-American joint venture for gold mining ("Zaravshan-Newmont") commenced operations, Uzbekistan was able to increase its gold production to 78 tons per year.

Uzbekistan is also following a path of evolutionary reform in agrarian relations. More than 19,500 peasant farms have been created, although forms of public ownership still dominate. The state still sets prices on agricultural products, including prices for which peasant farmers can sell their individual output. In brief, the government purchases about one-half of the cotton harvest at fixed prices; the balance is sold at prices established by officials at the oblast (provincial) level. This mechanism enables the state to control the redistribution of income in the agrarian sector (above all, from cotton production) and to channel these resources and thereby finance investment projects in industry and other state needs. However, the government has been gradually reducing the share of output that it purchases from the collective farms. It has also transferred 330,000 hectares of irrigated land from collective and state farms for allocation to the personal control of peasant farmers. As a result, the share of individualized private land has increased from 0.06–0.08 to 0.20–0.25 hectares. Altogether, today the peasant farms occupy 15 percent of the land.

Private land ownership is not permitted. In dealing with this situation, President Karimov has explained that the privatization of land in this country is impossible: "Given the special value of land under conditions requiring irrigated agriculture, given the present demographic situation, and given, most importantly, the requirements that contemporary agro-technology makes on the cultivation of cotton, it makes sense to keep land in state ownership and not to permit its sale. This is also true of water and the irrigation system. The transformation of land into a good would undermine the vital foundations of the population, give rise to speculation on land plots, and deprive the peasant farmer of confidence in tomorrow and in the fate of his children and grandchildren."[19]

Uzbekistan conducts a policy of ensuring self-sufficiency in grain by taking land that had previously been used to raise cotton and instead expands the areas sown to cereals. In 1991, the republic harvested 1.9 million tons of grain; it increased this output to 2.7 million tons in 1995 and to 2.3 million tons in 1996. It has, simultaneously, introduced more advanced technologies to preserve the former level of cotton production.

Uzbekistan ranks among the five largest producers of cotton in the world. In 1996, the collection of raw cotton amounted to 3.3 million tons. Along with gold and nonferrous metals, cotton continues to be the main export good from Uzbekistan.

Therefore, in the post-Soviet period, the economic structure of Uzbekistan is beginning to change in the direction of increasing the proportion of oil production and refining industry, developing certain industries (motor vehicle, light, and food-processing), achieving self-sufficiency in grain production, and modernizing the cultivation of cotton.

Uzbekistan is firmly and consistently implementing a strategy to replace imports by giving support to domestic industry and protecting it from competition by imported goods.

Uzbekistan is following a strict monetary and tax policy and, as a result, has significantly reduced the level of inflation. At the same time, the Uzbek sum has a highly limited degree of convertibility; the simultaneous existence of parallel exchange rates for the national currency (an official banking rate and a rate on the "black" market), given the severely limited number of juridical entities with the right to convert hard currency, does have a negative influence on economic development and reduces the investment attractiveness of Uzbekistan.

The deregulation of prices in Uzbekistan is proceeding very cautiously. Prices on consumer goods have been deregulated. However, the state continues to control the price of bread, flour, sugar, and vegetable oil.

As a result of the privatization process, the nonstate sector in Uzbekistan—which has 71.6 percent of the total labor force—accounted for 68.9 percent of the aggregate national income in 1996. This nonstate sector plays an especially significant role in agriculture, where it produced 97.7 percent of total output. Its role in industry was more modest, where it accounted for 53.5 percent of the output in 1996.

Kyrgyzstan

Kyrgyzstan has surpassed all the other Central Asian countries in the pace of its transition to a market economy. Following the collapse of the "ruble zone" in 1993, this republic became the first country in the CIS to introduce its own national currency, which has now become convertible. As a result of a radical privatization process, the population employed in state enterprises has fallen to just 40 percent of the total labor force.

Post-Soviet Kyrgyzstan is an agrarian-industrial country. In 1996, agriculture accounted for 46.6 percent of the total volume of GDP and has shown a tendency to increase. On the contrary, the share of output produced by industry has significantly declined.

To promote economic development, Kyrgyzstan has relied heavily on foreign investment. The Canadian company, Cameco Mining, has signed a contract with the Ministry of Gold Mining to develop and exploit the gold deposits in Kumtor; the American company, MK Gold, has jointed to found another joint-venture enterprise for gold mining. Experts believe that Kyrgyzstan has more than 2,350 tons of known and presumed reserves of gold. Until 1994, however, the republic had just one working gold mine, "Makmal." With the support of foreign companies, by 1998, Kyrgyzstan hopes to produce as much as 20 tons of gold per year.

Kyrgyzstan is also a supplier of other metals. Thus, it is the world's third largest producer of mercury; its output—700 tons per year—represents approximately one-fifth of total world production. It is also a major producer of antinomy; one combine at Kadamzhai produces up to 20,000 tons per year.

Kyrgyzstan also places great hopes on its extremely rich resources for the production of hydraulic energy and its well-developed hydroelectric infrastructure. All this makes it possible for Kyrgyzstan to become the greatest exporter of electric power.

But these hydroelectric resources are not without cost. Since acquiring independence, Kyrgyzstan has had to support, on its own and at the proper technical level, a powerful, integrated water power system and the complex of irrigation installations that were constructed during the Soviet era. This, however, is a major task, requiring substantial material, technical, and financial resources.

For the structural repair and the reconstruction of dams, canals, levees, and other water power installations, Kyrgyzstan has raised the question of assessing user fees from the Central Asian neighbors who ultimately draw upon its water. In particular, the upper house of the Zhogorku Kenesha (the Kyrgyz parliament) recently adopted a decree "on the inter-state water use from the water resources of Kyrgyzstan by Uzbekistan, Kazakhstan, and Tajikistan." This decree contains the claim that all water within the territory of the Kyrgyz Republic is its own property.

With respect to agriculture, in 1996 the share of output by peasant and farmer households rose from 14.8 to 23.8 percent of total production. However, the creation of farmer and peasant households has not generated an increase of the total volume of output. On the contrary, the production of the most important agricultural goods, with the exception of vegetables and potatoes, has steadily declined since 1993. As a result, the republic had to import about 45 percent of the food products it consumed.

Turkmenistan

The fuel and energy complex, which provides 60 percent of the income for the state budget, continues to belong to the state. A decrease in the production and export of natural gas has caused the country's financial situation to undergo a serious decline. Whereas, in 1991, Turkmenistan produced 84.7 billion cubic meters of natural gas, in 1995 this output had fallen to just 34.6 billion cubic meters. Furthermore, Turkmenistan can only ship its natural gas across the territory of the Russian Federation. However, because of the unfavorable terms for its contracts with the Russian firm Gazprom and because of the insolvency of its traditional buyers (Ukraine, Georgia, Armenia, and several other republics of the former USSR), Turkmenistan has cut its production of the "blue fuel" almost in half.

Instead, Turkmenistan is seeking to terminate this one-sided dependency in natural gas exports to the countries in the CIS—which, in fact, pay only 60 percent of the going price on world markets. Specifically, it is making plans to construct one pipeline through Iran and Turkey to Western Europe, and a second one to markets in China and Japan.

The process of privatization is proceeding in the spheres of consumer services, retail trade, public dining facilities, light and food-processing branches of industry, construction, and transportation. In 1997, in accordance with the "1,000 Day" Program of the President of Turkmenistan, the country began to carry out a privatization of middle-sized and large industrial plants.

In the judgment of Dzh. Bairamov (the director of the Institute of Economics, an agency directly subordinate to the Cabinet of Ministers), in 1993–96 more than 1,850 small and middle-sized enterprises have already been shifted to the nonstate sector of the economy. Altogether, the total number of enterprises in the nonstate sector rose from about 4,000 in 1992 to 24,000 in 1996; some 14,000 individuals were engaged in personal entrepreneurial activities. The private sector includes twenty brick-making plants (which produce 80 million kiln-baked bricks per year), three mills, twenty mini-mills, and eight canning plants.[20]

The Central Bank of Turkmenistan has limited autonomy and remains under the firm control of the president, who simultaneously wields all the powers as head of the government. But the country already has more than twenty joint-stock commercial banks as well as branches and offices to represent a number of foreign banks.

Turkmenistan has three parallel rates of exchange for hard currency: the general exchange rate, the official rate used in the sale of natural gas abroad, and an exchange for foreign transactions by enterprises.

Without question, the simultaneous existence of three different exchange rates for foreign currency does not create favorable conditions for an influx of foreign investment and for the general economic development of the country.

The right of private ownership to land is guaranteed by the Constitution of Turkmenistan. The legislation permits citizens to lease land plots up to 50 hectares in size and for no less than ten years, on the condition that the land is used for commodity production and later transferred to private ownership.

More than 900,000 hectares of land have been allocated for periods of at least ten years, and approximately 100,000 hectares have been converted to private property. More than 200,000 lessees are engaged in the production of grain and cotton.

With the assistance of foreign firms, Turkmenistan is constructing enterprises in light industry, food-processing, construction materials, machine-building and metalworking, chemical and oil branches, and electric power. At the beginning of 1997, some 150 plants (with a value of 800 million dollars) came on line; of these, 50 were built by Turkish firms at a cost of 400 million dollars. It is believed that these newly constructed enterprises will provide substitutes for imports and earn hard currency through an increase in exports.

Tajikistan

Tajikistan is primarily an agrarian country. More than 4 million of the 5 million inhabitants live in the village. The majority of industrial enterprises have ceased to operate. An aluminum plant in Tursunzade, which has a rated capacity of 517,000 tons of metal output per year, produced only 198,000 tons in 1996. The situation is no better in agriculture. The pride of Tajiksitan is cotton, but production has dropped to 40 percent of the level in 1990. As a result, Tajikistan is now producing less than 500,000 tons of cotton per year. More than half of what was grown must be harvested by hand, since many agricultural producers lack the funds to purchase cotton harvesters and spare parts.

The country introduced its own currency in May 1995. Since then, the Tajik ruble has been totally devalued; in a number of regions (especially in Khudzhent [Leninabad] Oblast and Badakhshan), the population prefers to use the Russian ruble. The foreign debt of Tajikistan has long since grown to more than 1 billion U.S. dollars.

The populace has been reduced to poverty. The average wage does not exceed 15 dollars per month. International experts believe that Tajikistan is even facing the threat of famine. Today, rationing has already been introduced into some rural areas, forbidding the sale of more than 1,000 grams per person a day. People in one strategically vital area—Gornyi Badakhshan—are essentially being sustained by Aga Khan IV, the head of Ismailis around the world, who regularly delivers flour and other food products to the region.

The fact that the state budget cannot support industrial enterprises and the social sphere has stimulated a market transformation in Tajikistan. Since September 1995, the country has embarked on the process of privatization. The state began to sell the stock for dozens of plants and factors, including branches in the export sector—cotton and mining. The new owners of the privatized enterprises, as a rule, are their former administrators. The majority of banks belong to the state. The securities market is only in an initial stage of gestation.

In the spring of 1997, in accordance with a decree by the president of the republic, 50,000 hectares of land were allocated to the peasants. The fertile soil of Tajikistan can produce up to three harvests a year. The transformation in the agrarian sector has enabled a certain improvement in the country's food situation.

Russia continues to maintain its own military presence in Tajikistan—the 201st motorized rifle division and border troops that guard the Tajik-Afghan borders. This is done in the conviction that whoever controls the situation in Tajikistan holds the key to all of Central Asia.

In the context of the current tensions between Tajikistan and Uzbekistan, and the complex process of national reconciliation in the country (which is proceeding with great difficulties and unexpected zigzags), Dushanbe essentially relies on the support of Moscow.

Moreover, the country's indebtedness to Russia for various credits is constantly growing. Tajikistan obtained these credits after it transferred its gold to the depository of Goskomdragmet Rossii [the State Committee of Precious Metals of Russia], and after the Tajik government acted to guarantee repayment of the credits through part of the book value of the Nurek Hydroelectric Station, aluminum, and cotton. Under these conditions, the independence of Tajikistan has long since become purely symbolic.

The domestic tensions in Tajikistan make this country unattractive to foreign investors. To be sure, there are some exceptions. For examto foreign investors. To be sure, there are some exceptions. For example, companies from South Korea and Italy have constructed plants to process cotton. Foreign investors—British and Canadian companies—are committing capital to the gold mining industry and working some gold-bearing deposits. Foreign firms have also shown a keen interest in the uranium deposits in the northern part of the republic. Nevertheless, the total amount of foreign investments in Tajikistan—just 50 million dollars per year—is the smallest of any Central Asian country.

State Power and Society

The existing political regimes in newly independent states, if one casts off all the camouflage generated by the image-makers, have nothing whatsoever to do with Western democracies. In terms of their authoritarian essence, they are similar to the Asian model democracy, as found in Singapore, Malaysia, and Indonesia. It is fair to say that this region is creating a Central Asian variant for the authoritarian democracies in the East.

Russian researcher, S. Panarin, holds that Central Asia has formed "an authoritarian model of political development in the form of a secular, national, unitary state." He identifies three of its variants:

- Kazakhstan and Kyrgyzstan: "An authoritarian model, but with real elements of democracy; a presidential republic with significant and constantly expanding authority for the head of state; a regime of soft or 'enlightened' bonapartism; a plebiscitary and edict-based administration in combination with a constitutional division of power."
- Uzbekistan and Tajikistan: "An authoritarian model with decorative features of democracy; a presidential republic with extremely large authority for the head of state; a regime of openly harsh bonapartism; in essence, a direct presidential rule in combination with constitutional, but purely formal division of power."
- Turkmenistan: "An authoritarian model with elements of monarchy (Asian despotism); a presidential republica with unlimited authority for the head of state; a regime of bonapartism that is simultaneously harsh and patriarchal; direct presidential rule in combination with a pseudo-democratization by means of referenda and 'elections,' comprehensive police control over the pop-

ulation, and populist gestures and the conscious inculcation of a cult involving the 'father of the nation'; a division of power is not established even at a constitutional level."[21]

In Kazakhstan and Kyrgyzstan, political parties and movements have been created and are now functioning. An opposition acts openly; human rights organizations are active; independent means of mass information exist. For the moment, the authorities are still tolerant of criticism aimed at themselves. To a great degree, these countries are open to the world.

The current Constitution of the Republic of Kazakhstan was adopted through a republic-wide referendum held on 30 August 1995. Its basic difference from the previous constitution of 1993 lies in a significant expanion of presidential authority. As political scientists B. Temirbulatov and A. Chebotarev have observed, "an analysis of the current constitution allows one to declare that the dominance of presidential-executive power over the legislative and judicial branches has been based on law, which, in political terms, can be regarded as a tendency to reassert the authoritarian principles in the system of a political power."[22] The authors have in mind the legal reinforcement of the president's political and legal instruments to exert pressure on the parliament and judicial system. This means, above all, the right of the president to convoke extraordinary sessions of parliament at his own initiative, on the recommendation of the chairpersons of the parliamentary houses, or at the request of at least one-third of the total number of deputies in Parliament. It also includes his power to veto laws adopted by Parliament, to dissolve Parliament, and to participate directly and exercise influence in the judicial process (including the appointment of judges).

In the case of Kyrgyzstan, a local researcher and political scientist, Zainidin Kurmanov, has described the political system in his country as an authoritarian regime of the liberal type. He writes that "Kyrgyzstan seemly has all the democratic attributes at hand. In fact, society does not understand that the presence of these democratic norms is pure window dressing, with the purpose of pleasing outsiders and playing up a democratic image for the Kyrgyz state . . . as a country that has such attributes as a government, parliament, parties and movements, press, and so forth, but it is not these things which govern society, but rather the family—kin, friends, regional clans, and money."[23]

In Uzbekistan and Tajikistan, the legislative branch is totally dependent on the executive. The party and political structure operates under the strict control of the state.

Turkmenistan has virtually no semblance of a party and political system. The existing means of mass communication are few in number and completely state-controlled. Censorship exists and has refused to register a number of newspapers and journals. The authorities are beyond criticism. Opposition is banned and must operate from outside the country. Human rights organizations are not tolerated. Of all the Central Asian countries, Turkmenistan is the most shut off from the external world.

The potential danger of domestic social and interethnic conflict dictates that the ruling elite not become tempted to introduce democratic models of political development. On the contrary, they have drifted toward the reassertion of an authoritarian model. Therefore, in the state and political development of Central Asia, the main emphasis has been on strengthening presidential and executive power both horizontally (with respect to the legislative and judicial branches) and vertically (by appointing the heads of oblasts rather than permitting local elections). This process has also entailed the enhancement of a well-developed repressive apparatus, tighter control over the means of mass information, and so forth.

It appears that the dominant tendency in state and political development in Central Asia is the formation and reinforcement of authoritarian political regimes. This includes a "strong presidential republic" in Kazakhstan, "an island of democracy" in Kyrgyzstan, "strong authorities and a strong state" in Uzbekistan, and the "Turkmenbashi" (Leader of the Nation) in Turkmenistan. Of course, the authoritarian regimes in Central Asia are based on the need to ensure social stability and harmony during the transition period.

These regimes, moreover, rely increasingly on the state bureaucracy, an emerging national bourgeoisie, and the constant buttressing of "the power structures" needed for order and repression. In ideological terms, these regimes actively use the conceptions of a national renaissance and the reinforcement of state sovereignty. In social psychological terms, they take advantage of the deeply embedded traditions of paternalism, obedience, respect for elders, patience, and tolerance.

The political economic essence of what is transpiring in Central

Asia is the formation of "bureaucratic capital"—that is, the fusion of a ruling elite with an emerging bourgeoisie. At this point, the merger is coming primarily in the spheres of trade and services; it is only gradually expanding to include the sphere of production itself.

The strategy of the ruling elite is concentrated on the creation of the most propitious conditions for their own further well-being and political survival. This means, above all, the reinforcement of the material and financial base (through the accumulation of property and money), the formation of political parties and movements that would lobby for their interests in society and especially in parliaments, establishment of control over the means of mass communication, and the creation and support of the requisite ideological myths.

A civil society is emerging in Central Asia, but at an exceedingly slow pace. One still finds a deeply inculcated paternalistic attitude toward the state and its institutions, a low level of political and legal culture. This is all compounded by the institutional backwardness of political parties and movements, nonstate public associations, and other agents capable of expressing and defending personal and civic interests.

Among the factors impeding the formation of a civil society, one should cite the persistence of tribal and other types of clan and regional divisions, the manifestation of ethnic nationalism, and the rebirth of religion after seven decades of dominance by proletarian internationalism and militant atheism.

Modernization, Westernization, and National Rebirth

Post-Soviet Central Asia, which was opened to the world after the breakup of the USSR, found itself in a zone of active cross-civilizational influences. Until the acquisition of state independence, the peoples of Central Asia were subject primarily to the cultural influence of Russia. After the destruction of the "iron curtain," when the post-Soviet space was thrown open to the influence of Western civilization, Central Asia became accessible to yet another influence—the neighboring Eastern civilizations of China, India, Arab Islam, Iranian Islam, and others.

In contemporary Central Asia, one finds several processes simultaneously unfolding: modernization, Westernization, and national rebirth. At present, it is difficult to judge which vector will prevail. In any case, it is highly unlikely that the region will return to the hegemony of Russian civilization, since Russia itself—in economic and cultural terms—has devolved from a donor-state into a receiver-state. Nor will westernization come to total dominance; the influence of Eastern civilizations in Central Asia is steadily growing. Indeed, the "winds from the East" are beginning to prevail over the winds from the West, with the twenty-first century being predicted to be the Age of Asia.

In all probability, Central Asia will continue to rekindle national cultures and languages, even while preserving an important role for Russian language and culture and even amidst the continuing "boom" in the study of the English language. In terms of economic development of this region, in the foreseeable future one can expect the dominant influence to come from the developed countries of the West, but amidst an ever growing role for the countries in the East.

S. Panarin has described this cultural dualism in Central Asia as follows: "The population of the Central Asian region is divided between the spheres of industrial and preindustrial (agrarian) civilizations. The former is found in the capitals, industrial cities, and areas with mechanized grain cultivation; the latter occupies the rest of the territory of the region. The habitat of the first civilization is a space for modernization; here one finds freely established social ties, liberal values, individualism, secular Weltanschauung, and cosmopolitan models of culture. The habitat of the latter civilization is the realm of tradition; powerful here are hereditary social bonds, patriarchal values, collectivism, religious sensibilities, and ethnic and subethnic models of culture."[24] Noting that the space of both these civilizations is very much like a mosaic, Panarin observes that the former sphere experiences a "greater internal predisposition toward the 'maternal' industrial civilization of Russia," while the latter is more inclined toward the "cultural traditions of the Muslim East."[25]

The process of Westernization in Central Asia entails the intrusion of a Western lifestyle, views, fashions, and recreational industry. In the cities, especially in the capitals, one finds a Western style in shops, restaurants, night clubs, casinos, and even golf clubs. The children of elite or just plain wealthy families are sent primarily to study in the institutions of higher learning not in Russia, but in the United States and Western Europe. The explosive increase in the study of English and other Western languages is particularly striking.

A decline in the economic power of Russia, along with the fact that Russian capital manifests little interest in Central Asia (in contrast to the intense activities of American, West European, South Korean, Japanese, and other firms), have meant both a decline in Russia's position (from the Soviet era) and a rising influence of other states.

The newly independent states of Central Asia no longer link their development to Russia, but rather to the countries of the West and of East Asia—which have long since surpassed Russia in terms of their economic and scientific-technological development.

A Unitary Central Asia?

As component parts of the USSR, the former Soviet republics of Central Asia had to deal more with the "center" than with each other. Regional cooperation was permitted, but under the strict control of Moscow, which made a determined effort to counteract any manifestations of regional separatism.

After obtaining independence, three of these five countries embarked on a process of integration in Central Asia. This process did not include Tajikistan (which, by 1992, was already mired in a bloody civil war and has only recently begun to seek national reconciliation) and Turkmenistan (which refrained from active participation in the integrationist processes both in the CIS and in Central Asia).

On 23 September 1993, the deepening ties of Kazakhstan, Kyrgyzstan, and Uzbekistan culminated in the signing of a treaty to create an economic union. On 10 February 1994, these countries proclaimed the formation of a "single economic space." On 8 July 1994, they created an Interstate Council, with an Executive Committee, to promote the formation of a single economic space in the region. This union is open to membership by the remaining states in the CIS.

The processes of integration in Central Asia go far beyond the framework of the economy alone. Other aspects are also coming to the fore—political, legal, humanitarian, informational, and of course regional security. A Council of Defense Ministers has been formed, with the charge of preparing concrete proposals on military cooperation. The decision to form a Central Asian peacekeeping force (under the aegis of the United Nations) is also being implemented; in September 1997, the force conducted training exercises on the territory of Kazakhstan and Uzbekistan. Another indication of the political will and willingness of these three states to expand the integration process was their decision to sign, on 10 January 1997 in Bishkek, a treaty on the eternal friendship of the Kyrgyz Republic, the Republic of Kazakhstan, and the Republic of Uzbekistan.

The states of Central Asia have much in common—in terms of their historic fate, culture, language, and religion. To be sure, integration here is impeded by the fact that their economies are basically similar, since all are primarily producers of raw materials. To achieve a higher level of cooperation for such resource-oriented economies is far from easy. Nevertheless, this process is already under way, giving rise to new proposals, which, however modest in scale, are fully sufficient to resolve problems of regional development and to enable these states to complement one another in various ways.

The problem of ensuring the unity of states in Central Asia is the most important strategic task. If this challenge is successfully met, it will provide the most favorable conditions not only for development but also for ensuring stability and security in the region. The historical past, including the Soviet legacy, and the realities of contemporary development are such that Central Asia has a rich potential for interstate and interethnic conflicts, competition, and the intervention of outside forces.

A source of intraregional conflicts can easily become disputes about the problems of sharing the water and land resources—which indeed are in acutely short supply. Competition for access to the richest natural resources, above all energy and fuel resources, can also lead to the intervention of other states, not only neighboring countries, but those located far from the borders of Central Asia.

If this region fails to make timely and substantial correctives in its strategy for development and if it does not enhance the unity of all five of the newly independent states, Central Asia could turn into the epicenter of the most acute conflicts, not only domestic but also international in scale.

Conclusion

In sum, historical forces in Central Asia are moving in the same direction as elsewhere in the world, only more slowly and not always in the immediate interests of the people. The newly independent states here have their own "dual economy": an emerging modern sector in the cities based on the marketplace, and a residual traditional (Soviet) economy in rural areas. The collective and state farm system, albeit in a modified variant, continues to thrive in Central Asia. Only in Kazakhstan has it been fundamentally demolished; here, a private, capitalist agriculture experiences the travails of birth pangs—and without any midwifery assistance by the state.

Given that the current strata of ruling elites in Central Asia is genetically derived from the former communist *nomenklatura* elite, there is a serious danger that this elite will exploit the transition period to promote their own selfish interests—both for their own enrichment and for the consolidation of their power. Hence, in conducting the privatization of property, it is highly tempting to circumvent the existing authority altogether and instead to give foreign investors untrammeled access to the natural resources of these countries.

Moreover, the present strategies for development do not adequately take into account the consequences of a deepening stratification of society—from the polarization into the rich and poor, and from mounting differences in developmental levels in the city and countryside and among individual regions. In the final analysis, this could lead to large-scale social convulsions.

"Independence is everything" declared, Kwame Nkrumah, one of the leaders of the national liberation movement in Africa in the 1960s. These very words have been engraved on a pedestal in his honor in Accra. Nevertheless, the realities of the subsequent independent development in most African states have shown that independence is far from being everything. The main thing is not independence, but development. Independence is only an important, necessary precondition for development. For the moment, the limited experience of the newly independent states of Central Asia only supports this harsh truth.

Notes

1. A.I. Iakovlev, "Sravnitel'nye zametki o preobrazovaniiakh v Turkestane i sovetskoi Srednei Azii," *Kentavr,* 1993, no. 2, p. 96.
2. Ibid., p. 104.
3. S. Zhukov, "Kazakhstan, Kyrgyzstan, Uzbekistan v sotsial'no-ekonomicheskikh strukturakh sovremennogo mira," *Mirovaia ekonomika i mezhdunarodnye otnosheniia,* 1997, no. 3, p. 47.
4. Ibid., p. 47.
5. Zh. Zaionchkovskaia, "Istoricheskie korni migratsionnoi situatsii v Srednei Azii," *Migratsiia russkoiazychynogo naseleniia iz Tsentral'noi Azii: prichiny,*

6. Mezhgosudarstvennyi sovet Respubliki Kazakhtan, Kyrgyzskoi Respubliki i Respubliki Uzbekistan. Ispolnitel'nyi komitet, *Obzor sotsial'no-ekonomicheskogo razvitiia respubliki Kazakhstana, Kyrgyzskoi Respubliki i Respubliki Uzbekistana,* 8 (Bishkek, 1997), pp. 12–13.

7. L.A. Fridman, "Rynochnaia ekonomika stran Tsentral'noi Azii (vzgliad s Zapada)," *Doklad na konferentsii "Regional'naia stabil'nost' i bezopasnost' v Tsentral'noi Azii"* (Ashkhabad, 12–16 May 1996).

8. Ibid.

9. Ibid.

10. S. Zhukov, "Kazakhstan, Kyrgyzstan, Uzbekistan," p. 53.

11. *Delovaia nedelia,* 20 June 1997.

12. G. Khuber and Zh. Davil'bekova, "Trastovoe upravlenie v Kazakhstane: opyt i problemy," *Al'Pari,* 1997, no. 2, p. 42.

13. Ibid.

14. *Kazakhstanskaia pravda,* 31 July 1997.

15. G. Kaliev, "Ob agrarnoi politike Respubliki Kazakhstan," *Aziia—ekonomika i zhizn',* no. 32 (August 1997).

16. Natsstatagenstvo Ministerstva ekonomiki i torgovli Respubliki Kazakhstan, *Kratkii statisticheskii ezhegodnik Kazakhstana* (Almaty, 1997).

17. N. Masanov, "Sovremennoe sostoianie skotovodstva v Kazakhstane," *Vremia po Grinvichu,* 25 June 1997.

18. I.A. Karimov, *Uzbekistan—sobstvennaia model' perekhoda na rynochnye otnosheniia* (Tashkent, 1993), pp. 37–38.

19. Ibid., pp. 93–94.

20. Dzh. Bairamov, "Problemy i perspektivy ekonomicheskogo razvitiia Turkmenistana v usloviiakh formirovaniia rynochnykh otnoshenii" (paper delivered to a conference on "Regional Stability and Security in Central Asia," in Ashkhabad, 12–16 May 1996).

21. S. Panarin, "Tsentral'naia Aziia: integratsionnyi potentsial i perspektivy migratsii," in *Migratsiia russkoiazychnogo naseleniia iz Tsentral'noi Azii: prichiny, posledstviia, perspektivy* (Moscow, 1996), pp. 29–30.

22. V. Temirbulatov and A. Chebotarev, "Problema stanovleniia instituta razdeleniia vlastei v Respublike Kazakhstan v perekhodnyi period," in *Obrazy budushchego Kazakhstana* (Almaty, 1996), p. 73.

23. Z. Kurmanov, "Kratkii kurs nezavisimogo razvitiia Kyrgyzstana: opyt analiza," *KutBilim,* no. 15 (13 June 1996).

24. S. Panarin, "Tsentral'naia Aziia," p. 25.

25. Ibid.

Part II

Economic Performance

4

Broader Parameters: Development in the Twentieth Century

Boris Rumer and Stanislav Zhukov

One cannot properly understand the most recent changes in the economy and society of post-Soviet Central Asia without an awareness of the historical background. That historical development can be most conveniently divided into three main periods: prerevolutionary, Soviet, and post-Soviet. The transition from one period to the next was accompanied by large-scale social, political, and economic tumult and disorder.

Pre-Revolutionary Background

Until the mid-1920s, the territory that subsequently came to form Kazakhstan, Kyrgyzstan, Tajikistan, Turkmenistan, Uzbekistan. Tajikistan and Turkmenistan formed part of the periphery of the Russian Empire. The level of economic and social development there was extremely low. The great bulk of the population engaged in a primitive form of agriculture that, in the case of the Kazakhs and Kyrgyz, amounted to nothing more than nomadic herding. At the end of the nineteenth century, the number of inhabitants of cities and towns represented just 12 percent of the total population; the most urbanized areas included Fergan, Samarkand, and Syr-Dar′ia oblasts. By contrast, the urban population in provinces that later came to comprise Kazakhstan and Kyrgyzstan could hardly have exceeded 4 to 6 percent. By the beginning of the twentieth century, only two cities in Kazakhstan had a population exceeding 20,000 inhabitants—Semipalatinsk (26,353) and the future capital of the country, then called Vernyi (22,982).

The territories that later came to form Uzbekistan undoubtedly had a higher level of development. Although the entire population was virtually illiterate, these areas had well-established trade centers. Thus, the 1897 census shows that, of the twenty largest urban settlements in Central Asia, eleven were found in the territory of modern-day Uzbekistan. The accelerated, centuries-old tradition of urban life and a relatively more advanced agriculture set apart the Uzbek territories from the rest of Central Asia. However, these advantages reflected not so much the high development there as the profound backwardness of the neighboring areas.

It should be noted that the backwardness of Central Asia can also be attributed, in part, to its geographical position as a peripheral area. Lacking access to the sea and being separated from the main trade routes of the time, this region had only sporadic contacts with the external world, and indeed these ties were restricted to a narrow stratum of elite groups.

In the first decades of the twentieth century, the military and economic requirements of the Russian Empire gave some impetus to development in this region. Nevertheless, the appearance of a few industrial enclaves and the growth of cities did little to change the face of Central Asia. An acceleration in the economic dynamics and improvements in the employment and production structure had not, as yet, acquired sufficient critical mass.

Soviet Period

There were significant changes after the Bolsheviks consolidated their power in the center of the former Russian Empire. Thus, since the 1920s, Central Asia has been forcibly included in the grandiose plans for Soviet modernization. It should be emphasized here that the analysis will focus only on the main results of development between 1920 and 1990, the sustainability and viability of this development, and the costs and efficiency that these changes entailed.[1]

The industrialization of Soviet Central Asia has been uneven and not guided by a long-term strategy. It has indeed run contrary to "the law of planned, proportionate development" that Soviet ideologists and political economists claimed as the foundation of the Soviet system.

Table 4.1

Growth of Industrial Production in the USSR, Uzbekistan, and Kazakhstan (in percent)

	USSR		Uzbekistan		Kazakhstan	
Five-year plan	Total growth	Per annum	Total growth	Per annum	Total growth	Per annum
First (1928–32)	202	15.0	157.0	9.4	—	—
Second (1933–37)	221	17.0	242.0	19.3	—	—
Third (1938–41)	145	13.2	131.0	9.4	—	—
Fourth (1946–50)	189	13.6	171.0	11.4	169[a]	11.1[a]
Fifth (1951–55)	185	13.0	161.5	10.0	316[b]	12.2[b]
Sixth (1956–58)	134	10.2	119.0	6.0		
Seventh (1959–65)[c]	—	—	178.0	8.7	164	10.4
Eighth (1966–70)	159	8.5	136.0	6.3	156	9.3
Ninth (1971–75)	143	7.4	151.0	8.6	127	4.9
Tenth (1976–80)	124	4.4	127.0	4.9	118	3.4
Eleventh (1981–85)	120	3.7	126.0	4.7	116	3.0
Twelfth (1986–90)	113	2.5	118.0	3.4	116	3.0

Sources: Promyshlennost' SSSR (Moscow, 1964), 34; *Narodnoe khoziaistvo Uzbekskoi SSR v 1970 godu,* p. 132; *Narodnoe khoziaistvo SSSR v 1970* godu, pp. 139, 141; *Narodnoe khoziaistvo SSSR v 1975 godu,* p. 203; *Narodnoe khoziaistvo SSSR v 1980 godu,* p. 132; *Narodnoe khoziaistvo SSSR v 1985 godu,* pp. 10, 101; *Narodnoe khoziaistvo SSSR v 1990 godu,* p. 357.
[a]Data for 1945–50.
[b]Data for 1950–60.
[c]Seven-Year-Plan.

The initial great leap came under the first two five-year-plans (1927–32, 1933–37)—a period when industrialization enveloped the entire territory of the USSR. Uzbekistan and Kazakhstan offer instructive examples: as the most industrially developed republics in Central Asia, they had to bear the full brunt of the accelerated industrialization that was then overtaking the USSR as a whole (see Table 4.1).

In the years immediately preceding World War II, however, the pace of industrialization slowed markedly. The reasons for this downturn were many; apart from the increased diversion of resources for military preparations, the sluggish growth rate was also due to the production-branch planning and administration of industry as well as the concentration of resources on new construction projects (chiefly in the old industrial centers of European Russia). The result was a steep decline in the growth of industrial output at the end of the 1930s.

Central Asia experienced its second surge of industrialization during World War II, when it acquired heavy industry—the result of the regime's decision to evacuate many industrial enterprises from the European part of the USSR eastward, much of it to Central Asia. Thus, machinery and equipment from more than one hundred industrial plants (in toto or in part) were shipped to Uzbekistan alone; this machinery—for metallurgy, coal mining, machine-building, and other branches of the economy—laid the foundation for forty-seven new industrial enterprises, more than half of which were located in Tashkent or its environs.[2] This development transformed Tashkent and the contiguous areas into the greatest industrial complex of Central Asia.

The magnitude of this forced relocation of heavy industry and its impact on the economy of Central Asia is evident from the data on Uzbekistan. Thus, during the period 1940–50, the output in machine building increased 653 percent, steel production jumped from 11,000 to 119,000 tons, coal output expanded from 3,000 to 1.5 million tons, and electric power generation rose from 481 million to 2,679 million kilowatt-hours.[3]

The formation of the economic structure of Kazakhstan, as part of the national economic complex of the USSR, was in fact driven by the demand of the industrial branches in the Urals and in Russia for various raw materials and foodstuffs. As a result, top priority was given to the extractive industries and agriculture. Hence the economy of Kazakhstan exhibited major differences in the level of development, as the traditional lines of local production coexisted with enclaves of high-tech production. In part, this uneven, checkered pattern of development—with scattered hotbeds of industrial development—was a legacy of World War II and the eastward evacuation of industrial complexes to Kazakhstan. These patterns were further intensified by the campaign in the 1950s to develop virgin lands and to bring them under cultivation. This peculiar configuration has remained largely intact until the present time.

The ethnic dimension here bears noting: the indigenous population has not exceeded 10 percent of all the employees in the industrial branches of the Central Asian republics. Hence, the entire industry of Central Asia represents a cluster of islands of technology, which are inhabited by immigrants from a society with a higher level of development. Thus, one can distinguish two disconnected, unrelated layers of the economy: one formed naturally on the basis of local conditions, the other established as the product of foreign influence (above all, Russia).[4]

In the first two five-year-plans following World War II, the growth rate of industrial production in Central Asia remained high, but lower than that in the USSR as a whole. Investment in the region's industries decreased, as virtually all the available resources were being concentrated on rebuilding the industries in European Russia that had been destroyed during the war.

In the second half of the 1950s, however, Central Asia experienced a marked decline in its rate of industrial growth. Several factors account for this. First, the wartime surge was so great that a relative fall-off was inevitable. Second, the industrial potential added during the war did not receive sufficient resources to finance further expansion or even proper maintenance. The result was a rapid depletion of fixed capital, which was not offset by replacement or repair and still less by upgrading.

Moreover, a significant portion of the equipment and machinery evacuated from the western regions was already badly worn at the time of installation. The assembly, installation, and construction of the requisite buildings, communications, and other components of the industrial infrastructure had to be completed under the acute pressure of the war, when every minute counted and no attention could be given to durability. The result was such massive deviation from standards that, to maintain production in the postwar years at previous levels, immense resources would have been required. The upshot was that, a decade after the war's end, the utilization of plant capacity had declined substantially.

Finally, narrow bureaucratic interest-group politics ("departmentalism") and centralized control of industry (and hence resources) dominated the first postwar plans. As a result, the interests of individual regions, especially those that had not suffered during the war, were relegated to secondary importance.

The third phase of accelerated industrialization in Central Asia came in the early 1960s. The primary impetus was Nikita Khrushchev's new system of *sovnarkhozy* (economic councils) to function as the key units for territorial economic administration (1957–65). For the only time in Soviet history, national regions were given a real opportunity to manage their local economies. The ensuing "regional autarky" contributed substantially to the creation of many new industrial enterprises, the expansion of infrastructure and the construction industry, and the development of the raw material and energy base. Although Moscow still exercised oversight, the sovnarkhozy independently managed many spheres of economic activity and used their new authority to expand the industrial base in their own region.

Significantly, these years also witnessed the creation of industrial enterprises unrelated to the processing of agricultural products or the exploitation of local minerals, raw materials, and energy resources. Specifically, in Central Asia the sovnarkhoz laid the foundation for new branches of industry (e.g., chemicals) and expanded the industrial capacity for construction materials and machine building. Particular attention was given to the chemical industry (on the basis of oil and gas processing and treatment) and nonferrous metallurgy; these emerged as the dominant sectors of heavy industry in Central Asia and began to play an even greater role in the industrial production of the region.

The sovnarkhozny thus provided the basis for accelerated industrial growth in later years. This legacy included the exploration and technical-economic assessment of natural resources, the improvement of construction materials and equipment, the expansion of schools for vocational training, and the development of a better transportation grid. Consequently, the period of the sovnarkhozy constitutes an important stage in the industrial development of Central Asia, and the momentum gained during these years had a long-term impact that outlasted Khrushchev's overthrow in 1964 and the dismantlement of sovnarkhozy the following year.

The five-year plan that followed the elimination of sovnarkhozy (1966–70) dealt a severe blow to the region's economy, as the organizational structure created in the past eight years was suddenly shattered. In a word, Moscow abruptly reversed policy, returned to centralized planning and management, and castigated the sovnarkhozy policy as narrow-minded localism *(mestnichestvo)*. The new Brezhnev leadership also bolstered the production-branch system and promoted vertical integration in territorial industrial planning. All this was the diametrical opposite to the decentralization pursued by Khrushchev with his network of local sovnarkhozy.

Inevitably, the new policy began to have a negative impact on the industrial growth of Central Asia, as was already apparent in the second half of the 1960s. Nevertheless, because construction and start-up are a protracted process (normally running from five to ten years), the full benefits of the sovnarkhozy investment programs did not become evident until the early 1970s.

Thereafter, however, Central Asia—as indeed the USSR as a whole—experienced a sharp contraction in the rate of industrial growth, once the sovnarkhozy projects had run their course and were not followed by new ones. Thus, industrial growth plummeted sharply during the tenth five-year-plan (1976–80), with no improvement in either the eleventh (1981–85) or the twelfth (1986–90). The same factors that caused this poor economic performance in the USSR were also at work in Central Asia; these have been extensively discussed in the literature and do not require a detailed elaboration here. However, each region of the former USSR has its own unique patterns and problems; it is important to identify those specific to Central Asia.

Although industrial production in Central Asia continued to grow at a significant pace for some time after the end of the sovnarkhozny period, it took on an entirely different character. Branch ministries, not regional planning organs, determined where and what kind of plants were to be built, giving scant regard to the need for complex, integrated development. The central ministries increasingly tended to concentrate industrial production in areas that already had well-developed infrastructures, where capacity could be expanded more quickly and at less cost. This concentration of industrial complexes in previously developed centers naturally meant a persistent tendency to neglect sparely settled areas.

The transformation of Central Asia over several decades of Soviet industrialization has had some broad consequences. First, in an incredibly short period of time, the indigenous populations of Kazakhstan and Kyrgyzstan were converted to a sedentary way of life. Second, because of the accelerated urbanization, the residents of cities and larger towns came to include nearly two-thirds of the population in Kazakhstan and about two-fifths of the population in Uzbekistan and Kyrgyzstan. Third, the indigenous population of Central Asia—especially in Kazakhstan and Kyrgyzstan—fundamentally altered its form of economic activity. By 1990, the nonagricultural branches accounted for 77.2 percent of the jobs in Kazakhstan, 67.3 percent in Kyrgyzstan, and 60.7 percent in Uzbekistan. At the same time, there were also far-reaching changes in the agrarian sector. The nomadic herders and small cultivators were "herded" into the institutional framework of the Soviet *sovkhozes* (state farms) and *kolkhozes* (collective farms). Moreover, there was also a large-scale expansion of agriculture in Kazakhstan and Kyrgyzstan. Finally, a network of relatively modern services was developed in the former Soviet republics of Central Asia. In terms of the development of education, public health, and life expectancy, these republics were among the most developed states, and that is confirmed by the index for the development of human potential.

Post-Soviet Period

At the end of the 1980s and early 1990s, Central Asia suffered a large-scale economic and social catastrophe. This catastrophe resulted both from the general crisis of the entire Soviet Union and from specific, purely local factors. If the general causes of the failure of the Soviet system have been rather meticulously examined in the scholarly literature, the specifics have plainly not been given sufficient attention.

A significant part of the local production, consumption, and capital investment consisted of financial and resource inputs coming from the other Soviet republics (above all, Russia). By the beginning of the 1990s, direct subsidies or grants for Central Asia had risen to become a substantial proportion of the GDP—one-fifth in the case of Uzbekistan, and one-seventh in Kazakhstan and Kyrgyzstan. Moreover, the grants represent only the visible share of the subsidies and do not include another hidden component, which was created through distortions in relative prices in the Soviet economy. For example, the prices on energy resources and industrial raw materials were fixed at artificially low levels, while the prices on foodstuffs and light industry products were inflated (measured in Central Asia levels). As a result, in 1991 the hidden price subsidies from Uzbekistan's trade with Russia were roughly 6.5 percent of its GDP; the analogous indicator was 7.3 percent for Kazakhstan and 1.1 percent for Kyrgyzstan. Obviously, when this significant influx of resources decreased, it was bound to trigger a downturn in economic activity in Central Asia.

Although the profound economic decline here was also true of the other former Soviet republics, the politicians and economists in this region attribute this crisis to the backwardness and disproportions in their economies. They also emphasize the dependency on foreign suppliers and the disruption of economic ties after the breakup of the Soviet Union. All this implies that these economic difficulties are due to objective factors, not to the policies and actions of the current leadership. To a considerable degree, such arguments do in fact correspond to reality.

But not entirely. Indeed, the economies of the Central Asian republics, at the point when they became independent, had far greater reserves for stability than is ordinarily assumed. Thus, it is a major exaggeration to assert that industrial enterprises were "helpless" because of the disruption of interdependent technology networks resulting from the catastrophic decline of production in 1992–94. Such claims fail to take into account that many enterprises, especially the larger ones, had substantial reserves, and that these reserves should have been sufficient to survive the period of crisis. One must also bear in mind that, throughout the entire Soviet period, every more or less large enterprise strove to achieve economic independence, to create many auxiliary shops and subunits. These facilities had to have the capacity to produce various parts, components, and construction materials and to repair and service equipment, and cover the plant's need for transport. They even included farming units capable of supplying the employees and plant cafeteria with food products. For such activities, enterprises accumulated "above-norm reserves" of materials in the form of metal, equipment, and so forth. By the early 1990s, audits revealed that this stockpile of materials was worth hundreds of billions of Soviet rubles and that a considerable share of such reserves were held by enterprises in Central Asia. Moreover, one must not forget the old, persisting tendency to conceal real productive capacities and to inflate the depletion of fixed capital. All this made it easier to fill the plan and to produce goods that, as output unreported in official statistics, could be used for barter and black market transactions. The scale of latent resources were so significant that many enterprises could stay afloat for a certain period of time and avoid a catastrophic decrease in production. That *could* have been the case if there had not been massive, uncontested stealing and if such resources had been sold off at dumping prices (mostly abroad). Thus, in 1992–94, there was a flow of various industrial goods from Kazakhstan to western China (Xinjiang), where they were sold at low prices or bartered for cheap, low-quality consumer goods.

In 1990–95, the GDP and industrial production of Kazakhstan fell by more than half and capital investment by four-fifths. During the same period in Kyrgyzstan, the GDP decreased by 50 percent, industrial production by 65 percent, agricultural output by 46 percent, and capital investments by nearly two-thirds. The pace of decline was much less precipitous in Uzbekistan (18 percent in the GDP). One must also bear in mind that some contraction was actually useful. It is no secret that, during the Soviet era, the economies of Kazakhstan and Kyrgyzstan (and, to a lesser degree, Uzbekistan) serviced the needs of the military-industrial complex, and—under the nonmarket economy of the USSR—that defense-oriented production did little to promote the country's material well-being. Nevertheless, the dimensions of economic contraction in Kazakhstan and Kyrgyzstan were so immense that it can hardly be explained by a demilitarization of the economy. Rather, the main dynamic of contraction in economic activity was a deep-rooted crisis in the civilian economy.

Many lines of production, even whole branches of the economy, in Central Asia depended heavily on migrant labor. From the 1930s to the 1960s, this region absorbed several million migrants, primarily from Russia, Belorussia, and Ukraine, and these migrants provided the labor input for the accelerated industrialization and collectivization. By the second half of the 1970s, however, the Central Asian republics were already beginning to report a substantial outflow of these nonindigenous inhabitants. And, from the late 1980s, this outmigration took on the character of a mass exodus: in 1989–94, approximately 2 million people—6.2 percent of the total population in 1989—left the region. As should already be apparent, it was precisely the most qualified and the most mobile part of the labor force that abandoned the region.

Central Asia also showed the artificiality of Soviet modernization and its limited impact on the local populace. To be sure, the gains of 1930–70 (in the conditions and character of labor, way of life, individual consciousness—all that Fernand Braudel called the structure of everyday life) were of revolutionary import for the overwhelming majority of the population. But any revolution, especially one superimposed from without, may well evoke a reaction. The first signs that the Soviet model of modernization had begun to falter in Central Asia and that a rejection syndrome had begun to set in, were already becoming apparent in the 1970s. This came in the form of a low rate of popular mobility, reduced recruitment of labor for the industrial branches, and a smaller rate of growth in labor productivity. By the late 1980s and early 1990s, the contradictions and problems that had grown steadily but beneath the surface suddenly burst into full view.

Specialists are deeply divided on the question whether contemporary Central Asian society is still essentially Soviet, traditional Muslim, or a traditional Muslim culture profoundly deformed by decades of Soviet rule. It is fair to say that contemporary Central Asian society is still poorly understood and that informed analysis is greatly impeded by the lack of reliable, objective information. Statistical data, especially in the social sphere, remain highly suspect. Sociological studies are very rare and fragmentary.

Still, some generalizations are possible. Post-Soviet Central Asian society consists of many different strata and, *au fond,* represents a unique fusion of the traditional culture of the Muslim East and the deeply rooted mentality of *Homo soveticus.* That is, it consists of two distinct, segregated components: an urban, "European," Russian-speaking, and Russified (Westernized) indigenous group and a rural, traditional, Turkic- or Persian-speaking one. By the late 1980s, the proportion between the first and second group in the region was approximately 2 : 3. As a whole, the general population—above all, the intelligentsia—is now searching for its own identity. A significant part preserves its common cultural bonds with Russia, which are manifested in many spheres of life, such as language, behavior, intellectual activity, work, and business. But the majority, and indeed a growing proportion of the population, belongs to the other camp, which is breaking with their "brothers around the former Soviet Union" and ever less inclined to identify with them in a cultural sense.

By the mid-1990s, Kazakhstan and Kyrgyzstan had acquired a somewhat different economic and social structure from that which they had inherited from the former Soviet division of labor. During the first half of the 1990s, they underwent a rapid process of "de-modernization" and signs of growing backwardness.

The downturn in modern production and de-industrialization, which accompanied a sharp reduction (in absolute and per capita terms) of production, consumption, and accumulation, was of course unavoidable for all the post-Soviet republics. However, in Central Asia (as in the Caucasus) de-modernization and the fall in the level of development have proven to be especially painful.

Although this process of economic regression in the Central Asian states is still not over, it is possible to offer a general characterization of the situation in these countries—their level and type of development as well as the structural peculiarities of individual national economies (see Table 4.2). Thus, the USSR bequeathed (in terms of sector balance) an "industrial-agrarian" economic structure in Kazakhstan, compared to an "agrarian-industrial" order in Uzbekistan and Kyrgyzstan.

Table 4.2

Main Characteristics of the Domestic Markets in Uzbekistan, Kazakhstan, and Kyrgyzstan

Country	Size of population[a] (millions of people)			Incomes of populace (millions of dollars) 1995		Expenditures of population (millions of dollars) 1995		Average wage (dollars)
	Jan. 1, 1996	2015	2025	Total	Per capita	Total	Per capita	June 1996
Uzbekistan	22.99	36.3	39.6	4,864	215	4,358	193	53
Kazakhstan	16.53	23.4	22	4,754	285	2,559	153	100
Kyrgyzstan	4.55	7.25	7	929	208	778	174	39

Sources: "Ekonomika stran Sodruzhestva nezavisimykh gosudarstv v pervom polugodii 1996 g.," *Delovoi mir,* 28 August 1996, p.4; Mezhgosudarstvennyi statisticheskii komitet Sodruzhestva nezavisimykh gosudarstv, *Statisticheskii biulleten',* 1996, no. 11, pp. 75–76; no. 13, pp. 56, 72; *Ekonomika i zhizn',* no. 4 (Jan. 1996), p. 2; "O prognoze chislennosti naseleniia SSSR," *Vestnik statistiki,* 1990, no. 10, "Finansy i statistika," p. 42; *Statistical Hamdbook 1995,* pp. 231, 271, 561; World Bank, *World Development Report 1994,* p. 210.

[a]Data for 1 January 1996, from Goskomstat SNG. The estimate for 2015 is a prognosis by the Goskomstat of the former USSR; this prognosis does not take into account, of course, the massive migration from Central Asia, which took the form of mass flight, in the early 1990s. The estimate for 2025 is that of the World Bank.

Significantly, however, these branch proportions corresponded to the larger Soviet framework for the division of labor; no heed was given to the scale of internal markets, transportation and labor costs, or the supply of raw materials and intermediate products. Once these countries acquired independence and began to form separate economies, the unified economic structure of the Soviet era was suddenly shattered. As a result, the proportions of production and employment in the Central Asian states are being increasingly determined by domestic factors—above all, by the size of the population and its purchasing power.

The small size of the domestic market, especially in the case of Kyrgyzstan, means that these countries cannot create an economic structure that is highly diversified and efficient, yet oriented primarily toward domestic demand. In that respect, only Uzbekistan has certain prospects, especially in the long-term perspective.

Nor can these states build an export-oriented manufacturing sector on a scale that would have a major impact on the macroeconomic proportions of their economies. The main obstacle here is the unfortunate geographic location: Central Asia is remote from the main centers of production and consumption in the world and until very recently did not have a developed infrastructure to access the main transportation arteries of the global economy. In addition, Uzbekistan not only lacks access to the sea but is encircled by countries that are also cut off from the sea. Furthermore, Russia and China, the countries closest to Central Asia and relatively more developed, are buffered by peripheral economic zones (Siberia and the northern Chinese provinces respectively). Given the inexorable process of internationalization and globalization, the problem of a disadvantageous geographic location can in principle be overcome. Still, it will undoubtedly continue to exert a negative impact on economic growth.

Notes

1. For an assessment of the consequences of Soviet modernization with respect to the Central Asian republics, see Boris Z. Rumer, *Soviet Central Asia. A Tragic Experiment* (London: Unwin Hyman, 1989).

2. Sh. Zakorov, *Problemy ratsional'nogo razmeshcheniia promyshlennosti Uzbekistana* (Tashkent, 1957), p. 77.

3. *Promyshlennost' SSSR* (Moscow, 1957), p. 77.

4. See Iu. Puzanov, *Kazakhstan: etapy ekonomicheskogo razvitiia* (Moscow, 1995).

5

Structural Changes

Boris Rumer and Stanislav Zhukov

Gross Domestic Product and Employment

The adaption to new post-Soviet conditions of development are reflected in the structure of production and employment. Moreover, the dynamics in the development of this structure bear distinctive characteristics in each of the individual states of Central Asia. The changes in the proportions of the main macrosectors of the GDP are determined by three factors: (1) the relative share held by sectors at the beginning of this period; (2) the change in relative prices on goods from these sectors; and, (3) the dynamics in the volume of output produced. The changes in the structure of GDP and employment are evident in Table 5.1 (pages 72–73).

As Table 5.1 shows, in Uzbekistan the structure of production had changed little by the mid-1990s. This rather "tranquil" rate of change in the structure of the GDP indicates that the relative prices for goods from the agricultural, industrial, and service sectors had changed at more or less the same rate. Production also contracted at approximately the same rates. It also bears noting that, in 1990, the proportional share of each sector was approximately one-third of the GDP.

The intensity of structural changes in the GDP was greatest in Kazakhstan. This is particularly evident if one examines the structure of production in current prices. Thus, between 1992 and 1996, agriculture's share of GDP fell from 23.4 percent to 12.6 percent;

conversely, the share of the service sector rose from 37.5 percent to 61.3 percent. The structure of the GDP (calculated in constant prices of the middle of the decade) did not suffer such significant changes, but does show an increase in the service sector. The sharp increase of prices on services and industrial goods has substantially exceeded the growth of prices in the agrarian sector, but the latter sector has also experienced a profound drop in output.

Kyrgyzstan has also experienced a fairly intense change in its structure of production. Although the share of the service sector in the GDP showed only an insignificant change, the proportion held by the agrarian sector increased, while that of industry fell drastically.

The situation in Tajikistan and Turkmenistan is more difficult to assess. In the case of Tajikistan, the share of industrial production in the GDP changed but little during this period. In general, the structure of production—at least, according to official statistics—changed but little. In Turkmenistan, official statistics obviously provide an inadequate picture of conditions; apparently, domestic prices there are completely divorced from any objective basis.

There were also significant changes in employment in the Central Asian states. Thus, three states—Kazakhstan, Kyrgyzstan, and Uzbekistan—reported a contraction in the proportion of those working in industry; this decrease was particularly pronounced in Kazakhstan and Kyrgyzstan. Kazakhstan also showed a fall in agricultural employment, but that decline was offset by increased employment in the service sector. The proportion of people working in the agrarian sector increased in Uzbekistan (6.5 percent), Kyrgyzstan (15.8 percent), and Tajikistan (11.4 percent). For its part, Turkmenistan showed a small increase of employment in agriculture, but in general the employment structure of that country had changed but little since the beginning of the decade.

Because monetary indicators in post-Soviet economies can be misleading, structural changes provide a more significant and precise indicator of the kind of changes now under way.

Profound change is also apparent in each of the macroeconomic sectors, with the development in industry being of particular interest.

Dynamics and Structure of Industrial Production

In the first half of the 1990s, industrial production took diametrically opposed lines of development in four Central Asian states (Kazakh-

Table 5.1

Structure of Gross Domestic Product and Work Force (in percent)

Country	Indicator	Sector	1990	1991	1992	1993	1994	1995	1996
Uzbekistan	Share of GDP	Agriculture	33.1	37.0	34.8	29.9	36.2	32.3	26.1
		Industry	22.4	22.4	26.1	26.1	24.0	17.9	19.7
		Construction	10.5	10.5	10.4	9.3	9.6	7.6	8.2
		Services	34.0	26.5	29.8	36.5	38.3	39.8	44.3
	Share of work force	Agriculture	39.3	41.9	43.5	44.6	44.3	43.7	43.5
		Industry	15.1	14.3	13.9	14.8	13.1	13.6	13.6
		Construction	8.9	8.2	7.2	·6.7	6.4	6.6	6.6
		Services	36.7	35.6	35.4	34.9	32.2	36.1	36.3
Kazakhstan	Share of GDP	Agriculture	34.5	28.1	23.4	16.1	14.8	12.8	12.6
		Industry		20.8	25.9	31.3	28.2	29.0	24.6
		Construction		12.0	10.0	7.8	10.5	10.8	6.4
		Services		32.7	36.0	37.5	45.2	45.4	56.2
	Share of work force	Agriculture	22.8	23.4	24.4	25.4	21.5	22.0	21.5[a]
		Industry		20.3	20.5	20.3	18.8	18.2	16.6
		Construction		12.0	10.3	10.1	9.0	7.3	5.6
		Services		44.9	45.8	45.2	46.8	53.0	55.8

(continued)

(Table 5.1 continued)

Country	Indicator	Sector	1990	1991	1992	1993	1994	1995	1996
Kyrgyzstan	Share of GDP	Agriculture	33.7	37.0	39.0	40.0	40.9	43.7	49.5
		Industry	27.0	28.5	33.0	25.7	30.9	16.8	12.7
		Construction	7.9	6.6	4.1	5.6	3.5	7.1	5.6
		Services	31.4	27.9	23.9	28.8	34.7	32.4	32.2
	Share of work force	Agriculture	32.7	35.5	38.2	39.0	42.0	42.0	49.2
		Industry	19.1	18.2	16.3	16.1	14.7	14.6	12.0
		Construction	8.8	8.4	6.2	5.3	4.7	4.7	3.9
		Services	39.4	37.9	39.3	39.6	38.6	38.7	34.9

Sources: Data from the national statistical agencies; S. Sazanov and B. Makhambetazhiev, "Sravnitel'nyi analiz ekonomicheskoi situatsii v Kazakhstane, Kyrgyzstane i Uzbekistane po itogam 1996 goda," *Aziia-ekonomika i zhizn'*, no. 22 (June 1997), p. 8; *Osnovnye pokazateli sotsial'no-ekonomicheskogo razvitiia Respubliki Uzbekistan v 1996 godu* (Tashkent, 1997), pp. 116, 151; Natsional'nyi statisticheskii komitet Kyrgyzskoi Respubliki, *Kyrgyzstan v tsifrakh. 1996* (Bishkek, 1996), p. 15; Natsional'nyi statisticheskii komitet Kyrgyzskoi Respubliki, *Kyrgyzstan v tsifrakh. 1994* (Bishkek, 1994), p. 13; *Statisticheskii biulleten'*, 1996, no. 2, pp. 82–85; no. 8, p. 101; no. 11, p. 87; no. 13, pp. 54–55, 70–71; *Statistical Handbook. 1996*, pp. 197, 199, 231, 233, 413, 415, 441–42, 503, 505.

Note: The table reflects the structure of gross added value. Given the inadequate reliability of data, Turkmenistan and Tajikistan have been omitted from the table.

[a]Estimates by the authors.

stan, Kyrgyzstan, Tajikistan, and Turkmenistan) and in Uzbekistan. In the first four countries, not a single branch of industry was able to avoid a most acute crisis; the contraction was especially salient in light industry, food processing, machine building and metalworking, and construction materials (see Table 5.2, pages 76-77). The smallest decrease occurred in electric power production. In addition, Turkmenistan reported a growth in the volume of production in metal working and light industry.

The situation in Uzbekistan was fundamentally different. Here a serious crisis beset only certain branches—metallurgy, the chemical industry, petrochemicals, and construction materials, which all reported a 33 to 47 percent drop in production from the 1990 levels. However, these decreases were offset by growth in fuels, light industry, and especially machine building and metalworking. As a result, the aggregate index for industrial production in 1995 was on the same level as it had been five years earlier. If one takes 1980 as the base year, industrial development in Uzbekistan has grown continuously and substantially for some twenty years.

This differential development in branch output has brought a major change in the structure of industrial production. The changes in relative prices have also had a substantial impact on the structure of industrial production. These factors have had their most beneficial effect on branches in the fuel and energy complex. In Turkmenistan, the aggregate share of fuel, energy, and electric power rose from 28.6 percent in 1985 to 55.3 percent in 1995. During the same decade, the proportion also increased in Kazakhstan (from 13.1 to 39.5 percent) and Uzbekistan (from 7.8 to 18.3 percent). Even Kyrgyzstan and Tajikistan, which do not have large hydrocarbon reserves, show an increase in the total production of fuel, energy, and electricity (mainly through an increase in the generation of electricity), with the same indicator rising from 4.4 to 21.0 percent in Kyrgyzstan and 4.8 to 20.7 percent in Tajikistan.

Another branch that has increased its share of industrial production is metallurgy. During the last decade, its proportion of industrial output rose from 7.6 to 37.8 percent in Tajikistan, from 17.4 to 26.7 percent in Kazakhstan, from 2.8 to 10.4 percent in Kyrgyzstan, and from 4.6 to 13.7 percent in Uzbekistan. Obviously, systematic deregulation of the fuel and energy market—an important production cost in metal production—will cause this indicator to rise.

Branches that have experienced a decrease in their share of industrial output include food processing and, especially, light industry. Specifically, the aggregate share of these branches fell in Uzbekistan from 53 to 29.2 percent, while increasing in Kazakhstan from 34.9 to 38.3 percent, in Turkmenistan from 52.8 to 22.2 percent, in Tajikistan from 62.2 to 23.6 percent, and in Kyrgyzstan from 54.1 to 38.6 percent.

One can draw the following general conclusions. First, with respect to the volume of industrial production, Kazakhstan, Kyrgyzstan, Tajikistan, and Turkmenistan have been thrown back several decades. The available statistical data make it possible to use 1985 for comparative purposes. However, to judge from considerable indirect evidence, the volume of industrial production in both countries has fallen to the level of the mid-1970s and, in some branches, even lower.

Second, the countries of Central Asia demonstrate a simplification of the branch structure of industrial production; a process that has been particularly salient in Kazakhstan, Kyrgyzstan, Tajikistan, and Turkmenistan. Thus, in Kazakhstan three branches alone—metallurgy, energy and fuels, and electric power—account for 64.6 percent of total industrial output. In Kyrgyzstan, the output from electric power, light, and food processing industries represented 59.4 percent of total industrial production in 1995. That same year, the energy and fuel industry, together with the electric power industry, accounted for 55.4 percent of gross industrial output. In Tajikistan, electric power and metal industries were responsible for 58.1 percent of total industrial production. By contrast, the industrial structure in Uzbekistan is relatively more balanced, with certain opportunities to develop not only the fuel and energy and metallurgical branches, but also light industry, food processing, and machine building and metalworking.

Third, the volume of industrial production in the Central Asian states remains very low in both absolute and per capita terms. Thus, the gross added value in industry was 4.117 billion dollars (248 dollars per capita) in Kazakhstan, 1.903 billion dollars (85 dollars per capita) in Uzbekistan, 1.106 billion dollars in Turkmenistan (247 dollars per capita), 0.242 billion dollars (54 dollars per capita) in Kyrgyzstan, and 0.213 billion dollars (37 dollars per capita) in Tajikistan.

Capital Accumulation

The extremely sharp economic decline in the states of Central Asia has also had a profound impact on the investment sphere. Because of the

Table 5.2

Dynamics and Structure of Industrial Production

Country	Branch	Structure of output[a] 1985	1995	Volume of production 1990 = 100
Uzbekistan	Electric power	3.8	7.5	87.0
	Fuel and energy	4.0	10.8	109.0
	Metallurgy	4.6	13.7	67.0
	Chemicals and petrochemicals	5.5	5.5	53.0
	Machine building and metalworking	11.2	8.9	145.0
	Construction materials	5.9	6.6	57.0
	Light industry	38.8	19.9	25.0
	Food processing	14.3	9.3	102.0
	Total Industry			101.6
Kazakhstan	Electric power	4.6	17.0	73.0
	Fuel and energy	8.5	22.5	60.0
	Metallurgy	17.4	26.7	67.0
	Chemicals and petrochemicals	6.0	3.9	23.0
	Machine building and metalworking	10.9	7.6	32.0
	Construction materials	6.1	3.9	18.0
	Light industry	16.2	27.9	16.0
	Food processing	18.7	10.4	30.0
	Total industry			47.0
Kyrgyzstan	Electric power	3.4	17.0	107
	Fuel and energy	1.0	4.0	52
	Metallurgy	2.8	10.4	80
	Chemicals and petrochemicals	0.6	0.2	13
	Machine building and metalworking	20.2	9.7	39

(continued)

(Table 5.2 continued)

Country	Branch	Source of output[a] 1985	1995	Volume of production 1990 = 100
Kyrgyzstan	Construction materials	4.3	3.7	47
	Light industry	27.9	17.7	41
	Food processing	26.2	20.9	56
	Total industry			57
Turkmenistan	Electric power	4.3	7.9	88
	Fuel and energy	24.3	47.4	46
	Metallurgy	0.2	0.1	77
	Chemicals and petrochemicals	3.6	2.9	42
	Machine building and metalworking	5.8	1.5	121
	Construction materials	6.5	3.7	71
	Light industry	39.2	16.2	109
	Food processing	13.6	6.0	88
	Total industry			66
Tajikistan	Electric power	3.9	20.3	95
	Fuel and energy	0.9	0.4	10
	Metallurgy	7.6	37.8	48
	Chemicals and petrochemicals	4.0	5.0	19
	Machine building and metalworking	9.0	3.8	33
	Construction materials	5.1	1.3	8
	Light industry	46.6	16.9	69
	Food processing	15.6	6.7	26
	Total industry			48

Sources for calculations: Statisticheskii biulleten', 1996, no. 2, p. 11; no. 8, p. 102; no. 11, pp. 96–97; *Statisticheskii sbornik*, 1993; World Bank, *Gosudarstva byvshego Sovetskogo Soiuza*, 1993, p. 736; *Statistical Handbook 1995*, pp. 261–62, 299–300, 589–90.
[a]In current prices.

contraction of subsidies from the former all-union budget and the breakdown of cooperation relations among enterprises that now found themselves on opposite sides of state borders, the level of capital investment in Kazakhstan in 1996 dropped to just 13.1 percent of its 1990 level. The equivalent indicator is 48.1 percent for Kyrgyzstan and 65.2 percent for Uzbekistan. As a result, the absolute volume of capital investments in 1996 barely exceeded 1 billion dollars in Kazakhstan and 4 billion dollars in Uzbekistan. Only Turkmenistan, if one is to accept the official statistics, managed to increase investment, but one can hardly assume that such investments were effectively utilized.

Unfortunately, the basic statistical data about capital accumulation and investments, which are of low quality at best, at times become positively phantasmagoric. Therefore any conclusions about the dynamics of the investment process in Central Asian states must remain highly tentative and approximate. And since it is not possible to construct long-term statistical series based on a single method, to a significant degree one must rely upon analogy and comparisons of parallel short-term series of different data sets.

These data indicate that the gross accumulation of fixed capital (a standard international category) is roughly approximate to the concept of "capital investment" that prevails in Soviet and post-Soviet statistics. In any event, in Kyrgyzstan (for which we have the most detailed set of data and which, undoubtedly, has gone the furthest in adapting its system of national accounts to generally accepted requirements) the difference between these two indicators in 1990–95 was only 2 percentage points of the GDP. The validity of this conclusion is confirmed by data for Kazakhstan in 1993. In Uzbekistan, however, the norm of capital investments that year was almost double the analogous indicator obtained from the standard international methodology. Thus, the statistics of national accounts in Uzbekistan are still remote from generally accepted standards. This conclusion is also confirmed by the significant discrepancies between various series of data for 1990–91.

In the first half of the 1990s, the norm of capital accumulation fell in all three countries. In 1991–94, it shrank to approximately 20 percent in Kazakhstan, and to 10 percent in Kyrgyzstan. In 1995, the situation in both countries began to move in opposite directions. Whereas Kyrgyzstan succeeded in restoring the investment level to that at the start of the decade, Kazakhstan experienced a sharp decrease—from 20 to 10 percent of the 1990 level. In Uzbekistan, where deregulation of the economy has been more limited than in the other two countries, the dynamics of accumulation have been highly contradictory. But one thing is clear: in the first half of the 1990s, Uzbekistan pumped a larger part of its GDP into investment than Kazakhstan and Kyrgyzstan were able to do. Indeed, in 1995 it succeeded in increasing this quotient to 27.5 percent.

Preliminary data for 1996 indicate that the volume of investments continued to increase in Uzbekistan and, especially, Kyrgyzstan, but fell by another 40 percent in Kazakhstan. The next few years will show whether the investment process in Uzbekistan and Kyrgyzstan in fact proves to be stable and enduring. For the moment, it appears likely that, in the case of Kyrgyzstan, the relative success of 1995–96 may remain unsurpassed in the near future, for that upsurge was due exclusively to an influx of foreign capital. Moreover, this capital infusion was directed largely at developing the large gold field of Kumtor; that single project consumes nearly half of all the investments from abroad. For the time being, however, the republic has no other investment projects of a magnitude comparable to that of Kumtor.

In Uzbekistan, until recently the investment process has relied primarily on internal sources. But one should take into account that this republic not only has created maximally favorable conditions for foreign capital, but also offers broad opportunities for profitable investment. Consequently, it seems reasonable to expect a sharp growth of foreign investments in the Uzbek economy and, hence, a rise in the norm of accumulation.

Foreign capital is also having a salient impact on the investment process in Kazakhstan. Suffice it to say that, in 1994, the proportion of direct foreign investments in total capital investments rose to 36.7 percent (compared to 27.6 percent a year earlier). According to data compiled by the experts at the National (Central) Bank of Kazakhstan, foreign sources provided financing for 48.7 percent of total capital investment in 1996. In view of the current economic situation and the economic policies announced for 1997–98, this indicator can be expected to increase.

At the same time, one cannot overlook the fact that, if in 1993–94 the absolute scale of capital investments in dollar equivalents in Kazakhstan and Uzbekistan was almost equal, in 1995 the correlation had shifted to 1.56 : 1 in favor of Uzbekistan. And this occurred notwithstanding the fact that, right until the mid-1990s, direct foreign investment in Kazakhstan substantially surpassed the level found in Uzbekistan.

Such a large gap is explained by the differences in the approaches used to mobilize domestic savings. Kazakhstan, like Kyrgyzstan, counted on a collective or group privatization and the formation of an Anglo-American scheme for mobilizing free monetary resources (through the mechanism of the stock market). In Uzbekistan, by contrast, the state continues to shape the investment flow by implementing numerous programs to sponsor branch and sector development. Moreover, the savings of the Uzbek populace are subject to significantly tighter regulation. On the one hand, administrative controls over the hard-currency market and massive prophylactic measures in the sphere of trade make it possible to restrict (at least substantially, if not totally) popular use of the dollar as legal tender or means of savings.

On the other hand, the government of Uzbekistan has designed several plans to link personal savings and capital accumulation in a single process. The most striking example here is the project to organize the assembly of passenger cars by a South Korean firm, Daewoo. Simultaneous with the launching of this large investment project, the government of Uzbekistan has authorized the commercial bank "Asaka" to extend long-term loans to individual purchasers. The credits are extended at a rate of 4 to 7 percent per annum for a term of up to seven years; the credit can amount to as much as 65 percent of the value of the automobile being purchased. This program, as part of the investment project, is thus creating additional purchasing power and demand; that will make it possible to achieve both recoupment of the project investment and to channel personal spending (i.e., savings) toward those branches given top priority in the state's investment policy. This is a typical example of a selective, targeted approach, which enables one to concentrate investments, production, and consumption on critical junctures in the economy. The experience of South Korea—from which Uzbekistan borrowed the strategy of a prioritized selective approach—shows that this approach may not necessarily be successful. However, the attempt to link production and consumption in a single process is undoubtedly more promising than no plan at all. In most post-Soviet states, consumer demand is satisfied by sources outside the national economy, thereby increasing the volume of imports.

It seems that this attempt to coordinate industrial and investment policy will prove successful. On the one hand, there is a strong demand for passenger cars in Uzbekistan. On the other hand, the production from this joint-venture (Uzbek–South Korean) enterprise will probably be exported to the neighboring Central Asian countries and Russia, for product price and characteristics will almost certainly give them a secure niche in the post-Soviet marketplace.

There is every reason to think that the role of local institutional factors in mobilizing domestic savings will continue to grow. At the same time, there are substantial differences in the potential volumes of domestic savings that these three states can mobilize. Thus, in 1993–95 the population of Kyrgyzstan succeeded in saving an average of 12 percent of their income (approximately 90 million dollars) per year, and these savings are dispersed among a large number of holders. The optimal mechanism for mobilizing these modest, scattered resources is a savings bank. In principle, Kyrgyzstan inherited such a banking system (with an extensive network of regional branch offices) from the former Sberbank. But the Kyrgyz Sberbank took no role in the investment process and instead followed a policy typical of the post-Soviet commercial banks; indeed, by the spring of 1996, it had become essentially bankrupt.[1]

This was already the second shock for depositors, who had not forgotten the confiscatory measures of the early 1990s. Revealingly, the confiscatory experiments of the last Soviet governments and the chaos that followed the breakdown of a single economic system in the USSR have undermined popular confidence in official banking institutions. Indeed, so much so, that in 1992–93 the population of Kyrgyzstan put nearly all its savings into the purchase of hard currency. The relative financial stabilization and the high interest rates for bank deposits have somewhat reversed this situation; as a result, in 1994, only 54.5 percent of personal savings were used to purchase hard currency. But, given that this indicator rose to 60 percent in 1995, it is questionable whether the depositors, especially those who are most active and mobile, and who hold the bulk of the savings, will retain their confidence in an uncertain financial institution. It is more likely that in 1998 the population will prefer the dollar, and that is entirely rational behavior given the low inflation, stable exchange rates, and mounting crisis in quasi-banking institutions.[2]

Kazakhstan, in contrast to Kyrgyzstan, has a norm of personal savings that is three times greater, amounting to 45–46 percent of their annual income. In a dollar equivalent, annual savings in 1993–95 amounted to about 1.3 billion dollars per annum. However, until 1994, the people here used up to 80 percent of the personal savings to purchase foreign currency. Thereafter, this indicator fell to 40.7 percent (1994) and then 21.8 percent (1995) of total savings. However, the reorientation of substantial means (in absolute and relative terms) to promote accumulation in the means of production (i.e., investments to create and support productive capacities) is impeded by the lack of specialized financial institutions, such as the development banks found in South Korea.

The opportunities for mobilizing personal savings in Uzbekistan are considerably more modest. The ratio of savings to income here fell to 10 percent in 1995. Given that Uzbekistan made a gradual and socially oriented transition to a market economy a chief priority, the incomes—and still more the savings—of the population will continue to grow, but slowly. In addition, the state does all that it can to prevent a sharp increase of the disparities in the income distribution, a policy that further retards the formation of investment potential.

One should also take into account that, the large Uzbek family has many children and hence special obligatory expenditures that devour a significant part of its savings. Above all, this concerns the dowry for brides and the minimum grant of material belongings given to a young man when he comes of age and leaves the parental home. Similarly, there are imperative (and substantial) ritual expenditures for birthdays, circumcision, death, and the like. All these factors inevitably reduce the role of personal savings as a basis for capital accumulation.

The preliminary plans on economic policy in 1996–98 make clear that an expansion of the domestic sources for investment cannot be expected. And this is particularly true in the case of Kazakhstan and Kyrgyzstan. The incomes of the population, to a still greater degree than earlier, will be used to pay for current consumption. This is all the more likely given the plans for a "shock" commercialization of the housing sector and the entire social sphere.[3]

To preserve the chosen variants of development in Kazakhstan and Kyrgyzstan, the hopes for a substantial increase in the state's investment role are rather illusory. In the course of convulsions of the first half of the 1990s, the government in both countries lost important sources of income. For example, the chaotic deregulation of foreign trade deprived both Kazakhstan and Kyrgyzstan of a traditional source of revenue. As a result, in 1995 the budget revenues of Kazakhstan fell to 18.4 percent of the GDP; in Kyrgyzstan the same indicator was 17.3 percent. As a result, both governments began to have a rising budget deficit. For example, during 1994–96, this deficit in Kyrgyzstan virtually never dipped below 5 percentage points of the GDP. Under such conditions, the only way for the state to expand its investment activity is to rely upon foreign loans.

The large-scale reduction of state expenditures for the social sphere may help somewhat to alleviate the budget deficit. In any case, such is the strategy countenanced by authorities in Kazakhstan. Nevertheless, this can at most be a modest level of cost-cutting; this re-channeling of resources to investment will amount to only 1 to 2 percent of the GDP, which cannot fundamentally change the situation.

In addition, the funds from such cost-cutting in Kazakhstan will be needed to support and maintain an economic and transportation infrastructure that is undergoing rapid degradation. A normally functioning infrastructure is a prerequisite for the transition to economic growth. But virtually all the components of the infrastructure are extremely capital-intensive, require a long period for recoupment, and—with very few exceptions—yield a low level of profit.

Thus, the unprecedented investment crisis in these countries in 1990–95 entailed not only a substantial decrease in the absolute scale of investments, but also in the sharp fall in the norm of accumulation (especially in Kyrgyzstan and Kazakhstan). Their economies not only lack the conditions and mechanisms to mobilize savings, but the savings are so meager that even their maximum utilization cannot provide substantial assistance in stimulating economic growth.

In part, the investment "famine" is alleviated by the influx of foreign capital, which has come to acquire growing influence in the process of capital formation in Central Asia.

This is due not only to financial-economic, but also technical-economic factors: none of the newly independent states of Central Asia produces capital goods and must import virtually all their machines and equipment. In Kazakhstan, the import of machinery and equipment amounted to 60–80 percent of all capital investment in 1994–95; the corresponding indicators in 1995 were 50 percent for Uzbekistan and 35 percent for Kyrgyzstan. The lower indicators in the latter two countries are due to the specific features of the investment projects being financed by foreign capital. Thus, the development of the Kumtor project in Kyrgyzstan, for example, demands substantial geological exploratory work, preparation of deposits for exploitation, and large-scale construction and infrastructure improvements. The cost of machinery and equipment in such projects is usually lower than the average level.

The available statistics on capital investment is fragmentary, but does show that the lion's share of new investments flowed into such sectors as electric power, oil, natural gas, and ferrous and nonferrous metallurgy. The proportion of capital channeled into manufacturing did not exceed 5 to 10 percent of total investments.

Even within the context of the economic crisis in Central Asia, this structure of capital investment is anything but optimal. For example, Uzbekistan is attempting to pursue a more or less conscious policy, in the investment sphere included. Nevertheless, the structure of its capital investments in 1996 does not, in our opinion, correspond either to the basic characteristics of the national economy or to the current economic situation.

First, a disproportionately large part of the investments went for non-productive construction (including housing), as well as transportation and communications. Indeed, the nonproductive sphere and the infrastructure consume over half of all the country's investments in fixed capital. This apparently reflects the inertia of the construction and investment complex that had developed in the Soviet era. To be sure, the social sphere and infrastructure are critically important for the economic development of a country. However, the extremely low level of personal income (and no growth can be expected here in the near future), together with the limited resources at the disposal of the state, do not allow Uzbekistan to divert so large a share of its investment capital to nonproductive construction.

Second, and most important, this investment policy discriminates against the agricultural sector as well as light industry (including textiles). As has already been noted, agriculture accounts for 26.1 percent of the GDP and 43.5 percent of the labor force in Uzbekistan. However, this sector received only 6.9 percent of the aggregate capital investment. Similarly, only 4.0 percent of the capital investment went for light industry and textiles. Paradoxically, Uzbekistan has some relative advantages in the agricultural sector, but has made scant attempts to exploit them.

Labor

Geography is a serious obstacle to linking Central Asia with global manufacturing, but it is not the only problem. In particular, one must not overlook the special characteristics of the local labor force. More-over, the work force in Kazakhstan and Kyrgyzstan is markedly differ-ent from that in Uzbekistan. Thus, in Kazakhstan and Kyrgyzstan (as elsewhere in most of the post-Soviet space), employees have gone through the "school of socialist labor" that essentially renders them unfit for working in export-oriented industries financed with foreign capital. Specifically, their inability to perform intense and monotonous work, their lack of a work ethic (essentially for performing work pre-cisely and on schedule), their disparaging and indifferent attitude to-ward product quality, the massive scale of drunkenness—all this had become typical of the Soviet labor force by the 1980s.

Moreover, the economic chaos of the late 1980s and early 1990s led to a disorganization and breakdown of the industrial labor force. The loss of traditional suppliers and sales markets, the years of undercapac-ity utilization (or complete nonutilization) of enterprises, the disinte-gration of branches in the military-industrial complex (where the employees were superior in terms of their qualitative characteristics)—all these factors have accelerated the degeneration of the labor force. This process was all the more intense because the years of economic catastrophe have been accompanied by a profound crisis in social cul-ture and worldview.

Nor should one nourish illusions about fresh labor resources that come to the workplace for the first time. In East Asia, and more re-cently in Indo-China, the success of export-oriented manufacturing conveyors is ensured by the merciless exploitation of a never ending stream of migrants from rural areas. At first glance, Central Asia might appear to enjoy the same potential. In fact, however, the Central Asian youths who reach working age and come to the city have not traversed the harsh school of family-based agriculture—the key trait of new labor in the newly industrialized and developing states of Asia. Even if the Central Asian family has an extensive household plot under culti-vation, that only plays a subsidiary role to work on the sovkhoz or kolkhoz.

The young generations in post-Soviet republics (and Kazakhstan and Kyrgyzstan are no exception) are further corrupted by the obliga-tory system of general education. This has long since turned into a profanation; almost automatically, it confers the stamp of "literate" without regard to individual intellectual efforts and successes. The massive exodus of specialists and teachers from Central Asia (most of whom come from the "nontitular"—that is, nonindigenous population), together with the massive reduction in budget expenditures, have dealt a devastating blow to the existing system of education.

The entire life experience of young people (as in the experience of older generations) tells them that one's success has absolutely nothing to do with individual effort. Hence it is difficult to entice them with the prospect of onerous, low-paid work on a modern industrial conveyor. The most active and energetic youths have found a high-income niche in the emerging private sector, in the branch offices of foreign companies and organizations, and—in the worst case—in the "shuttle trade." In a few years, this stratum will provide the managers and directors of modern capitalist enterprises. The problem, however, is that success in exporting requires a hard-working, disciplined labor force, not just managers and directors.

Nor can these problems even be offset by the relatively low cost of labor. Indeed, by the mid-1990s, the monthly wage in Kazakhstan has already surpassed 100 dollars on average and even the 200–dollar level in industry.

Under these conditions, Kazakhstan and Kyrgyzstan place their main hopes on the development of an export-oriented extractive industry. Kazakhstan, moreover, has become reoriented toward the exports from its ferrous and nonferrous metallurgy, where the output requires a low level of processing. In the first half of the 1990s, neither Kazakhstan nor Kyrgyzstan established any new lines of production. Nor do they seem likely to do so in the next few years, with two significant exceptions: (1) the gold field Kumtor in Kyrgyzstan, which, beginning in 1997, will extract 15 to 20 tons of gold per year; and, (2) the project of the American oil corporation Chevron to develop the Tengiz oil deposits in Kazakhstan.

Two current factors help to make this production competitive on international markets. First, as in the other post-Soviet republics, Central Asia has no meaningful ecological norms or requirements to prevent environmental pollution by enterprises. Given the lack of ecological costs in production, it is possible to produce goods that are significantly cheaper, even if environmentally harmful. Second, the current crisis encourages enterprises to exhaust their fixed capital, without any middle-term strategy or investment policy. This too substantially reduces production costs and, in the short term, makes production competitive.

Although the Soviet work ethic has also taken root in Uzbekistan, the work force there is better suited for the creation of an export-oriented manufacturing sector. Important factors here include the long culture of settled agriculture and the persistence of a traditional way of life; these served to prevent distortions in the "structure of everyday life" and the massive dissemination of drunkenness, especially in rural areas. Incidentally, the same is true of southern Kyrgyzstan, where the population has been historically bound to Islam and, until recently, engaged in agriculture. Paradoxical as it might seem, Uzbekistan can also draw on the experience of the Soviet era: for several months each year, the entire population over age fifteen is subject to compulsory mobilization to perform labor-intensive, unskilled work helping with the cotton harvest.

Although labor costs in Uzbekistan are still relatively low, it is not clear that this will compensate for the inauspicious geographic location and for the many other negative factors, such as the acute shortage of water resources.

Like the other two states, Uzbekistan is actively developing its extractive sector, above all, to mine gold and uranium ores. Together with cotton, these specialized products constitute the backbone of the national economy and ensure a flow of hard-currency earnings.

In short, notwithstanding some distinctive characteristics, the economy of Uzbekistan—in terms of main parameters—differs little from that of Kazakhstan or Kyrgyzstan. The domestic market in all three states is extremely small, and production is poorly diversified. That profile has persisted for a rather protracted period of time. In the more remote perspective, Kazakhstan plans to become a world-class exporter of hydrocarbons; Kyrgyzstan seeks to produce precious metals; and Uzbekistan aims to diversify its national economy and achieve a relatively balanced development of the agriculture, mining, and manufacturing sectors. But a number of objective and subjective factors impede the realization of these plans; in the best case scenario, they will not be realized anytime before the onset of the next century.

Demographic Growth and Employment

The dearth of domestic investment is hardly the only impediment to economic progress in the states of Central Asia: another key factor is the high rate of population growth. And because youthful strata predominate in the population structure, the working-age population is growing at particularly high rates.

Rough calculations indicate that, in the period 1995–2000, if these three republics are to provide jobs for newcomers to the labor market, they must annually create a huge number of new jobs—between 207,000 and 233,000 jobs in Uzbekistan, and between 64,000 and 76,000 jobs in Kyrgyzstan. To put these figures in perspective, in 1990–95 Uzbekistan was able to create only 45,000 jobs per year; the comparable figure for Kyrgyzstan was 21,500 jobs per year. In the period 2000–25, Uzbekistan will have to resolve a no less difficult task: create about 105,000 to 166,000 jobs per year. In Kyrgyzstan, however, the demand for new jobs will stagnate or gradually decrease (falling to 16,000 to 23,000 jobs per year).

Until recently, Kazakhstan has been in a relatively better situation in this respect. Thanks to the massive exodus of nonindigenous inhabitants, Kazakhs—in massive numbers—have taken over the most attractive of these recently vacated positions. It seems that the departure of the nonindigenous population will continue in the second half of the 1990s, though at a slower rate. In the most extreme variant, in the second half of the 1990s Kazakhstan will have to create at least 108,000 new jobs per year. But in the first half of the decade Kazakhstan lost more than a million jobs; hence the transition to a regime of expanding employment will be especially difficult here. In this regard, it is even advantageous for Kazakhstan to continue the massive emigration of the nonindigenous population. And, apart from everything else, this also accords nicely with the popular idea of a renaissance of the Kazakh nation and creating a state of Kazakhs.

In 1990–95, employment fell by 1,213,000 in Kazakhstan and by 108,000 in Kyrgyzstan. Only in Uzbekistan did the number of jobs increase (by 217,000). Moreover, in Kazakhstan and Kyrgyzstan, the scale of jobs lost and the level of official unemployment are significantly smaller than the decrease in production. In Uzbekistan, where GDP fell by 18 percent, the number of jobs actually increased by 3 percent.

The contribution of the main macrosectors to the growth, or contraction, of employment has been extremely uneven among the three countries over time. In Kazakhstan, during the first half of the 1990s (and for the whole period of 1980 to 1995), the decrease in jobs has been relatively evenly spread among industry, agriculture, and construction. Employment in the service sector, however, has sharply increased over the last fifteen years. For the period of 1990–95 in Kyrgyzstan, the decrease in employment mainly affected industry and construction. Employment in the agrarian sector, by contrast, increased. Altogether, during this fifteen-year period in Kyrgyzstan, two-thirds of the new jobs were in agriculture, with the remaining third being in the service sector. In Uzbekistan (during this same period, 1980–95), employment increased in all sectors, but the overwhelming mass of new jobs were in agriculture. Calculations also show that in Kyrgyzstan and especially in Uzbekistan, in the 1990s the agrarian sector substantially increased its role in absorbing new members of the work force.

These patterns in production and employment all point to mounting demographic pressure. And this labor surfeit comes amidst a profound decrease in production and a chronic deficit of investments. Taken together, these factors have a distorting impact on the structure and efficiency of the economy.

Above all, the excess employees at plants will contribute to the decline in labor productivity (measured as the volume of output per worker). In 1990–95, labor productivity in Kazakhstan fell by 46 percent in the economy as a whole, 28 percent in agriculture, 33 percent in industry, 88 percent in construction, and 56 percent in the service sector. In the same period, the same indicator for Kyrgyzstan dropped 54 percent in the economy as a whole, 49 percent in agriculture, 51 percent in industry, 29 percent in construction, and 40 percent in the service sector. In Uzbekistan, the decline in labor productivity was less substantial—some 20 percent for the economy as whole (with the decrease being concentrated in agriculture and construction). In industry and construction, labor productivity actually increased by 12 percent.

Foreign Economic Ties

There have also been profound changes in the interaction between the Central Asian states and the world economy. Unfortunately, the Soviet national economy was so constructed as to preclude any kind of rigorous, detailed comparison between the present situation and that earlier period, when republics formed part of a framework with a division of labor oriented toward the domestic Soviet market. In the best of cases, it is only possible to identify several basic tendencies.

By the beginning of the 1990s, the three Central Asian countries had

Table 5.3

Exports and Imports as Share of the GDP (in percent; based on current prices)

Indicator	Country	1990	1991	1992	1993	1994	1995
Exports	Uzbekistan	28.8	31.7	33.8	44.7	53.3	31.0
	Kazakhstan	16.8[a]	19.2[a]	53.1	33.1	26.6	31.1
	Kyrgyzstan	29.8	37.8	34.4	31.4	30.8	28.3
Imports	Uzbekistan	45.2	34.9	43.2	40.3	47.2	28.9
	Kazakhstan	28.9[a]	25.4[a]	62.1	39.4	28.8	23.9
	Kyrgyzstan	50.6	39.2	46.1	23.6	28.4	37.2
Balance	Uzbekistan	−16.4	−3.2	− 9.4	4.3	6.1	2.1
	Kazakhstan	−12.1	−6.2	− 9.0	−6.3	−2.2	7.2
	Kyrgyzstan	−20.8	−1.4	−11.7	7.8	2.8	−6.9

Sources for calculations: Statisticheskii biulleten', 1996, no. 13, pp. 55, 60, 65, 71, 76; no. 11, pp.75, 117; *Statistical Handbook 1995*, pp. 234, 276, 565; European Bank for Reconstruction and Development, *Transition Report* (London, 1994), p. 160.

[a]The indicators for Kazakhstan in 1990 and 1991 are calculated by experts from the European Bank for Reconstruction and Development; they are not entirely compatible with the other data.

an enormously unfavorable balance of trade: 20.8 percent of the GDP in Kyrgyzstan, 16.4 percent in Uzbekistan, and 12.1 percent in Kazakhstan (see Table 5.3). Attempts to correct this situation were undertaken, but in 1992 the excess of imports over exports was still running at 10 percent of the GDP. Only the onset of the Gaidar reforms in Russia (a key provision of which was to reduce the subsidies to former republics) forced the Central Asian countries to take serious steps to balance their foreign trade flows. To be sure, right up to 1994, this process was driven more by spontaneous actions than the impact of any system of well-considered measures. From time to time, trade wars erupted among the republics, further aggravating the contraction of interrepublic flows of physical resources. More important, they forced producers—confronted by the inability of their consumers to pay—to reduce sharply or to stop altogether the delivery of goods.

A number of factors forced the Central Asian states to seek solvent consumers outside the former USSR. Once enterprises were deprived of their traditional markets, many found that their sole hope for survival was to export to more effective markets. In addition, amidst the massive contraction of subsidies from the Russian budget, only the expansion of exports could enable the state to sustain a minimum level of critical imports, such as foodstuffs, medicines, and the resources to process agricultural crops. It bears noting, too, that these export-import operations also contributed to the instantaneous, personal enrichment of the party-soviet nomenklatura; the latter had become aggressively commercialized, consolidated their positions of power everywhere, and were thereby able to convert their power into foreign bank accounts. Finally, the efforts of all post-Soviet states to expand imports elicited maximum support from the International Monetary Fund (IMF) and the World Bank. These Breton Woods organizations have exerted a decisive influence on the economic policies in Kyrgyzstan since 1993 and in Kazakhstan since 1994, and their influence has substantially increased in Uzbekistan since 1995. Given that foreign loans and credits play an even greater role in the economy of these Central Asian states, stable export earnings become a reliable guarantee of repayment.

During 1992–95, the exports of Kyrgyzstan (for which the data are most complete) increased by 1.44 times, while the exports to markets outside the CIS rose by 1.82 times. As a result, the so-called far abroad (non-CIS countries) increased their share of total exports from 27 to 34 percent. In Kazakhstan, during these same four years exports to the non-CIS countries rose 1.68 times, as their share rose to 47.1 percent of total exports. In Uzbekistan, during the same period, exports to non-CIS countries rose by 2.06 times and came to constitute 57.6 percent of total exports.

Such a substantial increase in exports was not always reflected in the national statistics. In 1990–95, only Kazakhstan reported a substantial increase in the proportion of exports in the GDP; by contrast, the increase in Kyrgyzstan and Uzbekistan was insignificant. Such radically different dynamics was due to the substantial differences in the policy on exchange rates: the nominal exchange rate—the basis for calculating foreign trade flows in the national currency—in effect determines what kind of export and import quotas will result.

Kyrgyzstan offers a case where the policy of financial stabilization and suppression of inflation concentrates narrowly on a nominal exchange rate. The exchange rate is a key price in all post-Soviet economies. As a result, inflation in post-Soviet states depends heavily on the exchange rates. A combination of the fixed nominal exchange rate, low inflation, and an insignificant increase in exports leads to an apparent freezing of the share of exports in the GDP.

That was approximately the situation in Kyrgyzstan in 1994–95. The architects of stabilization placed the main emphasis on reducing the level of inflation, and in fact achieved their goal. At the same time, the price of such stabilization was restoring the export sector to its "donor" role. The artificially high exchange rate of the Kyrgyz *som* leads to a redistribution of profit from the export branches to an inefficient agricultural sector and to those industrial branches that service domestic demand. In addition to increasing the donor burden on exports, the high exchange rate stimulates imports: during 1992–95, Kyrgyzstan's import rose by 1.36 times, including an increase of nearly threefold from non-CIS countries.

Because the unfavorable balance of trade during this period amounted to about 100 million dollars per annum, Kyrgyzstan increasingly shifted from reliance on CIS subventions (mainly Russia) to support from international financial agencies. Apparently, the government assumes that by keeping the country afloat for a few years (through foreign credits and loans), it will succeed in putting an export-oriented extraction industry into operation. However, as has been pointed out, the prospects of expanding its exports in such a volume where it could both pay off its creditors and finance dynamic economic growth are exceedingly problematic.[4]

Although, the historical givens here may leave no alternatives, one cannot fail to be alarmed by the rapid growth in Kyrgyzstan's foreign indebtedness—both in absolute and relative terms. This escalating debt threatens to aggravate what is already a difficult macroeconomic situation. In 1994, its foreign debt reached 441 million dollars—a sum that equals 130 percent of annual exports and 17 to 40 percent of the GDP. One should also bear in mind too that once export incomes are corrected (by excluding barter and clearing transactions), the ratio of indebtedness to exports rises significantly.

Uzbekistan has also consigned exports to a "donor" role and indeed has made this integral to the basic logic of its economic reforms. It does this through a variety of devices. Thus, to a significant degree, the state has preserved its direct centralized control over export earnings. Another instrument is its policy on exchange rates. In 1994–95, Uzbekistan had several exchange rates, including the official exchange rate of the Central Bank, a special exchange rate for noncash transactions among commercial banks and their clients, a commercial rate for cash at exchange centers, and the going rate on the "black market." In the course of two years, the exchange rate of the Central Bank was 15 to 25 percent lower than the rate on the free market. At the same time, in contrast to Kyrgyzstan and Kazakhstan, in 1993–95 Uzbekistan had a favorable balance of trade. Its foreign indebtedness is also growing but, to judge from the ratio of indebtedness to exports and GDP, Uzbekistan does not assume a major risk and can, for the meantime, expand its borrowing on world financial markets.

The situation is somewhat different in Kazakhstan, where the exports in 1990–95 rose from 16.8 to 31.1 percent of the GDP. To be sure, part of the export incomes here is diverted to support other sectors of the economy. However, both the export sector itself (ferrous and nonferrous metallurgy; the oil industry) and the sectors that service them (above all, electric power) are in dire straits. The renewal of fixed capital (which has long since become obsolescent and depleted), the rationalization and modernization of technological processes, and indeed the simple need to maintain machinery for export-oriented production in working condition—all this demands large-scale capital investment, not to mention the expenditures for current operations. Kazakhstan can neither allow the looming collapse of its export sector, nor impose a substantial donor burden of supporting other sectors. The bulk of export income must remain directly in the export energy branches. These facts force the country to support a realistic nominal exchange rate for the national currency.

In 1994–95, the real exchange rate for the Kazakh tenge rose 1.65 times. At the same time, the country's foreign debt grew to nearly 3 billion dollars, which equals 15–22 percent of the GDP and 85 percent of exports. If barter and clearing deliveries are subtracted from the export totals, the ratio of foreign debt to exports amounted to 254 percent in 1994. To be sure, this index (to judge from preliminary data) subsequently fell to 128 percent.

The growth in the real exchange rate of the national currency is, during this period of transition economies, an organic part of the financial stabilization paradigm. Through the skillful manipulation of interest rates and through the use of complex financial instruments, the state can accumulate most of the hard-currency export earnings and use these to create hard-currency reserves. In Kazakhstan, for example, by 1 July 1996 the net international reserves of the National (Central) Bank amounted to more than 1 billion dollars; two years earlier, these had been virtually nonexistent. Naturally, the gold and hard-currency reserves of transition states are placed in first-class international banks. Thus, the growth in the value of the national currency in real terms solves the most important task of raising the country's credit rating on capital borrowing markets.

This situation is fundamentally different from what prevailed in the former USSR. In the Soviet economy, exports performed a donor role directly in branches that served the domestic market; this was done both directly (through a centralized redistribution of hard-currency earnings among top-priority branches and sectors) and indirectly (by establishing distorted prices that disadvantaged export producers). Now, the hard-currency earnings do go mainly to the real sector but are used for redistribution to importers and for reserves in the Central Bank. The viability of this strategy in the middle- and long-term perspective depends on whether the export sector is able to support the growing influx of imports and whether, without violating financial balances, it can satisfactorily provide the reserves needed for state solvency.

Midterm Perspectives

The process of forming national macroeconomic complexes in the Central Asian states is still not complete. Nevertheless, the available statistical data and other information make it possible to draw some tentative, interim conclusions. Given that the basic tendencies of development have achieved sufficient stability, one can construct a picture of the likely midterm economic prospects for each of these countries.

Kazakhstan, Kyrgyzstan, Uzbekistan, Tajikistan, and Turkmenistan have given different responses to the challenges of the 1990s. The situation in Tajikistan and Turkmenistan is by far the clearest and simplest. In the case of Tajikistan, the economy has been severely damaged by military conflict; for this reason alone, the economic prospects here are exceedingly gloomy. Moreover, because Tajikistan shares a common border with Afghanistan, the two countries essentially constitute a single zone of political instability and economic hardship. Given its small domestic market, the limited purchasing power of the population, and the lack of export opportunities (with few exceptions), this country is doomed to be the least developed state in the foreseeable future.

Nevertheless, Tajikistan does have certain favorable preconditions for economic growth. The military destruction notwithstanding, Tajikistan has essentially preserved the energy and irrigation systems that it inherited from the former USSR. Moreover, the military damage has mostly bypassed the most developed part of the country— Leninabad Oblast. This factor, together with the exceptionally hardworking ethos of the work force, creates a certain base for the development of agriculture and certain branches of processing industry.

Turkmenistan faces problems of a different sort. Surpassed only by Kazakhstan in level of development (as measured in per capita GDP), and blessed with colossal reserves of natural gas, this country nonetheless finds itself ranked as the least developed country. A substantial part of the economic activity in Turkmenistan is "virtual" and unrewarded, since the main consumers of its natural gas—Ukraine, Armenia, and Georgia—are insolvent and cannot pay for this energy. Under the best of circumstances, the gas is delivered through barter deals; for the most part, however, it is delivered on credit. Moreover, in Turkmenistan (the state playing the role of creditor), the vast majority of the population are living under conditions of extreme poverty. Given that the former Soviet republics cannot pay for these gas deliveries (at least, in the midterm perspective), the economic future of Turkmenistan depends entirely upon finding new access to world markets for natural gas. Even under the best of circumstances, this will not happen before the coming century, and for the next three to five years the situation here is unlikely to register any significant improvements.

A similar situation exists in Kyrgyzstan. Even after losing half of its GDP, this state does not have enough internal resources to sustain the existing productive base and social sphere. Notwithstanding all attempts to cut expenditures, the budget deficit still exceeds 10 percent of the GDP. The internal market is too small for an industrialization oriented toward domestic demand. In objective terms, Kyrgyzstan has limited opportunities to achieve any substantial increase in exports to competitive markets.

The government's sole hope, apart from obtaining foreign grants and loans, is to accelerate the development of the export-oriented gold-mining sector. To attract foreign capital to this branch, Kyrgyzstan has dropped virtually all restrictions and barriers, including ecological demands. Nevertheless, even under the most favorable scenario of development, future earnings from the export of gold and silver will hardly suffice to repay the national debts and to keep the infrastructure from degrading further.

As for Kazakhstan, by the middle of 1995 its midterm prospects had become clearly defined. By that point, the country faced the threat of a complete breakdown in the existing industrial structure; Kazakhstan itself had neither sufficient financial resources nor the technology to maintain and modernize this structure. As a result, the government took decisive steps to internationalize the country's industrial sector. In 1994–96, the largest metallurgical enterprises either became the property of foreign companies or were placed under their management. In 1996, the government began the sale of electric power stations to foreign investors, and has continued this policy to the present time. From the second half of 1996, the country privatized enterprises in the fuel industry, counting again mainly on the participation of foreign companies.

Thus, Kazakhstan has created an internationalized sector in its economy—a sector controlled by foreign capital and functioning in accordance with the price proportions and demand prevailing on world markets. It is not entirely clear how long lived and stable this new structure will prove to be. The key point is that the Cyclopean industrial giants of Kazakhstan were created to function in a nonmarket economy. The crucial question is whether it is possible to move these giants (such as Karmet, Zhezkazgantsvetmet, Balkhashmys, and others) into a market system, and the answer to that question is still unclear. One cannot fully discount a scenario whereby foreign investors, having drained the last resources from these expiring industrial giants, simply repudiate their grandiose projects for reconstruction.

But even in the optimal variant, the internationalization of the export-oriented and subordinate service branches is fraught with serious consequences for the rest of the economy. First, the scale of redistribution of export incomes (to support other branches and consumption) will be sharply reduced, since international capital now has control over these earnings. Second, the internationalized sector will accelerate the approximation of domestic prices to world levels. It is difficult to imagine a situation where foreign firms, having made huge investments in electric power and oil extraction, will agree to deliver oil and electricity at a loss to themselves and, still less, gratis (as currently is often the case). In turn, the price shock and establishment of average world price proportions will hasten bankruptcy for a significant part of industry and agriculture. Third, the economic development of Kazakhstan will be wholly dependent on unpredictable price fluctuations on world markets. And the markets for its main export goods—copper, lead, zinc, and rolled ferrous metals—are not distinguished by a high level of stability. For example, after the sharp fall in the price of copper (from about 3,000 dollars per ton in late 1995 to 1,800 dollars the following summer), the government not only encountered a contraction in export income, but also was forced to extend additional tax privileges to the South Korean corporation Samsung (which controls the largest Kazakh copper combine, Zhezkazgan).[5]

The sale of the choice units of industry in 1995–97 enabled Kazakhstan to obtain about 1 billion dollars of investment per year (see Table 5.4). In 1997–2000, Kazakhstan expects to attract more than 22 billion dollars from abroad, including 16.9 billion as direct foreign investment. Such a massive influx of capital (if indeed it transpires) will have a substantial effect on the macroeconomic indicators. Given that the GDP of Kazakhstan now stands at approximately 22 billion dollars, the influx of each billion dollar will generate 4 to 5 percent growth in the GDP.

At this point, it is impossible to estimate how realistic this scenario is for economic growth through the internationalization of the Kazakh economy. Reliable information is simply not available. In the authors' judgment, during the next three to five years (until the production funds of the metallurgical and oil enterprises can exert a presence), the economy will be dominated by offshore capital, by a few foreign firms, and by global financial speculators.

Even under the most auspicious turn of events, the capital stock and, especially, the natural resources can be redistributed in favor of strategic investors, who will come in the guise of transnational corporations. If this happens, Kazakhstan will begin in earnest to realize a development strategy already tested earlier by the rich oil-producing countries.

The main obstacle to the realization of this optimistic scenario is the global struggle for oil and gas resources in the Caspian Sea. In addition, there are also complex problems of a nonpolitical character. Are the Central Asian oil and gas deposits really competitive on a global scale? How will the appearance of new large-scale exporters of oil and gas affect world prices and world markets in general? What are the potential markets for Central Asian oil? These and other questions have yet to be answered.

Table 5.4

Influx of Foreign Resources to Kazakhstan (in millions of U.S. dollars)

Category	Type	1992	1993	1994	1995	1996	1997	1998	1999	2000	1996–2000
Received	Direct foreign investment	100	473	635	948	997					
Expected	Loans					235	578	888	1,271	576	3,549
	Credits					252	496	672	441	559	2,419
	Direct foreign investment					1,417	4,206	5,435	4,136	3,115	18,311
	Total					1,904	5,282	6,995	5,848	2,240	24,279

Source: Balance of payments of Kazakhstan; press-release by the Press Service of the Prime Minister of Kazakhstan (1997).

In the worst case scenario, after the productive capital of the metallurgical and oil industries are exhausted, exports from Kazakhstan will sharply contract. In turn, this will provoke the collapse of the local stock markets and, in the final analysis, the whole national economy. That kind of collapse can ensue from an unexpected fall in the price on Kazakhstan's main export goods—copper, zinc, lead, and oil. One cannot exclude the possibility that the International Monetary Fund (IMF) and world oil giants will create an emergency fund to save the Kazakh economy as in the case of Mexico in 1994, where similar processes were at work, and where the United States and the IMF offered extraordinary financial support for the collapsing Mexican economy. A similar situation emerged in southeast Asia in 1997. If events in Kazakhstan take a similar course of events, the hydrocarbon deposits could come under foreign control—for example, through a deal to exchange oil and gas deposits in exchange for emergency financial assistance.

According to a realistic scenario, in the next several years Kazakhstan will not become a major exporter of oil and natural gas. There are many reasons for this—above all, because of the more modest influx of investments (compared to expectations), difficulties in developing these deposits, the low quality of the raw materials, and failure to solve the transportation question. Hence the ambitious plans to expand the extraction and export of hydrocarbons are hardly likely to be realized. By the year 2005, the oil exports—in the best case scenario—will reach 30 to 35 million tons per year, a threefold increase over the current export level.

Whichever of the foregoing scenarios is realized, the development of Kazakhstan will be totally determined by the strategies of the transnational corporations dealing in oil and gas. The future of the country will fundamentally depend on decisions taken in the head offices of the oil giants and the world's financial-economic centers.

Despite the great differences in scale and concrete conditions, the Kazakh and Kyrgyz models of development represent a single kind. In both cases, the government has banked mainly on external factors. In Kyrgyzstan, it counts on assistance and credits, and also a possible flow of capital to the mining industry. In Kazakhstan, the government is relying on an influx of direct foreign investments in metallurgy, electric power, and oil production. Another common characteristic of such development is its concentration on a few industrial branches.

Capital-intensive projects for gold mining, oil production, and metallurgy will generate a relatively modest demand for labor. The latter will be forced to concentrate in already overcrowded sectors—either urban services (Kazakhstan) or agriculture (Kyrgyzstan). In essence, in the next five to ten years, economic growth in these two states—if it occurs at all—will bear distinctly "third world" qualities. A few pockets of progress, with limited direct ties to the national economy, will coexist with growing backwardness and immiseration.

Until recently, Uzbekistan has developed according to a somewhat different trajectory. In our judgment, this is the only Central Asian country (and one of the few in the CIS) that proved capable of laying the foundations for what is described as the "nation-state" in the literature on the development of capitalism and economic growth. Despite the lack or weakness of other attributes of the nation-state, the key and integral component in Uzbekistan has been a strong state authority.

In the late 1980s and early 1990s, this state authority succeeded in averting economic collapse. In no small measure this was due to two circumstances. On the one hand, the establishment of national control over gold mining and uranium exports enabled the regime to compensate for the contraction in the flow of financial and physical resources to the country. On the other hand, the basis of agricultural production in Uzbekistan was an industrial crop—cotton—that could, with relative ease, be redirected from Soviet to world markets.

Without denying the significance of conjunctures and incidental factors, one nevertheless cannot ignore their contributory role. The key factor in blunting the crisis in Uzbekistan was the carefully targeted actions of state authorities. To be sure, from a macroeconomic perspective, the main result of its efforts was to restore (or more precisely, to preserve) the "poor equilibrium" of the late Soviet era. The only difference was that now the levers of control over the economy and resource flows were firmly put under national control. It would be ridiculous to expect anything else under these circumstances. Uzbekistan did not succeed in finding an adequate answer to the main challenge—the rapid growth of its population and work force. The extreme fragility of the macroeconomic situation in the country was due to its almost total dependence on the demand for cotton on world markets. In 1992–95, cotton exports provided the lion's share of all export earnings in the country. The slightest fluctuation in prices and demand for raw cotton on world markets threatened to deal the republic's economy a devastating blow.

Equally unpredictable is the market for uranium. According to reports from the world press, Uzbekistan has succeeded in gaining access to this market: it has signed relatively large contracts with South Korea (1996) and the United States (1997).

In the coming years, Uzbekistan must prove that the country has created the preconditions to dismantle the "bad equilibrium" and to embark on a trajectory of rapid development. Otherwise, the preconditions created to accelerate economic dynamics will be simply absorbed through demographic growth. To stimulate economic growth, the country must solve two main tasks. One is to provide an increase in the flow of investment resources from abroad; the other is to embark on a more substantial liberalization of the economy and society than has hitherto been the case.

During the last year or year and a half, Uzbekistan has achieved a certain success in eliciting foreign capital. Numerous facts attest to the growing interest of private investors in the Uzbek economy. The same could be said about the expanding dialogue with international financial agencies. With respect to the second task, greater liberalization of the economy and society, the situation is less sanguine.

It is possible that, in a period of struggle with the real threat of economic catastrophe, the monopolistic position of the state—as the agent of development and the sole center for decision making—had its justification. However, the experience of the world shows that stable economic growth is the product of mixed state-private initiatives. Therefore, the development of a large private sector (whether in the form of structures analogous to those in South Korea or the relatively autonomous state companies of Taiwan) appears to be inevitable for Uzbekistan. Such is the case if, of course, it intends to avoid the standard "third-world" trajectory of development. Moreover, this will require a serious reconstruction of the existing mechanism for economic decision making.

An alternative to liberalization of the economic regime is the following variant: with private initiative repressed, the government itself remains the main partner of foreign capital and the mediator between the world market and the national economy. Although, in the midterm perspective, that variant is entirely viable, the trajectory of economic growth can quickly and imperceptibly give way to one of stagnation and decline.

Notes

1. T. Berger, "V Kirgizii byvshii Sberbank zhdet likvidatorov," *Interfaks-AiF*, no. 10 (11–17 March 1996), p. 11.

2. In both 1994 and 1995, the banking system of Kyrgyzstan operated at a loss, and the state was forced to intercede as its final savior. In the spring of 1996, however, the banking system began moving toward crisis and collapse.

3. See E. Karabekov, "Serpantin pered perevalom. Kyrgyzstan na puti k rynku," *Novoe pokolenie* (Almaty), no. 31 (9–16 August 1996), p. 5; E. Dudka, "Mezhdunarodnyi valiutnyi fond odobril srednesrochnuiu finansovo-ekonomicheskuiu programmu Kazakhstana na 1996–98 gody," *Panorama* (Almaty), no. 21 (26 July 1996), p. 2; "Zhilishchnaia reforma stala predmetom obsuzhdeniia na respublikanskom selektornom soveshchanii," *Panorama* (Almaty), no. 21 (31 May 1996), p. 2.

4. For details see S. Zhukov, "Economic Development in the States of Central Asia," in Boris Rumer, ed., *Central Asia in Transition: Dilemmas of Political and Economic Development* (Armonk, NY: M.E. Sharpe, 1996), p. 125.

5. V. Nikolaev, "Kazakhstanskaia med' na mirovom rynke. Okazhut li ei predpochtenie pokupateli?" *Kazakhstanskaia pravda*, 1 August 1996, p. 4.

6

Economic Integration in Central Asia: Problems and Prospects

Boris Rumer and Stanislav Zhukov

During the first stages of post-Soviet transition in the Central Asian states, it was widely believed that the shift to a market system could be coordinated or, at least, closely tied to integration at the regional level. The small scale of national markets, the lack of direct access to sea transportation, the cooperative links inherited from the old Soviet system—all this, it seemed, would impel these states to embark on intensive mutual cooperation and to coordinate their economic policies. Moreover, as specialists from the German Foundation for Economic Development (who prepared a specialized study of regional integration in Central Asia) concluded, in the early 1990s the states still shared a number of common characteristics that, in principle, should have served to facilitate large-scale cooperation. Specifically, they identified the following common features:

- a single Soviet past, whereby the experience of the Soviet era could serve as the basis for economic and social development in Central Asia;
- Russian language, as the *lingua franca* for all the countries of this region;
- similarities in the economic situation: despite considerable differences in details, none of the Central Asian economies had a

higher level of competitiveness, and all the states find themselves at approximately the same stage of development;

• the core of all the Central Asian economies is the production of primary goods for immediate export abroad; the creation of capacities to process these raw materials would help facilitate the process of market transition;

• the integrationist efforts in Central Asia could draw upon a common historical experience.[1]

The idea of integration has been supported by political steps as well. In addition to the participation in the CIS, which many post-Soviet leaders regarded as an intermediate step toward large-scale integration, three Central Asian states—Kazakhstan, Kyrgyzstan, and Uzbekistan—established the "Central Asian Union" in 1994. The main goal of the latter was to proclaim the creation of a single economic space for the participating states. In 1996, Tajikistan joined the roll of member states as an "observer" in the Union.

This chapter examines the problem of economic cooperation of the Central Asian states in terms of practical realities. It deals with a complex of interrelated questions: what factors determine the need for cooperation among these states and what are the practical results of this cooperation? What tendencies dominate in the Central Asian economic zone—centrifugal or centripetal? To what degree is each state dependent upon its neighbors? And, most important, to what degree can regional integration (more precisely, regional economic cooperation) become a catalyst for economic growth in Central Asia?

The Significance of Intraregional Trade in Central Asia

Amidst the continuous investment decline, ubiquitous low levels of internal savings, and the superabundance of labor resources, about the only form of cooperation in Central Asia is trade. In 1996, the total export of the five Central Asian states was 13.78 billion dollars, which represented an increase of 1.56 times over the level two years earlier. The corresponding figure for total imports was 11.84 billion dollars (an increase of 1.34 times from 1994). By contrast, *intraregional* trade volume decreased. Thus, intraregional exports shrank from 2.1 billion dollars in 1994 to 1.4 billion in 1995; according to estimates, it fell to about 1.0 billion dollars in 1996. Similarly, intraregional imports contracted, falling from 1.9 billion dollars in 1994 to 1.6 billion the following year.[2]

Uzbekistan and Turkmenistan were the main causes of the drop in intraregional exports. The former reduced its deliveries to the other Central Asian republics 4.4-fold (with an absolute decrease from 1.264 billion dollars in 1994 to 289 million dollars in 1996). Turkmenistan recorded a drop of 2.8 times (from 455.6 million dollars in 1994 to 161 million dollars in 1996). By contrast, the remaining three Central Asian republics—Kazakhstan, Kyrgyzstan, and Tajikistan—increased their exports to the region, but this growth could not offset the sharp contraction in exports from Uzbekistan and Turkmenistan.

As for imports, the total decrease (measured in value) was considerably less than in the case of exports. Indeed, four republics—Kazakhstan, Kyrgyzstan, Uzbekistan, and Tajikistan—reported an increase in imports from neighboring regional republics. Only Turkmenistan recorded a decline, as its intraregional imports fell from 103.3 million dollars in 1994 to 65.6 million dollars in 1996.

It bears emphasizing that the above indicators are based on the value of foreign trade in nominal dollars. If one takes into account the chaotic changes in domestic and foreign trade prices during 1991–96, the indicators for different years are not very comparable. The current statistical base does not enable one to reconstruct the dynamics of intraregional exports and imports for the first half of the 1990s in comparable prices and volumes; the requisite data are simply lacking.

Nevertheless, by the mid-1990s, the absolute volume of resources and goods in intraregional trade had clearly undergone a substantial decrease since the beginning of the decade. Thus, if one considers those branches that earlier constituted the basis of intraregional trade (such as electric power, natural gas, coal, and mineral fertilizers), the contraction in trade flows—if measured in physical terms—was ubiquitous. Thus, in the period of 1990–94, the intraregional trade in electric power fell from 60.3 to 13.3 million kilowatt/hours, that is, more than 4.5 times. Sharp drops were also registered for natural gas (1.6 times in 1992–94), mineral fertilizers (more than 4.2 times in 1991–94), and coal (3.5 times in 1991–94).

The instances of an increased value in exports and imports, given the decrease in physical volume of trade turnover, were thus due exclusively to the price factor.[3] Throughout the post-Soviet space (and in this regard Central Asia is no exception), foreign trade prices have gradually come to approximate those on world markets. Moreover, in most cases, the latter are higher than those that prevailed earlier within the USSR. Hence the growth in prices can compensate for the contraction in the physical volume of resources in the trade turnover. Although the road to equalizing internal and world prices is bumpy and twisting, it is clearly heading in that direction.

Given this fact, it is—in our judgment—pointless to talk about an increase of trade in post-Soviet space. Here one does not find a real growth in exports and imports but rather an increase in the monetary value of these foreign trade flows. By the end of 1996, the post-Soviet states have, essentially, applied world prices to their mutual trade. As a result, the monetary indicators for 1994–96 (almost without exception) are hardly comparable. Moreover, the more remote that they are from 1996, the less comparable they are.

The dependency of individual republics on intraregional trade varies considerably. Most dependent of all is Kyrgyzstan, but the situation is not much different in Tajikistan, which is especially dependent on its Central Asian neighbors for imports. In contrast to Kyrgyzstan (which depends, in roughly equal measure, on Uzbek and Kazakh deliveries), the Tajik imports come almost exclusively from Uzbekistan. In 1995, for example, Uzbekistan supplied 90 percent of the Tajik imports from the Central Asian Union and 75 percent of its total imports from the region as a whole. However, Tajikistan is far less dependent on intraregional trade for exports; in 1995, for example, it shipped less than 10 percent of its exports to Central Asian neighbors, with most of these goods going to Uzbekistan.

Uzbekistan, but especially Kazakhstan and Turkmenistan depend far less on intraregional trade. In 1994–96, the share of Kazakh exports to the Central Asian markets stabilized at a level of 6 to 7 percent, while the intraregional exports dropped sharply in the case of Uzbekistan (from 47.0 to 6.3 percent) and Turkmenistan (from 21.2 to less than 10 percent). These data demonstrate that Turkmenistan, which had been tightly integrated into the Central Asian economy (through natural gas and electric power deliveries), in recent years has reduced its trade with the neighboring states to a minimum. Kazakhstan moved in the same direction in the first half of the 1990s, and since 1995 Uzbekistan has done likewise.

This profound contraction in exports to neighboring markets is due to the disruption of the former deliveries of a noneconomic character as well as the reorientation of shipments to states capable of paying for such deliveries (for the most part, outside the former Soviet Union). For these reasons, there has been a sharp decrease in the share of intraregional imports of Uzbekistan and, especially, Kazakhstan and Kyrgyzstan.

What is the macroeconomic significance of intraregional trade for the individual countries of Central Asia? To answer this question, we have compared the export-import flows to the GDP of the individual states (calculated in U.S. dollars on the basis of official exchanges for the individual national currencies). Notwithstanding certain problems and shortcomings in these data,[4] they nonetheless make it possible to draw some interesting conclusions from an analysis of export-import quotients of GDP among the individual countries and regions.

It turns out that Tajikistan is the country most dependent on trade with its neighbors in the region. In 1995, the proportional share of Tajik exports sent to Central Asian markets amounted to 23.8 percent of its GDP, while its imports from this region were more than half its GDP. If one uses these data outright (without the requisite corrections), in 1995 both exports and imports exceeded the nominal dollar value of the GDP. In the case of imports, this situation had already become apparent the previous year.

Such a situation is obviously the consequence of the existing under-assessment of the GDP by the national statistical services. The local labor force, resources, and raw materials used to produce the final export goods (as well as the intermediate production) are all undervalued, while the final product is calculated essentially in terms of world prices.

At the same time, it would be wrong to reduce all this to technical shortcomings in the national statistics. Indeed, the situation with respect to export and import quotients of the GDP in Tajikistan is not simply a technical error, but reflects the special economic realities in the country. Namely, this country simply does not have a single national economy: its economic space is decentralized along regional and clan lines, with economic assets (including exports) openly serving criminal and offshore companies and organizations.

Foreign trade, under these circumstances, is completely isolated and detached from the domestic economy. The people who really control export enterprises (indeed, who are not necessarily the formal, legal heads of these businesses) are concerned only about enriching themselves in the shortest possible time and are willing to resort to any methods whatsoever. In using local resources and labor for export production, they in turn do not return the earnings to the national economy.[5] Export revenues simply flow into private bank accounts held abroad. It will be no easy matter to demolish this structure of social-economic interests and to reestablish export production as part of the national economic turnover.

Moreover, it turns out that the significance of intraregional trade is almost as small in Kazakhstan as it is in Turkmenistan. Thus, the regional exports (as a percent of the GDP) amounted to just 2.0 percent for Kazakhstan (1996) and 3.8 percent for Uzbekistan (1995); the analogous figures for imports were 1.8 percent for Kazakhstan and 1.6 percent for Turkmenistan. This is due to the dynamics of the dollar value of the Kazakh GDP, which grew much more quickly than did exports and imports. In Turkmenistan, one finds a substantial growth in the nominal dollar value of the GDP, set against a background of a decline in the absolute volume of trade, especially with former Soviet republics, including those in Central Asia.

Until 1996, Uzbekistan occupied an intermediate position between Kazakhstan and Turkmenistan on the one hand, and Tajikistan and Kyrgyzstan on the other. In 1996, the exports to Central Asian markets amounted to just 2.1 percent of the GDP, a figure that represents a tenfold decline since 1994. The import quotient of the GDP also fell to 2.0 percent of the GDP, a decrease of 4.5 times. In other words, Uzbekistan's dependence on intraregional trade has become as insignificant as in the case of Kazakhstan and Turkmenistan.

Therefore, the key question is whether the intraregional trade will help to create a regional economic bloc in Central Asia. The answer here is unqualifiedly negative. Indeed, things are now moving in precisely the opposite direction. A statistical indicator of this centrifugal dynamic is the ratio between the trade volumes among members of the Central Asian Union, on the one hand, and the aggregate export-import flows on the other. The authors have compiled such data for the years 1994–96.[6]

These data clearly sustain several important conclusions. First, whatever group of Central Asian states one examines, the main tendency is the same: the significance of intraregional trade is decreasing, especially with respect to exports. Given the growing determination of national producers to reorient toward markets with the capacity to pay for their goods, one could hardly expect anything else. It can be said that the global ties of the Central Asian states increasingly take precedence over regional connections.

Second, Central Asia—taken as a whole—constitutes undoubtedly a more integrated trading association than the Central Asian Union (Kazakhstan, Kyrgyzstan, and Uzbekistan). The latter is the most fragile trading association in the post-Soviet realm. Moreover, the trading ties among the Union's members, which were of little significance at the outset, have tended to decline even further. If in 1994 the proportion of mutual exports among these three countries constituted 12.2 percent of total trade, in 1996 it had fallen to 6.9 percent. A similar decline is apparent in imports, which fell from 10.4 to 7.9 percent during the same period. For Central Asia as a whole (for the years 1994–95), intraregional exports fell from 21.1 to 13.5 percent of total trade, with a smaller decrease in the same indicator for imports (dropping from 20.8 to 17.9 percent).

Third, despite the breakup of a single Soviet economic space and the contraction of bilateral economic relations, the CIS continues to represent a rather closely linked trade bloc.

What are the immediate prospects for commercial cooperation of the Central Asian states? Have the centrifugal tendencies of the early 1990s run their course and given way to the reverse tendency?

An examination of the branch structure of foreign trade in Central Asian states shows that the main exports from Kazakhstan, Tajikistan, and Turkmenistan consist of oil and natural gas, oil distillates, electric power, and ferrous and nonferrous metals. In 1996, these goods accounted for 68.7 percent of the aggregate exports from Kazakhstan, 72.8 percent from Turkmenistan, and 69.2 percent from Tajikistan. The main export from Uzbekistan is cotton, followed by electric power and natural gas. Only in Kazakhstan are exports more or less diversified so as to include agricultural products as well as goods from the food processing and textile industries.

Moreover, the structure of exports of these five states remained stable during the period of 1994–96. Because of the continuing investment crisis in the region, it is difficult to imagine that this structure will change in any fundamental way in the next five or ten years.

It is entirely obvious that the potential for expanding trade among the Central Asian states is impeded by the similar structure of their export products. To repeat, these states produce approximately the same set of goods; hence their economic structures are not mutually complementary. Moreover, the potential for expanded imports from neighboring countries is inhibited by the limited purchasing power and even the outright capacity to pay for goods and services.

At the same time, one must take into account a very important circumstance: exports and imports of the five Central Asian states are rather tightly bound to a limited number of markets. Thus, in 1996, the three main export partners of Kazakhstan accounted for 57.1 percent of the country's aggregate exports.

However inconsequential the deliveries to neighboring countries might be, all five of the Central Asian states (including Kazakhstan, Turkmenistan, and Uzbekistan) nonetheless make it a high priority objective to retain these export markets. And two countries—Kyrgyzstan and Tajikistan—have no realistic alternative to the development of intraregional trade.

Revealingly, the official statistics fail to capture and report certain commercial transactions among these countries. It is well known, for example, that mutual trade flows can be established in either of two ways: either on the basis of data from the exporting country, or on the basis of data from the importing country. Ideally, one should create both sets of data, with one side being the mirror image of the other. In other words, the data on exports from Kazakhstan to Uzbekistan should be identical to the data on imports to Uzbekistan from Kazakhstan. In the case of the Central Asian republics, however, the two sets of data do not coincide and indeed reveal a substantial gap. A similar situation obtains throughout the entire post-Soviet realm. Thus, in the trade of Central Asia with Russia, the official statistics for these two countries "loses" about 1 billion dollars.

Extra-legal—and extra-statistical—is the turnover in the underground channels of intraregional trade in Central Asia, a "shadowy sphere" representing about 15 to 20 percent of the officially registered indicator. For all practical purposes, this turnover has involved almost exclusively unregistered financial-commercial and industrial groups, and it does not appear in the flows of resources and goods reported by the national statistical services. A significant factor in the trade turnover of the shadow economy also belongs to the so-called "shuttle traders" *(chelnoki)*—the hundreds of thousands of people who regularly journey abroad, including neighboring states, to engage in such trade.

Some idea of the absolute scale of unregistered exports and imports can be gleaned by comparing official statistics with the data on balance of payments (which, in fact, provide a more accurate picture of export-import flows). In Kazakhstan, for example, in 1996 the statistics on customs showed an export volume of 6.23 billion U.S. dollars, but the balance of payments reported 6.32 billion dollars; official records on imports listed 4.26 billion dollars, but the balance of payments amounted to 7.09 billion dollars. Thus, to quantify these results, the case of imports reveals that official records captured only 60 percent of total imports.

It is difficult to say whether the shadow imports will continue to run at such a high volume. If the national governments are able to establish strict control over this informal shadow trading, it is likely that the volume will sharply decrease. It is no secret that, from a macroeconomic point of view, uncontrolled trade flows are inefficient and often unprofitable. They exist only as a mechanism for diverting national resources and budget revenues into private hands.

The Central Asian Union: Economic Cooperation

In 1996, the trade turnover among the members of the Central Asian Union—Kazakhstan, Kyrgyzstan, and Uzbekistan—stood at 1.4 billion U.S. dollars. The three trade partners had roughly equal shares of this trade: of the Union's trade turnover, 34.7 percent belonged to Kyrgyzstan, 34.5 percent to Kazakhstan, and 30.8 percent to Uzbekistan. In general, the dynamics of trade turnover for 1994–96 show a stabilization in the mutual export-import flows of the three members of the Union. In terms of the bilateral shares of trade, in 1996 the trade of Kazakhstan and Uzbekistan accounted for 44.1 percent of the Union's total turnover, Kazakhstan-Kyrgyzstan trade represented 31.8 percent, and Uzbekistan-Kyrgyzstan amounted to 24.1 percent.[7]

A closer analysis of Kazakhstan's trade with the other two members—about three-fourths of all export-import transaction in the Union—provides a clear picture of the flow of goods among the three states. The lion's share of trade turnover belongs to fuels, grain, and electric power. Thus, in 1996, grain, flour, and groats accounted for 34.5 percent of the Kazakh exports to Uzbekistan, with another 18.3 percent belonging to salt, sulphur, and lime. That same year, Kazakhstan's exports to Kyrgyzstan consisted mainly of fuel and petroleum products (47 percent), followed by grain, flour, and groats (18.6 percent). In turn, two-thirds of Kazakhstan's imports from Uzbekistan consisted of natural gas, fuel, petroleum distillates, and electric power. Its imports from Kyrgyzstan consisted mainly of electricity, beverages, sugar, and confectionary products.

Although the mutual deliveries of petroleum products and grain have significantly decreased within the framework of the Central Asian Union, the mutual dependency for electric power and water has remained important. And the exchange of water, electricity, natural gas, and coal are all closely interrelated.

Ever since the Soviet era, the electric power plants of Kyrgyzstan—with its hydroelectric complex on the Naryn River—have coordinated their operations with the agricultural cycle of Uzbekistan and Kazakhstan. In the fall, winter, and early spring of each year, the largest reservoir (Toktogul) accumulates its water reserves, which are then sent in the summer to the plantations in the Uzbek part of the Fergan Plain and to the rice fields of Kazakhstan (Kzyl-Ordin and Iuzhno-Kazakh Oblasts).[8] For its part, Uzbekistan purchased electric power from Kyrgyzstan and in return delivered natural gas; Kazakhstan paid for its water by delivering coal from the Ekibastuz coal fields. Coal and natural gas, in turn, enable Kyrgyzstan to generate electricity at thermal power plants during the winter.

Such a complex system of mutual deliveries takes into account the specific and differing interests of the partners. By the mid-1990s, Uzbekistan was using 59 percent of the electric power generated from the Naryn hydroelectric plants, and Kazakhstan took another 27 percent. As a result, Kyrgyzstan itself used only 14 percent of the power that it was producing.[9]

In the first years after the breakup of the USSR, this system of mutual deliveries—which had been built up over many years—suffered serious disruptions. Kazakhstan and especially Uzbekistan continued to receive water from Kyrgyzstan, but periodically failed to deliver coal and natural gas, citing their own internal difficulties. Both states also cut back sharply on purchases of electric power from Kyrgyzstan.

That forced Kyrgyzstan to reply in kind. During the summer, the Toktogul hydroelectric station—rather than cut back on the production of electricity and accumulation of water—continued to work at full capacity, utilizing water resources intended for the irrigation of crops. The result was a situation fraught with unpredictable consequences.

The Toktogul reservoir is the key artificial body of water in the Naryn and Syr-Daria hydroelectric system; it is also a reservoir for long-term regulation of water flows. In other words, the volume and level of water in this reservoir determines the situation at all the hydroelectric stations lower on the Naryn and Syr-Daria, as well as the functioning of the agricultural sector in Uzbekistan and Kazakhstan.

Simultaneously, Kyrgyzstan raised the issue of charging fees for the use of water resources. In the middle of 1996, the parliament of Kyrgyzstan dispatched a special message to its counterparts in Kazakhstan, Uzbekistan, and also Tajikistan—that is, those states that draw water from the Syr Daria and smaller streams in its basin. This note pointed out that because of the unequal distribution of water resources in the region, the bulk of these resources were concentrated in Kyrgyzstan (in the mountainous mass of Ala-Too); it is in these mountains that the Syr-Daria begins, forming the water resources for four states, including the densely populated Fergan Valley. Of the 47 billion cubic meters of water collected in the territory of Kyrgyzstan, only one-quarter is used within that country; the remaining 75 percent goes to Uzbekistan, Kazakhstan, and Tajikistan. Yet Kyrgyzstan alone has had to devote substantial resources—at least 70 million dollars per year—to maintain the complex hydro-technical, irrigation, and hydroelectric plants and facilities. In addition, complained Kyrgyzstan, there are various indirect costs as well as opportunity costs (e.g., some 46,000 hectares of fertile land had to be flooded to create these reservoirs). In short, the large water reservoirs like Toktogul, Andizhan, Papan, Kerkidon, Kirov, Orto-Tokoi, and Kasansai are located in the territory of Kyrgyzstan but service mainly the neighboring states of Uzbekistan and Kazakhstan. Moreover, during the winter months, the Naryn hydroelectric complex—rather than produce electricity—accumulates water to supply the fields of the neighboring states for the following summer. Kyrgyzstan estimated the total losses and profits foregone at 60 million dollars. The neighbors, by using these water resources, have increased their cultivated land area by more than 7 million hectares. Given these circumstances, Kyrgyzstan proposed that all the water consumers of the region share this burden[10] and, in effect, raised the question of monetary fees for the use of transnational rivers. As the first step in this process, Kyrgyzstan began to levy fees for water use within its own territory.[11]

The ensuing discussions resulted in a compromise. To pay for its use of water, Uzbekistan increased (or, more precisely, restored to the 1993 levels) the delivery of natural gas to Kyrgyzstan, and at prices substantially lower than those prevailing on world markets.[12] A mutually acceptable compromise was found, after difficult confrontations, for other residual problems.

Some foreign observers maintain that, in 1992–95, Uzbekistan sought to exploit the dependence of its neighbors in the sphere of fuel and energy to exert a certain pressure in political matters as well.[13] They argue that this pressure, while not publicly advertised, took the form of Uzbek pretentions to exercise leadership in the region. These pretentions are usually seen in terms of Uzbekistan's overt attempts to supplant Turkmenistan as the main supplier of natural gas in the region.

The present authors, however, hold a somewhat different view of the mutual relations in the complex issue of natural gas and energy. Turkmenistan, which aspired to become a "second Kuwait" in the Central Asian framework, sought to abandon insolvent consumers who, in effect, could pay for large deliveries of natural gas only through some form of barter. By early 1994, Kazakhstan's debts to Turkmenistan for natural gas deliveries had already come to exceed 60 million dollars.[14] Moreover, even these payments in kind were irregular, being neither in full nor on time. Frequently, Turkmenistan had to resort to extreme measures to obtain what it was due. It is highly revealing, for example, that Kazakhstan agreed to extinguish its debts to Turkmenistan (amounting to 24.3 million dollars) through the delivery of asbestos, phosphorus, lead, copper rods, and various other barter goods in March 1997.[15] In addition, Turkmenistan already had analogous problems in its relations with Ukraine and the Caucasus republics, which continue to be large-scale users of natural gas but are in no position to pay for it. However, Turkmenistan was unable to shut off Kazakhstan completely from natural gas deliveries for the simple reason that the pipeline to Europe (which can pay for what it consumes) passes through the territory of Kazakhstan.

Under the circumstances, it was entirely natural to substitute Uzbek gas for that from Turkmenistan. That is all the more appealing because the natural gas pipeline that runs through the Central Asian republics also passes through Uzbekistan, and that republic is far more dependent on trade with its neighbors than is the case with Turkmenistan. If Uzbekistan had any political calculations behind this decision, these were only an auxiliary factor to the basic economic considerations. It is quite another matter that, almost immediately, Uzbekistan found that neither Kazakhstan nor Kyrgyzstan was able to pay for the gas deliveries. By the end of 1994, Kazakhstan's debts for Uzbek gas had already mushroomed to 138 million dollars.[16] Kyrgyzstan's debts for the delivery of Uzbek gas constantly ran in excess of 1 million dollars.[17] Such a high level of indebtedness was due to the fact that Uzbekistan was constantly seeking to raise the price to world market levels. In 1994, Kazakhstan obtained its natural gas at the price of 80 to 84 dollars per thousand cubic meters—compared to 100 dollars on world markets.[18]

In an effort to force its debtors to pay, Uzbekistan began to interdict, on a regular basis, its deliveries of natural gas.[19] Naturally, Kazakhstan and Kyrgyzstan promptly resorted to countermeasures. For Kyrgyzstan, the most powerful economic argument in its dialogue with Uzbekistan was of course the latter's dependence on its water. Moreover, these two countries have concluded agreements on payments, which provide for a mixed form of payment consisting of money and clearing deliveries.[20]

For its counterarguments to Uzbek pressure, Kazakhstan used the indebtedness of Uzbek firms that shipped freight on the Kazakh railway lines, as well as Uzbekistan's debts for grain imports. For example, in February 1996, the Uzbek debt for rail services was estimated at 160 million dollars.[21] Until recently, Uzbekistan has also remained highly dependent on Kazakhstan for grain imports, parts of which were used for clearing transactions in bilateral intergovernmental agreements.[22] As a result, Kazakhstan forced the Uzbek government to cut the export price of natural gas to 50–55 dollars per million cubic meters.[23]

The problems describe above, along with many similar difficulties in mutual accounts, cannot be resolved on the level of indirect producers and users, the majority of whom have a limited capacity to pay. At the same time, throughout the post-Soviet realm one finds that end users do not pay for the delivery of electricity and energy. To settle the interstate claims that over time have accumulated, it is necessary for states and presidents to intercede directly; only they are in a position to control the flows of financial and physical resources at the macro level by taking decisions to liquidate natural gas debts against the debts for rail freight services, or by reaching agreements for clearing on terms that deviate substantially from world prices. The transitional character of the Central Asian economies, which (for a number of reasons) will continue for several years, makes the intervention by political authorities necessary. Sooner or later, however, such political intercession will have to abate and disappear.

Since 1996, the government of Kazakhstan, for example, has finally renounced any responsibility for users' failure to pay for natural gas. As a preventive measure, in November 1995 Uzbekistan sharply curtailed the export of natural gas in order to avoid a situation where it was unclear who, in the final analysis, will pay for its gas deliveries.[24]

In strategic terms, palliative and extra-market measures to regulate bilateral economic relations run counter to the very logic of reforms now being adopted in both Kazakhstan and Kyrgyzstan. Even without these measures, both countries had long since surpassed Uzbekistan in terms of economic liberalization and institutional restructuring through privatization, but in 1996–97 they took additional decisive measures for the final demolition of a planned, distribution economy based on the Soviet model.

Recently, there has been a striking upsurge in the scale of Kazakh-Kyrgyz ties. It is tempting to interpret this either as a covert struggle for regional leadership between Kazakhstan and Uzbekistan, or as an attempt by Kyrgyzstan to compensate for its relative weakness in the dialogue with Uzbekistan. While both motives must not be discounted, the present authors believe that the formation of the Kazakh-Kyrgyz tandem has a solid economic basis. In terms of the type of economic policy and the institutional structure taking shape in both states, these two countries are without question far more similar to each other than to Uzbekistan, which has deliberately chosen a separate, unique line of development. Kazakhstan and Kyrgyzstan are also drawn closer by the fact that their political regimes are far more democratic and distinguished by complete openness and transparency.

As for the influence of politics, the close cooperation among the Central Asian states depends not only on regional, but on the larger schema of post-Soviet forces and interests. The demonstrative closeness of Kazakhstan and Kyrgyzstan, which have formed a customs union, began to gain momentum in response to the closer ties between two other members of this union, Russia and Belarus. Given their critical dependence on trade with Russia, neither Kazakhstan nor Kyrgyzstan is particularly interested in reinforcing that dependence through political or, especially, military-strategic ties. Hence the formation of a dual Slavic alliance precipitated the formation of a Central Asian tandem. As Nursultan Nazarbaev unambiguously declared: "If a center of consolidation is created in the European part of the CIS, we will strengthen the Central Asian Union."[25]

The closer ties between Kazakhstan and Kyrgyzstan do not signify, however, that their bilateral relations are devoid of contradictions and competition. From time to time, Kyrgyzstan exploits the fact that Uzbek natural gas flows to Kazakhstan through a pipeline passing through Bishkek: namely, it claims part of the Kazakh quota of gas delivers—much as Ukraine does on Russian gas destined for Europe.[26] In 1995, the two sides conducted difficult negotiations on the question of extinguishing Kazakhstan's debt of 45.5 million dollars for electricity from Kyrgyzstan. On the basis of mutual concessions, Kyrgyzstan agreed to reduce the price on this electricity by almost half (from 3.5 to 1.9 cents per kilowatt/hour).[27] Only under open pressure from Kyrgyzstan did Kazakhstan agree to consider the question of creating a single energy pool for the two countries and to participate in the construction of electric power plants on Kyrgyz territory.[28]

One cannot overlook the fact that Kazakhstan, with transparent envy, looks askance at Uzbek-Kyrgyz plans to construct a rail line from Andizhan (Uzbekistan) through Osh and Irgeshtam (Kyrgyzstan) to Kashgar (China). This new line will not only link China to Central Asia (and, then to Europe) but will do so by skirting the territory of Kazakhstan.[29]

As the above data show, relations in the Central Asian Union (and in the region more generally) are far from idyllic. From time to time, the members of the Union become locked in serious disputes over the payment and use of natural resources. In principle, a similar picture exists all across the post-Soviet realm.

Fundamentally, all the states of the region, with the exception of Tajikistan, for obvious reasons aspire to make themselves self-sufficient in energy resources. Without doubt, they will do this as soon as they have the requisite financial resources. To be sure, the mutual trade in the region and the cooperation in production (at the level of individual enterprises) will not entirely disappear. Still, this trade will be based on purely market terms and on a significantly smaller scale than is now the case.

The growing openness of Central Asian economies to world markets will gradually efface the force of intraregional dependencies. For example, in 1995–96, Uzbekistan became reoriented toward the purchase of grain from sources outside the CIS and thus began to replace imports from Kazakhstan. The reason is that, on world markets, it obtains certified grain of high quality on incomparably more favorable terms than those offered by Kazakhstan.[30]

Central Asia is perfectly aware of these new tendencies. It is revealing, for example, that Serik Primbetov (first chairman of the Executive Committee of the Inter-State Council of the Central Asian Union) should have made the following statement: "One should not measure everything in terms of economic parameters alone; our union represents more a union of spiritual values."[31]

The Central Asian Union is engaged not only in resolving disputes that periodically erupt or in regulating questions that date back to the Soviet era, when Central Asia as a whole (and, in part, Kazakhstan) functioned as a single economic complex. At the level of presidents and governments, they have created a concrete program for cooperation that involves more than fifty new joint, collaborative projects.

The realization of these new projects, however, requires investment. To attract this capital, the participants of the Central Asian Union have created a "Central Asian Bank for Cooperation and Development" (*Tsentral'noaziatskii bank sotrudnichestva i razvitiia,* or TsABSR). This bank is to play the role of an informational and analytic center, but above all to function as an investment mechanism and thereby convert integrationist rhetoric into practical reality.

At this point, the bank has granted several small credits. These include 300,000 dollars to an Almaty corporation "Saiman" (to produce electric meters), 300,000 dollars to the Uzbek firm "Farmprom" (to organize the production of blood products), and 300,000 dollars to a Kyrgyz corporation "KEMZ" (to manufacture household and industrial-grade electric motors).[32] The volumes of financing demonstrate clearly that these joint collaborative projects have basically a symbolic character. Nor can one expect any signal breakthroughs from this bank in the immediate future, for its investment potential is exceedingly modest. Significantly, by January 1997, the participating countries had given the bank only about two-thirds of its charter capital—which, indeed, was already modest to begin with.[33] In short, it resources are absolutely inadequate for meeting the investment needs of Kazakhstan, Uzbekistan, and Kyrgyzstan.

This bank has neither become (nor is it likely to become) a serious channel capable of drawing unencumbered means from world financial markets for investment in Central Asia. That role is far more likely to be exercised by established institutions like the World Bank, the Asian Development Bank, and the Islamic Development Bank.

In April 1997, Uzbekistan openly expressed disillusionment with the work of the Central Asian Bank for Cooperation and Development.[34] That disenchantment derived from two main considerations. First, the bank—as a commercial bank—requires state guarantees for projects that it funds. The government of Uzbekistan, however, contends that its contribution to the charter capital should be treated as its state financial guarantee for loans. Second, because of the special characteristics of the hard-currency system of Uzbekistan, for all practical purposes Uzbek enterprises cannot make use of credits from this bank: the latter issues credits in freely convertible currency and demands repayment in the same. Whereas borrowers in Kazakhstan and Kyrgyzstan have no difficulty converting their earnings from the national currency into dollars, enterprises in Uzbekistan encounter serious obstacles to turning their profits into hard currency.[35]

In general, the fundamental incompatibility in the differing national systems for currency regulation constitutes a formidable barrier to the development of Uzbekistan's cooperation with Kazakhstan and Kyrgyzstan. Despite the constant pressure of its partners in the Central Asian Union, Uzbekistan categorically refuses to sign an agreement on mutual convertibility of national currencies.[36] In the autumn of 1996, as Uzbekistan encountered serious difficulties in its balance of payments (and hence in its capacity to support the official exchange rate on the *som*), Uzbekistan reduced transactions through correspondent accounts that financial institutions of CIS countries had opened in banks on its territory. Naturally, the National (Central) Bank of Kazakhstan responded by suspending quotations on the exchange rate between its tenge and the Uzbek som.[37]

The incompatibility of macroeconomic policy and structural factors also makes it difficult for Kazakhstan and Uzbekistan even to reach agreement on the terms for bilateral trade. Thus, Kazakhstan regards commercial relations with Uzbekistan within the framework of most favored nation status, while Uzbekistan wants a system of free trade.[38]

Desiring to marketize the barter trade (at least formally), in April 1996 the presidents of the member countries of the Central Asian Union authorized their state banks (the National Bank of Kazakhstan, the National Bank of Kyrgyzstan, and the Central Bank of Uzbekistan) to establish and run clearing chambers in Almaty ("Kazakhstan-

Kyrgyzstan-Uzbekistan"), in Bishkek ("Kyrgyzstan-Kazakhstan-Uzbekistan"), and in Tashkent ("Uzbekistan-Kazakhstan-Kyrgyzstan"). Moreover, it was expected that these chambers, in a short period of time, would develop branches in other cities of these republics.[39] Given the factors cited above, however, one cannot expect any substantial results from this agreement.

In Kazakhstan, for example, the domestic prices on natural gas and grain have been almost totally deregulated and are now regulated by the market. In addition, the state has declined to subsidize either producers or consumers. Hence it is virtually impossible to create special, quasi-market (but in reality centralized) systems of cooperation (with their own prices and terms for delivery); this applies to transactions with any state, including Uzbekistan. Thus, Kazakhstan's grain is freely available for purchase on the exchange, along with all the requisite licenses for export. In 1996, Uzbekistan came to rank as the second largest buyer—after Russia—of grain at the International Kazakhstani Agro-Industrial Exchange.[40]

Evidently, the idea of creating a mechanism for investment cooperation to stimulate the development of commercial ties in new spheres, while basically a sound conception, has nonetheless foundered. There were two main reasons for this. First, and fundamentally, not a single member of the Central Asian Union has the unencumbered investment resources to allocate for such general development. Second, confronted by a collapse of investment, all three countries adamantly insist that the Central Asian Bank for Cooperation and Development allocate resources proportionate to their individual contribution to the bank's charter capital. Amidst the acute shortage of capital, no one intends to use his scarce resources to help someone else. Hence the profitability of concrete projects, and their significance in the middle or long term, are not taken into account.

A close analysis of the collaborative projects shows that this program has done nothing more than mechanically combine the proposals of numerous ministries and state agencies. In fact, this amounts to a mere list of possible spheres of bilateral and trilateral cooperation that happened to be under official review at the time the program was prepared. It is clear that considerations like economic efficiency and significance for regional development did not play a role in the preparation of this program. It is no accident that some of the officials involved in multilateral cooperation have expressed serious doubts about the feasibility of some of these cooperative projects.[41] Even the most important projects have gone unrealized. Thus, the construction of the natural gas pipeline "Gazli-Bishkek-Almaty" in 1995–96, for lack of funds, could not be undertaken; to complete this work on their respective territories, Kazakhstan needs 10 million dollars and Kyrgyzstan 5 million dollars.[42]

For these same reasons, prospects for the creation of transnational companies and financial-industrial groups in Central Asia are not promising. For example, more than thirty Kyrgyz, Uzbek, and Kazakh enterprises have announced plans to create an industrial group called "Tsentrazelektron," which would combine enterprises from the electronics, radio, and instrument-manufacturing industries that had, in the Soviet era, been part of the military-industrial complex.[43] However, in seeking to establish relations on a market basis, these enterprises have inevitably encountered the problem of mutual payments, an issue that cannot be resolved at the micro level, but rather requires compatible macroeconomic policies by the states involved.

In principle, the prospects are brightest for those enterprises in the region that have been created by foreign capital and that form a vertical chain of production. For example, the South Korean company Daewoo created an auto assembly plant in Uzbekistan and included (or plans to do so) several Kazakh and Kyrgyz enterprises into a single production cycle.[44] However, so long as the member states of the Central Asian Union have substantial differences in currency controls, foreign capital is forced to resolve problems of interenterprise payments by lobbying directly at the highest instances of political authority. And the very fact that such projects bear the imprint of exclusiveness and subjective treatment means that they cannot become the locomotives of development for the national economies.

Turkmenistan and Tajikistan: Central Asian "Outsiders" and Regional Economic Integration

Turkmenistan

This republic holds a special place in the post-Soviet and Central Asian division of labor. As in the Soviet era, natural gas continues to be its main item of export. Moreover, the earlier pipeline system serves to make Turkmenistan, for the time being, totally dependent on Russia. In practice, Turkmenistan does not have the opportunity to act independently in shipping its natural gas to end users.

Cooperation with Uzbekistan and Kazakhstan is significant for Turkmenistan mainly because the pipelines that deliver natural gas to the Russian system (and, subsequently, to Europe) pass through the territory of these two Central Asian states. In addition, both coun- tries (but especially Kazakhstan) are still rather large-scale users of Turkmenistan's natural gas. However, in the coming years, Turkmenistan will apparently continue to pursue a policy of reducing deliveries to those countries that have a limited capacity to pay for the natural gas.

It is thus no accident that the share of Central Asian countries in Turkmenistan's aggregate exports plummeted from 21.5 percent in 1994 to 8.6 percent in 1995. Almost all of this export goes to the members of the Central Asian Union; only an insignificant share goes to Tajikistan. It is important to note that in 1994–95 Turkmenistan reduced the absolute volume of exports to the Central Asian region by nearly threefold. The exports to Uzbekistan showed a particularly strong decrease, and by 1995 this country had already dropped off the list of the top ten export markets for Turkmen goods. In 1994–96, export deliveries to Kazakhstan fell twofold; that country dropped from second to fifth place in the list of export markets for Turkmenistan.

The reason for such changes lies in the fact that natural gas represents the lion's share of Turkmenistan's exports to Central Asian markets. However, as has already been pointed out, Turkmenistan—faced with the inability of its users to pay—has consistently rancheted down the volume of its gas deliveries.

At the same time, Central Asia supplies less than 5 percent of the total imports to Turkmenistan, and in 1994–96 the absolute value of such imports did not exceed 70 million dollars. Most of these goods come from Kazakhstan and Uzbekistan. Because Turkmenistan has constantly had a favorable balance of trade with these countries, it has sometimes been forced to engage in barter deals and in clearing commercial transactions.

Turkmenistan's cautious posture toward regional cooperation is also due to natural and geographic factors. Thus, whereas the discharge of Syr-Daria (the largest water artery of the region) is shared by four Central Asian states (Kyrgyzstan, Uzbekistan, Kazakhstan, and

Tajikistan), Turkmenistan draws its water from the Amu-Daria basin. Although the republic depends almost entirely on river discharges that are formed on the territories of other republics, the only potential for disputes over the use of this water involves Uzbekistan.

The key component of the water system on the Amu-Daria is the Nurek water reservoir, located on the territory of Tajikistan. Its role in the water cascades formed by the Amu-Daria and a number of smaller rivers in Uzbekistan and the Karakum Canal (in Turkmenistan) is analogous to that played by the Toktogul reservoir in Kyrgyzstan. In principle, Turkmenistan finds it relatively easy to come to an agreement with Tajikistan about the terms for water usage, since the latter is keenly interested in obtaining natural gas from Turkmenistan. The main stumbling block is Uzbekistan, which itself is interested in supplying natural gas to Tajikistan in exchange for water, electricity, and aluminum. Whereas Turkmenistan reduced natural gas deliveries to Kazakhstan and Kyrgyzstan at its own initiative, in the case of Tajikistan this was due mainly to competition from Uzbekistan.

Until 1996, Uzbekistan had claims to the entire hydraulic engineering system of Turkmenistan. It justified such claims by the fact that this system was allegedly constructed with funds from the Uzbek SSR and by Uzbek builders.[45]

Given these circumstances, for a long time Turkmenistan preferred to resolve questions concerning water usage through an Interstate Coordination Commission on Water, not through direct bilateral negotiations. Turkmenistan is perfectly satisfied by the fact that each state on the commission has equal rights and the same number of votes. Especially in its initial phase, the commission relied heavily on past practices with respect to the division of limits and quotas on water use. It is no accident that the president of Turkmenistan, Sapamurad Niiazov, is so hypersensitive and hostile to proposals by international organizations to make certain corrections in how water use is regulated at the regional level: "This sharing [of water] has been a vital issue throughout history, and the World Bank should exercise caution. . . . The point is to ensure more efficient utilization of water resources."[46]

There is yet another factor predisposing Turkmenistan to prefer multilateral diplomacy in resolving questions of water usage. Namely, it is the only country in Central Asia (or even in the CIS) that did not reduce the land area under cultivation, but actually increased this sown acreage by some 20 percent in the first half of the 1990s.[47] Given the natural and climatic conditions in Turkmenistan, this expansion was only possible through an increase in water consumption by the agrarian sector. Given the limitations on water resources in the region, this growth amounted to a de facto redistribution of water in favor of Turkmenistan.

It was only in early 1996, at a meeting between presidents Karimov and Niiazov, that bilateral agreements were signed to regulate the utilization of water discharges.[48] It is possible that, in exchange for Uzbek concessions on the use of water resources, Turkmenistan had to abandon its claims to the Kokdumalak oil fields—the largest petroleum reserves in Uzbekistan, but on territories contiguous to Turkmenistan. The latter, for a while, had insisted on holding discussions about "the fair division of hydrocarbon reserves."[49]

On the other hand, Turkmenistan is the only country in the region that, in theory, does not need to cooperate with its neighbors to construct new export avenues to world markets. In addition, at least hypothetically, Turkmenistan could build new gas pipelines in collaboration with either Iran or with Afghanistan and Pakistan. In September 1995, Turkmenistan and Iran signed an agreement to commence construction on a gas pipeline from the deposits in Koperdzh (Turkmenistan) to the Iranian point Kurt-Kui, a total length of 140 kilometers and with a load capacity of 8 billion cubic meters per year. The gas should then go to the Iranian distribution network in the northern part of the country. Iran has agreed to purchase all 8 billion cubic meters. The cost of building the pipeline is estimated to be 215 million dollars, and Iran has assumed responsibility for 80 percent of this sum.[50]

The Turkmen-Iranian pipeline project may grow into something still larger. It is known that, as far back as 1994, Turkmenistan, Iran, and Turkey agreed to construct a large pipeline following the route of Turkmenistan, Iran, Turkey, and Western Europe. The project would cost 7 billion dollars and have a load capacity of 28 to 30 billion cubic meters of natural gas per year. In theory, it could be built in six or seven years.[51]

Commentaries usually underscore the geopolitical dimensions of the question: while realization of the Turkmen-Iranian agreement opens Central Asia to world markets, it also frees Iran from the international isolation superimposed by the United States. However, the interests embedded in these projects are, first and foremost, of a geoeconomic character. It is far from clear why Iran, itself a major producer and exporter of natural gas, should want to open world markets to its own competitor.

Superficially, the most promising project is the route running through Turkmenistan, Afghanistan, and Pakistan. This project involves plans to construct a pipeline from the Dauletbad reserves in Turkmenistan to the city of Sui in central Pakistan and also to the Pakistani town of Multan, with the possibility of further shipment to India.[52]

However, the Pakistan-Indian route raises a plethora of purely economic questions. Thus, to what degree are the plans by Pakistan (and, later, India) to purchase large volumes of natural gas backed by a capacity to pay? What volume of investment is needed for these two countries to build the power stations that keep the natural gas flowing through the pipelines? What will be the final cost of constructing such a pipeline in a region intersected by high mountains and subject to seismic activity? And, most important, if these large scale projects are realized, what will be the net profit for the suppliers of hydrocarbon resources?

However these questions are answered, Turkmenistan is cognizant of the fact that the neighboring states in Central Asia are in no position to make any substantial contribution to the resolution of these tasks. As a result, it has chosen to pursue a policy that distances it from any regional unions and prointegrationist associations. It follows the same policy, moreover, with respect to the CIS. Thus, Turkmenistan has not signed the Tashkent military agreement concluded in May 1992 by the majority of member-states in the CIS. It is also highly revealing that, in 1995, it downgraded its original status as a member of the CIS to that of an associate member, and indeed it has come to regard the whole CIS as merely a consultative mechanism.[53] Ashkhabad has made neutrality the basis for its foreign policy, and in December 1995 the General Assembly of the United Nations formally granted Turkmenistan the status of "permanent neutrality."[54]

Turkmenistan is the only Central Asian state that, officially, does not regard the Taliban movement of Afghanistan as a threat to its own security. Even after February 1997, when the Taliban movement established control over two-thirds of the Afghan territory and impelled Uzbekistan, Kazakhstan, and Kyrgyzstan (together with Russia) to countenance the possibility of a large-scale war in Central Asia, Turkmenistan demonstratively refused to participate when the defense ministers from those other states met to make plans for a military response to the Taliban threat.[55]

Evidently, Turkmenistan has some economic calculations behind this special foreign policy. Having colossal reserves of natural gas as well as a sufficiently well-developed industrial complex to extract this resource (a fact of critical importance), Turkmenistan seeks to secure several alternative routes—or, at a minimum, one such route—to world markets. To realize this goal, it needs to maintain balanced relations with all those states that, potentially, might provide new routes for a pipeline to world markets.

Turkmenistan's attempt to distance itself from the Central Asian region, as well as its efforts to construct an alternative pipeline, can hardly evoke the support of its neighbors. For example, Uzbekistan makes no secret of the fact that it looks askance at the proposal to build a Turkmenistan-Pakistan pipeline.[56] President Islam Karimov of Uzbekistan regards the rapprochement between Turkmenistan and Iran in 1992–95 in terms of an attempt by the "Islamic revolution" to penetrate the Central Asian region. In one interview, Karimov openly declared that the intensification of Turkmen-Iranian contacts threatens to subject his country to the fate of Tajikistan, and in general represents a menace for all states in the region.[57]

Behind such declarations is an economic subtext. Having relatively large reserves of natural gas, but being rather ill-situated in the very center of this region, Uzbekistan fears that it will be left out of large international projects to ship its hydrocarbons to world markets.

To be sure, each of the potential exporters is waging a political struggle on every possible front. Thus, the very same Uzbekistan does not categorically preclude participation in a Turkmenistan-Pakistan pipeline. In May 1996, the presidents of Turkmenistan, Uzbekistan, and Iran—in the presence of their colleague from Pakistan—signed a memorandum of mutual understanding on the construction of an international pipeline. Iran assumed the role here as the foreign guarantor for Afghanistan, since the latter is still torn by internal strife and warring factions. Moreover, Islam Karimov proposed the construction of a highway and railway that would run alongside the new pipeline.[58]

Hence it is not entirely precluded that, in the event Turkmenistan, Uzbekistan, Afghanistan, and Pakistan come to a firm agreement, and the requisite investment capital can be raised, the first pipeline from Central Asia will go to the Pakistan city of Karachi. Incidentally, in the summer of 1996, Kazakhstan began to hold discussions with Pakistan about the possibility of laying a pipeline from the Kazakh deposits to ports on the South Seas.[59]

Tajikistan

An exceptional situation has come to prevail in Tajikistan. At the present time, this country is not even a unified state, but rather consists of several different zones. Some of these are under the control of the central government; some are ruled by power groups at the regional level; others have no formal authorities at all, but are simply subject to the depredations of field commanders and armed bands.

The main zones, which are partly under the control of formal state authorities, include Dushanbe and the contiguous oblasts, Leninabad Oblast, and Gornyi Badakhshan. Dushanbe itself is ruled by the central government of Emomali Rakhmonov (or the "Kuliab clan"); the northern territories centered in Khudzhande (formerly Leninabad) are under the control of the so-called "Leninabad (Khodzhent) clan," which is traditionally oriented toward Uzbekistan. Gornyi Badakhshan is the focus of a fund created by the spiritual leader of Ismailis, Aga-Khan IV, who regularly sends flour, medicines, and other humanitarian assistance to the region.[60]

The central government under Rakhmonov is primarily sustained by economic and military assistance from Russia. According to the estimates published by the Tajik opposition, in 1992–95 Russia provided more than 600 million dollars in aid and credits—not to mention the costs of maintaining border troops and the 201st Motor Rifle Division.[61] Other states and international organizations—including such unlikely bedfellows as the United States and Iran—are also helping the central government to stay afloat. By mid-1995, the aggregate foreign debt of Tajikistan was estimated at 731 million dollars, which in fact exceeds that country's GDP as measured in terms of the official exchange rate.[62]

Gornyi Badakhshan, which embraces 44.5 percent of the territory of Tajikistan, is cut off from the rest of the country by major mountain ranges. A strategic, year-round highway links the center of Gorno-Badakhshan Oblast (the city of Khorog) with Osh in Kyrgyzstan. This artery carries the most of the freight and, in the winter, when the mountain route becomes impassible, it maintains the link between Gornyi Badakhshan and the external world.

Leninabad Oblast is the most developed region in Tajikistan and produces a significant part of that country's GDP. Even a fleeting glance at a map shows that northern Tajikistan, like a wedge thrusting into the Fergan Valley, is economically oriented toward Uzbekistan and Kyrgyzstan, not to the regions of its own country located on the other side of a major mountain range.

Hence it is hardly surprising that, among the Central Asian states, Uzbekistan is the primary economic partner for Tajikistan. In 1995, for instance, Uzbekistan accounted for 90 percent of its exports and about 80 percent of the imports.[63] Moreover, in 1994–96, these bonds between Uzbekistan and Tajikistan noticeably intensified. Indeed, Uzbekistan ranks among the top three export markets for Tajikistan, while being the main source of imports to that country.

As to the profile of Tajik exports to Uzbekistan, electric power comprises about 90 percent of total exports, followed by unprocessed aluminum (6.7 percent). In turn, Tajikistan obtains mainly natural gas and electric power. This large-scale mutual flow of electric power dates back to the Soviet era. To be sure, if the balance is now in Uzbekistan's favor, earlier Tajikistan was the "donor" of cheap hydroelectric power. It was only in the winter, when the volume of water in mountain streams fell, that Tajikistan's seasonal shortage of electric power had to be covered through deliveries from Uzbekistan.

At present, Uzbekistan remains a major supplier of electric power. Users include the Tajik aluminum plant in Tursunzad, which accounts for more than 50 percent of that country's exports and, apparently, for more than 80 percent of export earnings in freely convertible currency.[64]

This critical dependence of Tajikistan on Uzbekistan is apparent in other spheres as well. Thus, the only railway line linking the Tajik aluminum plant with the foreign world passes through Uzbek territory.[65] Furthermore, natural gas from Turkmenistan comes to Tajikistan through Uzbek territory, which uses this fact to put pressure on its neighbor. In theory, Uzbekistan in turn is critically dependent on Tajikistan for water. In fact, however, the irrigation systems in Leninabad and Khatlon oblasts of Tajikistan form a single network with the contiguous territories of Uzbekistan. Hence Tajikistan cannot exploit this factor in its negotiating position with Uzbekistan.

In general, the relations between these two states can best be described as those between a "leader" and the "led." Notwithstanding all the mutual dependency of their national economies, the role of leadership unquestionably belongs to Uzbekistan. De facto, this leader/follower relationship was already in place in early 1995, when Uzbekistan agreed to restructure the Tajik debt (198.96 million dollars) for repayment in the year 2000. That debt, as acknowledged by Tajikistan, included an Uzbek credit to cover its unfavorable balance of trade for 1995 (amounting to 77.19 million dollars).[66] In the beginning of 1996, Tajikistan confirmed that it owed Uzbekistan 199.802 million dollars; that debt was again restructured so as to defer repayment until 2003.[67]

Tajikistan was compelled to join Uzbekistan in exploiting the Altyntopkan gold fields, which are located at the juncture of Leninabad and Tashkent oblasts. Although the main mine and shafts are located on territory of Tajikistan, the latter shares the profits from the extraction of precious metals on equal terms with its neighbor. The enrichment of ores is performed at the Almalyk mining-metallurgical combine in Uzbekistan.[68]

Given these and other factors, close cooperation with Moscow provides the leadership of Tajikistan with a certain counterweight to the influence of Tashkent. Were it not for Russian assistance, Tajikistan would have quickly fallen to the status of a vassal subordinate of Uzbekistan.

One must also note the special role that Tajikistan plays in criminal and extra-legal dealings within Central Asia and the CIS. The last state in the region to establish its own national currency, Tajikistan continued to circulate rubles bearing 1991–93 imprint dates until 10 May 1995.[69] Taking advantage of this fact, its neighbors and other states in the CIS used Tajikistan to dump ruble holdings, including those of dubious origin. This literally bled the country's economy dry, since virtually all its output and products were exported in exchange for these rubles. The inundation of traders from neighboring countries (above all, Uzbekistan) was further abetted by the fact that Tajikistan received part of its interstate credits from Russia in the form of cash.[70]

Some data indicate that Tajikistan, even afterward, continued to be involved in money laundering. In any case, some observers claim that in 1995–96, in Gornyi Badakhshan and Leninabad Oblast, the primary currency in circulation was still the Russian ruble, not the Tajik's own currency.[71]

One cannot understand the economic realities of Tajikistan without taking into account the factor that this country became an important transit stop on the movement of narcotics from Pakistan and Afghanistan to Russia (and then on to Europe). The population of Gornyi Badakhshan, on a massive scale, has become directly involved in the drug business.[72] In recent years there is mounting evidence that drug crops are attracting ever broader strata of the population and from all regions of the country.[73] In essence, Tajikistan is replicating the path of certain Latin American states, where the lack of other resources is making narco-business into the backbone of the national economy.

From time to time, the Tajik and Russian press publish ambitious plans for the economic rebirth of Tajikistan. The core of these plans is to complete construction of the Rogun hydroelectric station, which will enable the republic to become a major supplier of cheap electric power for the neighboring states of Central Asia, but also Afghanistan, Pakistan, and even India.[74]

It is our view, however, that such plans are not very realistic. First, to complete the construction and to erect a temporary dam and other necessary engineering installations, it is necessary to invest at least 3.5 billion dollars.[75] Even if one overlooks the improbability of attracting such huge investments in a country torn by civil war and located in a highly explosive and unstable region, it is far from clear just how many years will be required for the recoupment of such massive infusions of capital. Second, the capacity of the Central Asian and other contiguous states to pay for this electricity is far more modest than the authors of such fantastic projects assume. And, finally, the delivery of electric power over long distances, amidst the new system of costs and relative prices (which are approximated to those on world markets) can prove to be uneconomic and inexpedient.

To be sure, one cannot foreclose the possibility that the transformation of Tajikistan into the main source of electricity in Central Asia would enable these states to optimize their economy at the general regional level.

Common Water Resources: A Situation Pregnant with Conflict

Central Asia is a region with complex natural and economic conditions. More than half of the territory of these Central Asian states consists of deserts, semi-deserts, and arid steppes. The average annual precipitation in Kyrgyzstan, Tajikistan, Turkmenistan, Uzbekistan, and southern Kazakhstan amounts to 120 to 250 millimeters per year.[76]

Water is a resource of critical importance for supplying the needs of the population and for supporting agriculture.

But the principal source of water comes from surface sources, chiefly rivers. As Table 6.1 indicates, underground water supplies are limited and poorly developed; they supply from 2 percent (Turkmenistan) to 18 .percent (Kyrgyzstan) of the average annual aggregate water consumption in the various Central Asian states.[77]

The main water systems of the region consist of the two transnational rivers, the Amu-Daria and the Syr-Daria, which have an annual discharge of 69.5 and 37.0 cubic kilometers, respectively.[78] The total discharge of these two rivers, along with some smaller ones, is approximately equal to the annual water usage in Uzbekistan, Kyrgyzstan, Turkmenistan, Tajikistan, and southern Kazakhstan (with the remaining areas of Kazakhstan being part of the natural climatic zone of Siberia and drawing water from such sources as the Irtysh, Ishim, Ural, and other rivers).

As Table 6.2 indicates, the river resources are distributed very unevenly. Annual averages for several years show that only in Kyrgyzstan (and, to a lesser degree, Tajikistan) is the river discharge formed mainly on their own territories. In Kazakhstan 47.3 percent of the discharge comes from its own territory, and the proportions are much smaller in Uzbekistan (12.3 percent) and Turkmenistan (0.7 percent). In other words, the water consumption of Turkmenistan, Uzbekistan, and Kazakhstan (to a lesser degree and primarily in its southern part) comes from the territories of their neighbors.

The Amu-Daria basin envelops Tajikistan, Uzbekistan, and Turkmenistan, while the Syr-Daria basin includes Kyrgyzstan, Uzbekistan, Kazakhstan, and Tajikistan. It is therefore only natural that the division of water discharge from these transnational rivers should be a central issue in the interstate relations of Central Asia. Without agreements by contiguous states to regulate the quotas on water consumption, the agriculture of Uzbekistan, Turkmenistan, and southern Kazakhstan would quickly collapse, and raise the shortage of potable water—already felt in these countries—beyond any tolerable level.

The severity of the water question is intensified by the highly complicated water management system that the Soviet regime constructed in Central Asia. That system involved a unified natural-production cycle, water resources, colossal artificial installations for water control and irrigation, and also numerous hydroelectric plants. This general

Table 6.1

Basic Characteristics of the Water Economy in the States of Central Asia (average annual indicators in cubic kilometers)

Indicators	Kazakhstan	Uzbekistan	Kyrgyzstan	Turkmenistan	Tajikistan
Water consumption	30.3	52.4	9.0	19.8	12.0
Estimated subterranean water	47.3	30.0	14.0	1.2	6.4
Confirmed reserves of subterranean water	13.1	5.2	3.4	1.0	2.1
Subterranean water currently used	2.5	5.72	1.63	0.44	1.82

Sources: Mezhgosudarstvennyi statisticheskii komitet SNG, *Sodruzhestvo nezavisimykh gosudarstv v 1994 godu. Statisticheskii ezhegodnik* (Moscow, 1995), pp. 285, 404, 441; Gosudarstvennyi komitet po prognozu i statistike, *Narodnoe khoziaistvo Respubliki Uzbekistan v 1993 g. Statisticheskii ezhegodnik* (Tashkent, 1994), p. 283; Gosudarstvennyi komitet po statistike i analizu, *Statisticheskii ezhegodnik Kazakhstana* (Kazinformtsentr, 1992), p. 166); I.S. Zektser, "Resursy podzemnykh vod i ikh ispol'zovanie," in *Rol' vodnykh resursov v zhizni strany* (Moscow, 1987), p. 24; *Gidroenergetika i kompleksnoe ispol'zovanie vodnykh resursov SSSR* (Moscow: Energoizdat, 1982), p. 41.

Note: Most data come from the mid-1980s. In those instances where information is lacking, the authors have used indicators to earlier or later periods. However, given the force of inertia in natural and water systems, these data provide a reliable guide to the situation in the 1990s.

Table 6.2

River Discharge in Central Asia (average annual amount in cubic kilometers)

Indicator	Kazakhstan		Uzbekistan		Kyrgyzstan		Turkmenistan		Tajikistan	
	Volume	Percent	Volume	Percent	Volume	Percent	Volume	Percent	Volume	Percent
From domestic rivers	53.5	47	12.2	12	48.7	99.2	0.46	0.7	52.2	60
From rivers in CIS	35.5	32	87.3	88	0.37	0.8	59.9	94.9	19.1	22
From rivers outside CIS	24.0	21	–	–	–	–	2.8	4.4	15.4	18
Total	113.0	100	99.5	100	49.1	100.0	63.1	100.0	86.7	100.0

Sources: See Table 6.1.
Note: See note in Table 6.1.

system creates a closely interrelated cycle for the natural discharge of rivers, the operation of canals, dams, sluices, hydrosystems, reservoirs, irrigation complexes, and the operation of hydroelectric power plants.

Moreover, the functioning of this system—which is partly natural, but for the most part artificial—is coordinated with the agricultural cycle. In turn, the cultivation of agricultural crops in contiguous Central Asian states is closely linked to water and irrigation capacities.

This highly interdependent system functions within a tightly constricted set of temporal and technical constraints. Thus, both the Amu-Daria and the Syr-Daria derive water from the melting of glaciers. Consequently, water for these rivers (or for the reservoirs and irrigation systems based on them) can only be done during strictly regulated times of the year. To cite another example, if the water from the reservoirs of Kyrgyzstan is released at the wrong time, this will paralyze the agricultural sectors of Uzbekistan and Kazakhstan that depend on these water resources.

The USSR had regulated water, energy, and agrarian questions within the framework of a centrally planned system and a single state. After the formation of five independent states in Central Asia, questions of water supply were shifted to the level of interstate relations. On 18 February 1992, these states established the Inter-State Commission for the Coordination of Water Management in Central Asia. The commission has, *inter alia,* the task of coordinating replenishment and water levels in reservoirs, as well as the discharge of the Amu-Daria and Syr-Daria rivers.[79] The commission is not an open public body; to judge from press reports, however, the Central Asian states resolve problems of determining the limits on water consumption in an atmosphere of acrimonious disputes and controversy.[80]

Amidst an acute economic crisis, it is inevitable that the question of a redistribution of resources to support the water-irrigation system be raised. This is all the more true since, in many cases, the newly independent states encounter a situation where the expenditures to support canals, reservoirs, pipelines, and the like are borne by one state, but the water resources thereby obtained are used by other countries.

A host of unforeseen problems, however, is involved in the assessment of fees for the use of water resources. Unless such fees are introduced (including assessments for the water used in field irrigation), it is not possible to resolve the problem of a redistribution of water discharges from the transnational regional rivers. But, because the enterprises and populations have little or no capacity to pay, the imposition of new production costs for water usage threatens to aggravate the problems that already beset the agricultural sector. Evidently motivated by such considerations, in 1995 Uzbekistan established an assessment from agricultural producers that covered only half of the costs of providing water for their fields.[81]

Moreover, only the states can figure as the contracting party to settle mutual accounts. For one thing, all the countries involved leave an important resource like water under the exclusive control of central authorities. Moreover, it is difficult for a single state to collect the water assessments even within its own territory. Thus, in 1995, Kyrgyzstan established a water levy on agricultural producers at essentially a symbolic level—1.5 tyin (0.14 cents) per cubic meter. If one takes into account the fact that the minimal expenditure of water in the agrarian sector amounts to 5.5 million cubic meters, the total amount due is approximately 70 million som (about 6.5 million dollars). In reality, however, the government succeeded in collecting only 9 million som (about 832,000 dollars).[82] The arrears were due to the simple inability of agricultural producers to pay.

As the economic transformation intensified, one fundamental problem assumed decisive significance: to what degree should the existing energy, water, and agricultural system be adjusted to market realities? In the Soviet period, the dominance for gross output indicators (for electric power, grain, and cotton) justified any costs and expenditures. Only this can explain the colossal scale of resources that were expended on waterworks and irrigation projects, despite their rather modest end results. The area of irrigated land in Central Asia, by the beginning of the 1990s, had increased nearly fourfold since the beginning of the Soviet regime (see Table 6.3).

The newly independent states have inherited the energy, water, and agricultural system of the former Soviet Union, but this can only continue to function if massive infusions of capital are periodically made. In purely market terms, however, such investment is basically inefficient. But this system supports the life and work of the population, and it also serves as the basis for agricultural production. The loss of external sources of financing (i.e., from the all-union center in Moscow) together with the inability of the Central Asian states themselves to keep this system in working order (at least on the earlier scale) leave essentially two lines of development:

Table 6.3

Land Area Under Irrigation in the States of Central Asia
(millions of hectares)

Country	Before 1917	1974	1989
Kazakhstan	696	1,539	2,294
Uzbekistan	1,339	2,825	4,164
Kyrgyzstan	425	1,000	1,034
Turkmenistan	307	744	1,259
Tajikistan	211	543	691
Total	2,978	6,651	11,442

Sources: Narodnoe khoziaistvo SSSR v 1989 g. Statisticheskii ezhegodnik (Moscow: Finansy i Statistika, 1989), p. 456; N.G. Ovsiannikov, *Vodnye resursy SSSR, ikh ispol'zovanie i okhrana* (Tomsk: Izdatel'stvo Tomskogo universiteta, 1980), pp. 123, 126, 131–32, 135.

- The inherited system will self-destruct and degrade to a minimal, marginal level; given the economic crisis and a shortage of financial resources, this variant appears quite probable.
- A process of partial dismantling and adaptation to the new conditions will proceed under the more or less organized control of the interested states, which, however, will be required to make significant investments.

As developments in recent years indicate, *both* processes are now at work.

The water factor is also of critical importance for the agrarian evolution of the Central Asian states. The introduction of private property on land itself, constitutes a complicated process, decides very little. Water was and is the main factor of production for agriculture. The simultaneous reform of land and water usage threatens to unleash mass chaos and destabilization in the region. The risk of decisive measures can only be borne by those countries that do not have a shortage of water resources—that is, Kyrgyzstan and the northern part of Kazakhstan (those areas amply supplied by the natural climatic system of Siberia). For Uzbekistan and Turkmenistan, rapid privatization in the agrarian sector—if the water factor is left out of account—would be akin to suicide.

The knotty issues involving the Aral Sea are hardly any less complicated. In 1994, the five states of Central Asia established an international fund to save the Aral Sea; drawing resources from initial contributions by the participating states. But annual allocations amounted to just 0.3 percent of each country's GDP; as a result, by March 1997, the fund had accumulated only 2.12 million dollars. As might be expected, the only states to pay the full amount due were Kazakhstan, Turkmenistan, and Uzbekistan—that is, the countries that border directly on the Aral Sea. Tajikistan and Kyrgyzstan, by contrast, made no payments whatsoever.[83]

The states of Central Asia obviously do not even have the wherewithal to cope with the enormous problems caused by the fall in the water table and surface area of the Aral Sea. Rather, the fund was created mainly to evoke an international resonance to these problems. Convinced that it is impossible to devise a common, unified approach to the Aral problem and lacking the requisite resources, the Central Asian states are increasingly disposed to follow their own separate policies.

Thus, in January 1997, Kazakhstan completed the construction of a dam that divided a single hydraulic plane into two parts—one in the East (Kazakhstan), another in the West (Uzbekistan). The waters of the Syr-Daria ceased to flow into the western part of the Aral Sea, but the water level in its eastern part slowly began to rise.[84] Apparently, from a practical point of view, this was the only proper solution. One can now hope for a stabilization at least in that part of the Aral belonging to Kazakhstan. At the same time, this was a politically sensitive decision, since it separates the Uzbek part of the Aral from the Syr-Daria. Obviously, this decision will further complicate the difficult social-economic and demographic situation in Uzbekistan's Karakalpakstan. In this respect, the regular meetings of Central Asian leaders on the Aral issue embody a certain prophylactic character, enabling them to discard mutual claims and to devise compromises in a civilized manner.

Transportation as an Integrating Factor

The mutual dependence of Central Asian states also derives from the integrity of the transportation infrastructure. The first major transportation system in the region was the Turkestan railway line; built at the beginning of the twentieth century, and for a long time it was the sole link to the Russian Empire and the outside world. From the 1930s to the 1980s, the Soviet Union built here—and virtually from scratch—a network of highways and rail lines. Although it built this system within the framework of a centrally planned economy, military strategic needs often took precedence over purely economic considerations. That is because Soviet military doctrine treated Central Asia and Kazakhstan as a bastion to defend against China and the southern flank of NATO.

As a result, the network of highways and rail lines are directed not toward the interior of the region itself, but to Russia, which thus became the main focus of foreign economic relations for Central Asia. Moreover, transportation links were often better developed between countries than inside individual states. For example, northern and southern Kyrgyzstan are linked by a single highway, and even that roadway is poorly constructed and leaves much to be desired, especially in the winter. For all practical purposes, Gorno-Badakhshan Oblast of Tajikistan—so far as its infrastructure is concerned—is separated from the rest of the country. The transportation system of northern Kazakhstan is integrated with the contiguous areas of Russian Siberia, but has poor links to Central Asia.

The situation in Central Asia is not something exceptional: the inadequate development of the transportation infrastructure and the relatively high level of development of the regional and interregional networks are typical for backward states. Nevertheless, this trait—along with others—constitutes a barrier to the formation of integrated national economic systems.

It is therefore not surprising that ever since the Central Asian states achieved independence, they have attempted (or at least made plans) to correct the most flagrant deficiencies in their transportation infrastructure. However, projects involving the infrastructure are capital-intensive and require a long period for recoupment of the investments. Therefore, almost all the transportation projects in the region rely mainly on foreign loans and credits. Particularly noteworthy here is the contribution of Japan and the Asian Bank of Development to the improvement of the transportation infrastructure within individual countries. Thus, their credits have made it possible to modernize and complete construction of the railway junction "Druzhba" (Kazakhstan), to build a bridge over the Irtysh River (near the city of Semipalatinsk in Kazakhstan), and to construct a year-round highway linking southern and northern Kyrgyzstan. Moreover, the Asian Bank of Development is examining the possibility of financing a highway to link Alamty, Karaganda, Akmola, and Borovoe.[85]

But the main transportation projects in the region involve a global dimension. Until very recently, Russia was the sole link between the states of Central Asia and the external world. As the foreign economic ties shifted from Russia and the former Soviet republics to other markets, this region has begun to construct railway lines and highways to circumvent Russia and to establish access to global transportation networks.

In recent years, the creation of a pan-Asian and pan-European transportation corridor has been a subject of active discussion and debate. In 1993–95, a commission of the European Union allocated more than 30 million European Currency Units (ECUs) to develop regional programs for a transportation complex called "Europe-Caucasus-Asia," which would include the construction of sea, railway, and highway systems in the Central Asia corridor.[86]

Inclusion of Central Asia in the global transportation network involves not only a latitudinal East-West but also a longitudinal North-South dimension. The Central Asian and, especially, the Russian press treats these essentially as competing, not complementary, lines of development. However, from the midterm and especially the long-term perspective, both the latitudinal and the longitudinal should be seen as complementing one another. The leading world centers of economic activity could, as circumstances warrant, use the special advantages that each has to offer. For example, the East-West corridor gives producers and consumers in European Russia the shortest access to the Chinese market (through Petropavlovsk, Akmola, and the railway junction Druzhba). Meanwhile, the North-South axis provides the Volga region of Russia with its shortest access to the lively trade routes of the Persian Gulf. It is another matter that such links could isolate, in terms of transportation webs, areas like the Russian Far East and the Trans-Siberian railway.

In the final analysis, the choice of the most convenient and economically rationale route will be taken amidst a fierce competitive struggle, and a decisive role in this will be played by shipping rates, freight volumes, quality of service, and so forth. So far as the Central Asian countries are concerned, the critical issue is the sequence for realizing these global projects.

The first to be developed has been the latitudinal route—a railway line, opened in 1990, that links the railway junction at Druzhba (Kazakhstan) with Alakanchou (China). In 1995, this line carried 1.17 million tons of freight, and the following year that figure had risen to more than 2 million tons.[87] The key points in the latitudinal East-West route include the Central Asian cities of Almaty, Bishkek, Dushanbe, and Ashkhabad.

The main nodes in the longitudinal North-South corridor include the following: Astrakhan (Russia); Makat, Beineu, Eralievo, and Bektash (Kazakhstan); Turkmenbashi, Gazandzhik, and Gyzyletrek (Turkmenistan and Azerbaijan); and, Gazandzhik, Tedzhen, and Serakhs (Azerbaijan, Turkmenistan, and Iran). In other words, a meridional route unites the railway lines and sea communications of Russia, Kazakhstan, Turkmenistan, Azerbaijan, and Iran. On 12 May 1996, the railway line Meshkhed-Serakhs-Tedzhen (with a length of 320 km) commenced operations, linking the rail system of Turkmenistan (and in turn the entire Central Asian region) with that in Iran. Once this line achieves full capacity, it will carry up to 7 million tons of freight per year.[88]

Of all the Central Asian countries, Turkmenistan is bound to profit from these projects, whatever their configuration, since it is strategically located on both the latitudinal and longitudinal axes. Kazakhstan and Uzbekistan represent a certain competitor for the latitudinal routes if Tashkent, in competition with Kazakhstan, succeeds in establishing a transportation route to China without passing through Almaty. This latter project involves a highway linking Andizhan (Uzbekistan), Osh (Kyrgyzstan), and Kashgar (China); running 940 km in length, the undertaking is more than half-finished. There are also plans to build a parallel rail line along the same route; such construction could not build on any existing lines and hence must be built from scratch. According to the original rough estimates, the volume of freight capacity can reach 10 to 12 million tons per year.[89] Kazakhstan has responded to these plans with unconcealed envy and claims that this new branch will not help to reduce the line between Asia and Europe.[90] The real backdrop to these differences is the ongoing struggle among states in this region to occupy the main points in the emerging network of global transit routes.

Nor is Kazakhstan especially interested in creating the so-called "Trans-Caspian Corridor" running through Tashkent, Ashkhabad, Baku, Tbilisi, and Poti. Nevertheless, in May 1996, the presidents of Uzbekistan, Turkmenistan, Georgia, and Azerbaijan signed an agreement to coordinate their efforts to build this new corridor. Almost simultaneously, Georgia announced that it was beginning construction to join the Georgian and Turkish rail lines.[91] For Uzbekistan, this new route runs approximately 3,000 km—about 1,000 km shorter than the traditional routing through Russia and Ukraine (with the port of Il'ichevsk).[92]

Although Tajikistan has been largely uninvolved in these plans for new transportation routes, it too is seeking to obtain direct access to Asia. In mid-1995, the Fund of Akha Khan signed an agreement with Tajikistan to cooperate in building a highway to the Karokorum highway, which links this region with China, Pakistan, and Afghanistan.[93] In May 1997, Iran expressed its support for an analogous project and announced its willingness to invest 28 million dollars to construct a Kuliab-Kalaikhumb road if the Tajik government would provide matching funds.[94]

One must keep in mind that the global project for a pan-Asian and pan-European corridor gives the Central Asian states only a passive role in transit links. A comparison of the efficacy of the various transit routes will enable the European and Asian countries (and companies) to choose the optimal route. Central Asia, for its part, will only provide the territory needed to realize this project. To be sure, countries in the region will gain from the fact that they will obtain shorter and, possibly, somewhat cheaper access to world markets. Moreover, the very construction of massive infrastructure projects and their subsequent operation will stimulate economic growth in the contiguous territories. In general, however, the mainsprings for this growth will come from outside the region itself.

The focus of intraregional disputes continues to be the overt and hidden contradictions among the Central Asian states themselves. For all their gravity, such differences cannot prevent the realization of global projects. In the final analysis, one must not forget that the Great Silk Route had several branches in Central Asia and hence was able to satisfy the special interests of local areas.

There is good reason to think that the export of hydrocarbons from Central Asia will follow these future transportation corridors. The volume of investment required is so immense that investors prefer to insure each other and to share the risks. The simultaneous realization of huge oil, natural gas, and other infrastructure projects will make it possible to reduce individual constructions costs. The parallel realization of hydrocarbon and transport projects is also dictated by technical considerations: the development of new oil and gas deposits, especially in the shelf zone, requires an enormous amount of heavy-tonnage equipment, and this can only be delivered if the requisite rail lines have been built.

In any case, the global infrastructure projects in Central Asia will not be realized anytime soon. Apart from everything else, they will require that the states in this region replace virtually all of the existing transportation infrastructure and rolling stock. The width of rail tracks in Central Asia is 1.520 mm, not the standard 1.435 mm used in China, Iran, and Europe.[95] The double reloading of cargo or a double switch over in wheel base (i.e., upon entering and leaving the region) will significantly increase the cost of shipping freight. Moreover, the existing fleet of locomotives and rail cars is basically worn out and requires almost complete replacement. For example, by the end of 1996, two-thirds of the diesel locomotives and one-third of the rail lines in Kazakhstan were in a state of severe dilapidation.[96] Similarly, Uzbekistan needs to replace some 40 percent of the railway ties and fleet of locomotives.[97]

In conclusion, it bears noting that the construction plans for a pan-Asian and pan-European corridor have, until now, been confined to the realm of hypotheses. Even if one disregards the problem of maintaining stability in the region (which is beset by a mass of extremely acute economic, social, and ecological problems), it is not entirely clear who, and under what conditions, plans to finance these multibillion dollar projects. So far as the authors know, the question of financing such plans has not yet been even posed at the practical level.

Is the Economic Integration of Central Asia Realizable?

A complex of fundamental economic preconditions that would favor the development of regional economic integration in Central Asia does not exist at the present time. This is evident from the following considerations:

1. In the course of the continuing economic decline, the five states of Central Asia have evinced a clear tendency to develop similar national economies. As a result, they lack the need for integration, or even for closer cooperation, so as to complement the national economic complexes of the individual states.

2. The Central Asian states have approximately the same set of production factors. In particular, they all suffer from an abundance of

labor resources. Moreover, because of the high tempos of demographic growth, the absolute and relative surplus of labor resources will rapidly increase. At the same time, all these countries suffer from another common, critical problem: an extremely acute shortage of domestic savings and capital accumulation.

3. The emerging strategy of national development—in explicit or implicit form—makes import substitution an integral element in their economic policy. This import-replacement strategy results from both the largely similar structures of their natural (and especially energy) resources and from the attempt to reduce a negative balance in its trade and payments.

4. Peculiarities in the institutional environment generate serious obstacles to the coordination of efforts in the economic sphere. On the one hand, all fives states (though to a lesser degree in the case of Uzbekistan and Turkmenistan) have experienced a restructuring of industrial organization at the micro level. On the other hand, the states of Central Asia follow economic strategies (especially with respect to allocating roles to various economic agencies) that, to a large degree, are incompatible. Whereas Kazakhstan and Kyrgyzstan carried out a policy of deliberately dismantling the state as an institution (which, in turn, had a far-reaching impact on the whole process of social-economic development), Uzbekistan has pursued a contrary course, assigning the state an ever greater role in the economy. In Turkmenistan, the state structure and economic policy have taken the form of a voluntaristic, Eastern variant of the "Leader-ism," as in Tajikistan, where the state has been paralyzed and disabled by civil war and the interclan conflicts.

It should thus be painfully evident that this institutional discordance can hardly contribute to the process of drawing these five states closer together. Indeed, precisely the contrary obtains, as the five grow further and further apart.

If one takes into account these and many other related factors, it is difficult to expect any major breakthrough toward regional integration. It is not even so much a question of the difficulties attending the transition period, when immediate and pressing problems take precedence over attention to mid- or long-term prospects for development. The foregoing factors lead one to conclude that Central Asia, as yet, does not possess the objective foundation for a fundamental, broad-based economic integration. This does not mean that economic cooperation between these countries is doomed to disappear entirely. On the contrary, such cooperation will unquestionably develop both within the framework of the single economic system inherited from the former USSR, and also in certain new areas and spheres. Those elements bequeathed by the Soviet past—a unified or highly interdependent system of energy, oil and natural gas pipelines, transportation and water systems—continue to constitute the main foundation for mutual economic assistance in Central Asia. One cannot fail to observe that in a number of cases this is an obligatory form of cooperation based on a simple lack of alternatives.

It bears noting that Kyrgyzstan and Tajikistan are more interested in regional cooperation than the other states. Moreover, as far as Kyrgyzstan is concerned, both Kazakhstan and Uzbekistan are approximately of equal significance. Tajikistan, especially its northern part, is primarily oriented toward Uzbekistan. Kazakhstan and Uzbekistan assign the highest priority to their own mutual relations, but the relative significance of this economic nexus was substantially diminished during the period of 1994–96.

In principle, Turkmenistan shows a lesser need and interest in expanding regional mutual cooperation. Significantly, its exports flow almost entirely to destinations outside this region; this is the only country that does not require the cooperation of its neighbors for purposes of constructing new pipelines to ship its natural gas to world markets.

In sum, there is good reason to conclude that, at least in the foreseeable future, Central Asia is hardly likely to create a regional economic association like that in the European Economic Community, the North American Free Trade Agreement (NAFTA), or even the Association of Southeast Asian Nations (ASEAN). The maximum that is likely to appear here is a fragile association, something similar to the Council for Cooperation of Persian Gulf States. Moreover, this will occur only in the event that Kazakhstan, Turkmenistan, and (in part) Uzbekistan succeed in becoming major, world-class exporters of oil and natural gas.

The need for such an association is determined by geography and the special characteristics of the newly independent states. Lacking direct access to the sea, neither Kazakhstan nor Uzbekistan can expect to become major exporters of hydrocarbons without the close cooperation of their neighbors. But only external forces, coming from outside the region, can serve to cement such association ties. The Central Asian states, whether individually or collectively, lack both the opportunities and resources to finance multibillion dollar projects to extract and transport oil and natural gas.

Moreover, one should keep in mind that each of the states of the Persian Gulf has its own direct access to the sea (and hence to world trade routes), thereby making them independent of each other. Furthermore, the general situation in Central Asia is far more difficult. The coordination of economic strategies and the political course of such landlocked countries (indeed, especially at a time when they find themselves in acute economic crisis) constitutes an incomparably more complex task.

The triple union of Kazakhstan, Kyrgyzstan, and Uzbekistan (joined, in the second half of 1996, by Tajikistan as an observer) is intended to compensate—at least partly—for the weakness of the national statehood of its participants and to reinforce their negotiating position in dialogues among themselves and with the external world.

Above all, this pertains to cooperation with Russia, which remains the main economic partner for all the Central Asian states (the sole exception being Turkmenistan). Given this critical economic dependence on the Russian market, the countries of Kazakhstan, Kyrgyzstan, and Uzbekistan are seeking to create a system of political balances and counterweights that can create greater equity in their relations with Russia. It is no accident that a principal objective of the Central Asian Union is to create a more or less coordinated position for the three countries as they prepare for the summits of the CIS.

In principle, the Central Asian Union strengthens the position of Kazakhstan, Kyrgyzstan, and Uzbekistan in their mutual relations with Turkey, Iran, and also within the framework of the Organization for Economic Cooperation (OEC) and the Commonwealth of Turkish-Speaking States. Although ranking substantially lower than these neighboring states in terms of economic potential, the three members of the Central Asian Union are nevertheless merciless in blocking any attempt by more powerful neighbors to assume the role of "older brother" in the region.

The accelerated politicization of regional cooperation in Central Asia is also nourished by a constant threat of destabilization from Tajikistan (beset with civil war) and Afghanistan (which, for all practical purposes, has broken down into individual territories).

One must also take into account the fact that the Central Asian

Union is neither the sole nor the most important "proto-integrationist association" in the region and in post-Soviet space. Apart from the fact that Uzbekistan, Kyrgyzstan, and Kazakhstan are participants of CIS, it bears noting that Kyrgyzstan and Kazakhstan are members of a Customs Union with Russia and Belarus. The economic significance of this association for Kazakhstan and Kyrgyzstan is markedly greater than that of the Central Asian Union. Thus, whereas the relative significance of trade within the Central Asian Union generally decreased in 1994–96, the trade with Russia developed at higher rates.

In the authors' opinion, trade cooperation at the regional level does not in the least contradict the development of relations between the Central Asian states and Russia. Without going into prolix speculation about this issue, one can say that these two dimensions of cooperation serve more to supplement than to block each other. Moreover, if one takes into account the structure of economic cooperation that had already developed in the Soviet era, the development of trade between Central Asia and Russia will apparently also serve to promote a growth of trade within the region as well.

At the same time, there are other impulses favorable to integration. One comes from the explosive instability of the region: the indeterminacy and insecurity of each of these new independent states in post-Soviet space, together with the fragility and volatility of the situation in the region (which could explode in the event that Tajikistan disintegrates or the instability of Afghanistan spills over into the region). Hence, the simultaneous entry into various unions (bilateral, and multilateral interstate associations) can be fairly seen as an attempt by Central Asian elites to find a certain exogenous compensation for the economic and political vulnerability of the newly independent states.

However, in the longer term, the prospects of the region are almost exclusively determined by the degree to which it can be successfully integrated into the world economy. Cooperation at the regional and supraregional levels cannot give the Central Asian countries the dynamic inputs needed for economic take-off. In essence, the sole theoretical possibility for sundering the tentacles of backwardness and poverty is to transform Kazakhstan, Turkmenistan, and Uzbekistan into major suppliers of hydrocarbons and other raw materials in high demand on world markets.

Notes

1. G. Diter, "O neobkhodimosti regional'noi integratsii v Tsentral'noi Azii," in *Regional'naia integratsiia v Tsentral'noi Azii,* Tsentr ekonomicheskogo i sotsial'nogo razvitiia, Nemetskii fond mezhdunarodnogo razvitiia (Berlin, 1995), pp. viii–x.

2. Data on foreign (including intraregional) trade of the Central Asian republics here is taken from the following sources: National Statistical Agency of the Republic of Kazakhstan, *Statistical Bulletin,* no. 4 (Almaty, 1997), pp. 47–54; Natsional'nyi statisticheskii komitet Kyrgyzskoi Respubliki, *Sotsial'no-ekonomicheskoe polozhenie Kyrgyzskoi Respubliki. Ianvar' 1997* (Bishkek, 1997), pp. 21, 23; World Bank, *Statistical Handbook 1996: States of the Former Soviet Union* (Washington, DC, 1996), pp. 210–11, 248–49, 423–24, 453–54, 520–21; Mezhgosudarstvennyi statisticheskii komitet SNG, *Sodruzhestvo nezavisimykh gosudarstv v 1995 g.* (Moscow, 1996), p. 79; Mezhgosudarstvennyi statisticheskii komitet SNG, *Vneshneekonomicheskaia deiatel'nost' gosudarstv Sodruzhestva v 1994 g.* (Moscow, 1995), pp. 25–26, 313, 328; Natsional'nyi statisticheskii komitet, *Kratkii statisticheskii sbornik* (Bishkek, 1995), pp. 156–57; unpublished, preliminary data compiled by the national statistical agencies of the various Central Asian republics for 1996.

3. To judge from fragmentary, preliminary data for 1995–96, the contraction of the physical volume of trade turnover, particularly for fuel and energy, has substantially slowed. Moreover, in the trade among some of the Central Asian republics, there has even been a certain increase in deliveries. For example, in 1995–96, Uzbekistan almost doubled its exports of natural gas to Kyrgyzstan, and in 1995 Tajikistan increased its exports of electric power to Uzbekistan. In general, however, the region has still not witnessed a stable tendency to increase the physical volume of intraregional trade.

4. One must, however, treat these indicators with due caution—in the first instance, because the nominal dollar volume of GDP largely depends on policies with respect to the official exchange rate, which can be subjected to unpredictable changes. Thus, for example, Uzbekistan and Turkmenistan regulate the exchange rate through administrative measures; hence it is impossible to predict how the Uzbek *som* and the Turkmen *manat* will behave in the event of liberalization. In 1994–95, Kyrgyzstan essentially fixed the nominal exchange for the *som,* which was used as an anchor in its anti-inflationary policy. However, the rate set for the *som* against the dollar was unduly high; lacking the support of a favorable balance of trade and payments, it relied more on foreign loans.

5. For example, according to some sources, the largest enterprise and main source of hard-currency earnings in Tajikistan is the aluminum plan in the city of Tursunzade, which is under the control of corrupt elements. The republic budget receives only 10 percent of the plant's earnings; the rest is distributing among its real bosses—Ekaterina Sytaia and Takhir Dzhalilov. "Srok ul'timatuma Sodirovu istek," *Nezavisimaia gazeta,* 21 March 1997, p. 3.

6. These data are calculated from the following sources: World Bank, *Statistical Handbook, 1996: States of the Former Soviet Union* (Washington, DC, 1996),

pp. 210–11, 206–9, 240–45, 248–49, 419–22, 423–24, 449–52, 453–54, 512–17, 520–21; Mezhgosudarstvennyi statisticheskii komitet SNG, *Vneshneekono-micheskaia deiatel'nost' gosudarstv Sodruzhestva v 1994 g.* (Moscow, 1995), pp. 20–22, 24–27, 177, 209, 220, 250, 313, 328, 339; *Statistical Bulletin,* no. 4, pp. 61–66; Natsional'nyi statisticheskii komitet Kyrgyzskoi Respubliki, *Kratkii statis-ticheskii sbornik* (Bishkek, 1995), p. 158.

7. Data here are drawn from the sources cited above, in endnotes 1 and 5.

8. Iurii Razguliaev, "Energetika Kirgizii: problemy i perspektivy," *Aziia-ekonomika i zhizn'*, no. 10 (Sept. 1995), p. 19.

9. Iu. Razguliaev, "Lednik v karmane ne unesesh'," *Aziia-ekonomika i zhizn'*, no. 37 (Sept. 1996), p. 22.

10. Iu. Razguliaev, "Lednik v karmane," p. 22.

11. Iurii Razguliaev, "Voda techet mimo polei," *Delovoi mir,* 1 June 1996, p. 2.

12. *Delovoi mir,* 15 January 1997, p. 2.

13. See, for example, Bruce Pannier, "The Gordian Knot of Energy," *Transition* (Open Media Research Institute, Prague), 21 Feb. 1997, pp. 36–39; R. Dzhevdetov, "Kazakhstan zhdet deshevogo uzbekskogo gaza," *Segodnia,* 11 May 1995, p. 8.

14. Vadim Nekrasov, "Grozit li Kazakhstanu 'gazovaia blokada?" *Al-maatinskii biznes vestnik,* no. 19 (8 March 1994), p. 2.

15. "All over the Globe," *Vremia po Grinvichu* (Almaty), no. 22 (21 March 1997), p. 2.

16. *Panorama,* no. 14 (12 April 1995), p. 5.

17. Larisa Lozovskaya, "Kyrgyzstan Cuts Gas Deal with Uzbekistan," *Kyrgyzstan Chronicle,* no. 10 (13–19 March 1996), p. 2.

18. Ibid.

19. R. Dzhevdetov, "Kazakhstan zhdet deshevogo uzbekskogo gaza," *Segodnia,* 11 May 1995, p. 5.

20. *Delovoi mir,* no. 10 (6–12 September 1996), p. 4.

21. "Zheleznaia doroga—ne doinaia korova," *Aziia-ekonomika i zhizn'*, no. 7 (February 1996), p. 17.

22. Boris Kuz'menko, "Respublika [Kazakhstan] peresmatrivaet svoiu agrarnuiu strategiiu," *Business MN,* no. 13 (30 March 1994), p. 9.

23. *Panorama,* no. 14 (12 April 1995), p. 5.

24. Karlygash Ezhenova, "Anatolii Lobaev, Minneftegaz: 'My v sostoianii obespechit' naselenie kazakhstanskim gazom'," *Panorama,* no. 44 (15 November 1996), p. 9.

25. Vasilii Iugov, "Labirint soiuzov," *Vek,* no. 13 (11–17 April 1997), p. 6.

26. "Zamerzaiut u moria tepla," *Delovoi mir,* 21 November 1995, p. 2.

27. *Panorama,* no. 14 (12 April 1995), p. 5.

28. Aleksandr Tarakov, "Dvustoronnemu sotrudnichestvu zadan novyi impul's," *Kazakhstanskaia pravda,* 9 April 1997, p. 1.

29. Ergali Bail'dinov, "Investitsionnaia privlekatel'nost' Kazakhstana zavisit ot sovershenstva nalogovogo zakonodatel'stva," *Panorama,* no. 5 (7 February 1997), p. 4.

30. "Novyi finansovyi menedzhment pozvolit reshit' mnogie strategicheskie i takticheskie zadachi," *Panorama,* no. 12 (28 March 1997), p. 9.

31. Karlygash Ezhenova, "ES gotov peredat' nou-khau ekonomicheskoi integratsii Kazakhstanu, Uzbekistanu i Kyrgyzstanu," *Panorama,* no. 17 (April 1995), p. 3.

32. "Potentsial vzaimovygodnogo sotrudnichestva dolzhen byt' ispol'zovan spolna," *Azaiia-ekonomika i zhizn',* no. 24 (December 1995), p. 1; no. 1 (June 1995), p. 14.

33. "Otchet Tsentral'noaziatskogo banka sotrudnichestva i razvitiia po vypolneniiu reshenii Mezhgosudarstvennogo soveta Respubliki Kazakhstana, Kyrgyzskoi Respubliki i Respubliki Uzbekistana," *Aziia-ekonomika i zhizn',* no. 5 (February 1997), p. 3.

34. Iurii Galymov, "Problematichnyi kapital," *Delovoi mir,* 3 April 1997, p. 3.

35. Although the Central Bank of Uzbekistan formally conducts such conversions at the official exchange rate, in practice this transaction must overcome a host of administrative and, especially, arbitration hurdles. As a result, conversion of earnings to hard currency even represents a problem for the daughter firms of transnational corporations. Predictably, small and medium-sized domestic producers are virtually excluded from such conversion transactions.

36. Karlygash Ezhenova, "Soglasheniia o partnerstve i sotrudnichestve stanut osnovnym instrumentom politicheskogo dialoga s gosudarstvami Srednei Azii," *Panorama,* no. 30 (9 August 1996), p. 6.

37. Karlygash Ezhenova, "Natsbank Kazakhstana prekratil kotirovki tenge k uzbekskomu sumu," *Panorama,* no. 45 (22 November 1996), p. 8.

38. "Torgovo-ekonomicheskoe sotrudnichestvo Kazakhstana s tsentral'noaziatskimi respublikami," *Aziia-ekonomika i zhizn',* no. 43 (October 1996), p. 6.

39. A. Sukhonos, "Voz sdvinetsia s mesta," *Delovoi mir,* 29 May 1996, p. 2.

40. "Analiticheskii obzor eksportnykh kontraktov, zakliuchennykh na Mezhdunarodnoi kazakhstanskoi agropromyshlennoi birzhe za desiat' mesiatsev 1996 g.," *Aziia-ekonomika i zhizn',* no. 48 (November 1996), p. 13.

41. M. Mamarazakov, "Edinoe ekonomicheskoe prostranstvo gosudarstv Tsentral'noi Azii: etapy realizatsii sovmestnykh proektov," *Panorama,* no. 43 (8 November 1996), p. 4.

42. Ibid.

43. Iurii Razguliaev, "Ekonomika lomaet granitsy," *Delovoi mir,* 10 September 1996, p. 2.

44. Oleg Khe, " 'Uzdeuavto' planiruet vypuskat' avtomobili iz komplektuiushchikh, proizvedennykh v Tsentral'noaziatskom regione," *Panorama,* no. 38 (4 October 1996), p. 11.

45. Dmitrii Aliaev, "Spor Ashkhabada i Tashkenta razreshitsia v arkhivakh Moskvy," *Kommersant-Daily,* 28 September 1995, p. 4.

46. Iaroslav Razumov, "V stolitse Kazakhstana zavershilsia sammit glav tsentral'no-aziatskikh gosudarstv po problemam Azii," *Panorama,* no. 9 (7 March 1997), p. 5.

47. "Ekonomicheskoe polozhenie v agropromyshlennykh kompleksakh gosudarstv-uchastnikov SNG v 1995 g.," *Data Medium* (supplement to *Delovoi mir* [weekly]), no. 7 (18 July 1996), p. 2.

48. M. Bektasov, "Vodnyi balans na regional'nom urovne," *Aziia-ekonomika i zhizn',* no. 6 (February 1996), p. 19.

49. Aliaev, p. 4.

50. *Finansovye izvestiia,* no. 79 (20 October 1995), p. 1; *The Moscow Tribune,* 7 September 1995, p. 8; *Turkmenskaia iskra,* 1 September 1994, p. 1.

51. Andrei Danilov, "Gazoprovod Turkmenistan-Evropa obeshchaet gigantskie pribyli vsem uchastnikam proekta," *Turkmen-Market,* no. 8 (12 October 1994), p. 8.

52. *Segodnia,* 16 May 1997, p. 4; Sergei Dukhanov, "Na trube soshelsia klinom belyi svet," *Delovoi mir,* no. 22 (29 November–5 December 1996), p. 8; *Interfaks-Aif,* nos. 6/7 (14 August 1995), p. 10.

53. Grigorii Kolodin, "Trekhstoronniaia diplomatiia Ashkhabada [interv'iu s ministrom inostrannykh del Turkmenistana Borisom Shikhmuradovym]," *Nezavisimaia gazeta,* 30 April 1996, p. 3.

54. Saparmurad Niiazov, "My ostavim potomkam v nasledstvo protsvetaiushchee demokraticheskoe svetskoe i neitral'noe gosudarstvo," *Nezavisimaia gazeta,* 31 July 1996, p. 5.

55. Iurii Chernogaev and Il'ia Bulavinov, "Afganskaia voina mozhet perekinut'sia na territoriiu SNG," *Kommersant-Daily,* 26 February 1997, p. 2.

56. Azer Mursaliev and Khasan Mustavaev, "Tikhaia voina za aziatskie kommunikatsii," *Moskovskie novosti,* no. 21 (26 March–2 April 1995), p. 12.

57. Mikhail Gerasimov, "Tegeran i Ashkhabad nalazhivaiut kontakty," *Segodnia,* 1 July 1994, p. 4.

58. Azer Mursaliev, "V obkhod Rossii," *Kommersant-Daily,* no. 18 (21 May 1996).

59. Nursultan Nazarbaev, "Ia s bol'shim optimizmom smotriu na budushchee otnoshenii Kazakhstana s Rossiei," *Nezavisimaia gazeta,* 28 July 1996.

60. Semen Bagdasarov, "Moskve grozit 'aziatskii tseitnot'," *Nezavisimaia gazeta,* 15 May 1996, p. 3; Anatolii Sukhonos, "V 'strane gor'," *Delovoi mir,* 27 February 1996, p. 2.

61. Svetlana Sokolova, "Tadzhikskii tseitnot vse real'nee," *Obshchaia gazeta,* no. 20 (23–29 May 1996), p. 5.

62. Stiv Levin, "Budushchemu natsional'noi valiuty Tadzhikistana ugrozhaet razval ekonomiki," *Finansovye izvestiia,* no. 33 (16 May 1995), p. 3.

63. Calculated on the basis of data from sources cited in footnotes 1 and 5.

64. Sergei Puntus and Kirill Vishnepol'skii, "Tadzhikskie metallurgi ne streliaiut v sograzhdan," *Kommersant-Daily,* 26 October 1996, p. 8; *Vneshneekonomicheskaia deiatel'nost' gosudarstv Sodruzhestva v 1995 g.,* pp. 166–69.

65. Ekaterina Sytaia and Takhir Dzhalilov, "Srok ul'timatuma," p. 3.

66. Irina Gribovba, "Uzbekistan i Tadzhikistan nalazhivaiut ekonomicheskie sviazi," *Segodnia,* 12 January 1995, p. 4.

67. Irina Gribova, "Tadzhikistan polnost'iu zavisit ot postavok uzbekskogo gaza," *Segodnia,* 24 January 1996, p. 9.

68. Artem Gorodnov, "Uzbekistan i Tadzhikistan podelili zolotorudnoe pole," *Segodnia,* 7 June 1996, p. 8.

69. "Ukraina i gosudarstva Srednei Azii sozdaiut sobstvennye finansovye struktury," *Finansovye izvestiia,* no. 53 (27 July 1995), p. 3; Andrei Grigor'ev, "Tadzhikistan zamenil rubl' na rubl'," *Segodnia,* 11 May 1995, p. 4.

70. Anatolii Sukhonos, "Dorogi vedut k integratsii," *Delovoi mir,* 22 September 1995, p. 2.

71. Grigorii Sanin and Stepan Dvornikov, "Karavany idut na Sever," *Segodnia,* 14 August 1996, p. 7.

72. Umirserik Kasenov, "Zatiagivanie protsessa dostizheniia natsional'nogo primireniia chrevato dlia Tadzhikistana raspadom, a dlia Rossii-ukhodom iz Tsentral'noaziaatskogo regiona," *Panorama,* no. 50 (27 December 1996), p. 4.

73. See, for instance, the following accounts: Mumin Shakirov, "Geroin nashego vremeni," *Novaia gazeta,* no. 29 (12–18 August 1996), p. 5, and no. 30 (19–25 August 1996), p. 5; *Izvestiia,* 21 March 1995, p. 1.

74. For example, see Anatolii Maksimov, "V Rogune opiat' zagovorili po-russki," *Delovoi mir,* 11 February 1995, p. 5.

75. Feliks Patrunov, "Vakhsh-reka dikaia," *Delovoi mir,* no. 2 (9–15 January 1995), p. 13.

76. A.A. Bostandzhoglo and A.A. Tushkin, "Vodnye meleoratsii," in *Rol' vodnykh resursov v zhizni strany,* ed. G.V. Voropaev and S.L. Venderov (Moscow: Nauka, 1987), p. 53.

77. Calculations based on the data in Table 6.1.

78. S.L. Venderov, "Resursy poverkhnostnykh vod i ikh ispol'zovanie," in *Rol' vodnykh resursov v zhizni strany,* p. 91.

79. *Kazakhstanskaia pravda,* 18 February 1997, p. 1.

80. For example, see Marstam Bektasov, "Vodnyi balans na regional'nom urovne," *Aziia-ekonomika i zhizn',* no. 6 (February 1996), p. 19.

81. UNDP, *Uzbekistan. Otchet po chelovecheskomu razvitiiu, 1995* (Tashkent, 1995), p. 18.

82. Based on the authors' estimates and the data in Iurii Razguliaev, "Voda i zemlia: problem zdes' poka khvataet," *Aziia-ekonomika i zhizn',* no. 27 (June 1996), p. 4.

83. Iaroslav Razumov, "V stolitse Kazakhstana zavershilsia sammit glav tsentral'noaziatskikh gosudarstv po problemam Arala," *Panorama,* no. 9 (7 March 1997), p. 5.

84. *Sel'skaia zhizn',* 21 January 1997, p. 1.

85. *Kazakhstanskaia pravda,* 1 May 1997, p. 3; Maksim Andriushin, "Stal'noi perekrestok v tsentre Azii startuet v XXI vek," *Kazakhstanskaia pravda,* 18 April 1997, p. 1; *Panorama,* no. 34 (September 1996), p. 7.

86. Gabriel Namtalashvili, "Transportnyi koridor 'Evropa-Kavkaz-Aziia' mozhet uskorit' razvitie iuzhnykh respublik," *Finansovye izvestiia,* no. 6 (10–16 February 1994), pp. 1–2.

87. S.E. Atymanov et al., "Zheleznye dorogi respubliki vsegda byli rentabel'nymi," *Aziia-ekonomika i zhizn',* no. 41 (October 1996), p. 23.

88. *Segodnia,* 14 May 1996, p. 1.

89. Nigina Baikabulova, "Vorota na Vostok," *Pravda vostoka,* 29 April 1997, p. 1.

90. Sergei Borisov, "Transportnye marshruty po vsem azimutam," *Aziia-ekonomika i zhizn',* no. 8 (February 1997), p. 24.

91. Azer Mursaliev, "V obkhod Rossii," *Kommersant-Daily,* no. 18 (21 May 1996).

92. "Transport i sviaz' v Uzbekistane" (mimeograph; 1996), p. 14.

93. *Kommersant-Daily,* 30 May 1995, p. 5.

94. *Delovoi mir,* 13 May 1997, p. 2.

95. Serik Primbetov, "Vozrozhdenie drevnego Shelkovogo puti," *Aziia-ekonomika i zhizn',* no. 47 (November 1996), p. 1.

96. Beisbek Nurgaliev, "Vse rezhe i tishe begut sostavy," *Kazakhstanskaia pravda,* 6 November 1996, p. 2.

97. "Transport i sviaz' v Uzbekistane," p. 3.

7

Between Two Gravitational Poles: Russia and China

Boris Rumer and Stanislav Zhukov

Among the many countries seeking to participate in the division of the Soviet legacy, Russia and China have special economic and political interests. And although investment by the West and the "Asian tigers" is today of greater importance for the economic recovery of Central Asia, the survival of the new states in this region—both in economic and political terms—depends upon their relations with these two powerful neighbors.

Russia

Notwithstanding the large-scale contraction in its economic ties with Central Asia, Russia is still the main trade partner for the region. Moreover, in the case of Kyrgyzstan and especially Kazakhstan, Russia is the dominant trade partner. In 1996, for example, the Russian market absorbed a substantial proportion of total exports from these countries—44.5 percent in the case of Kazakhstan and 30 percent in Kyrgyzstan. In turn, Russia accounted for much of the total imports to Kazakhstan (55 percent) and Kyrgyzstan (26.4 percent).

Since the breakup of the Soviet Union, the economic relations between Russian and Central Asia went through two stages of development. In the first phase (lasting from 1992 to 1994), Russian policy toward this region was rather closely tied to resolving the fundamental task of making the transition from a command-mobilization economy to one based on market principles. From the beginning of the market transformation in January 1992, the principal goal of Russia's economic policy—all across the post-Soviet realm—was to reduce its role as donor. It therefore adopted a whole complex of measures: (1) improvement in trade terms with the "near abroad" (i.e., former Soviet republics) by making export and import prices closer to average prices on world markets; (2) reduction in the physical volume of resources delivered to states with limited purchasing power; (3) tightening of terms for the grant of credits; and, (4) dissolution of a single ruble-based monetary system and encouraging the newly independent states to introduce their own national currencies and policies of currency exchange. These policies soon began to take effect; in 1993–94, for example, the prices on the main set of Russian goods shipped to members of the CIS came significantly closer to those on world markets.

Purely pragmatic considerations underlay Russia's decision to dissolve a single ruble zone. Significantly, it had to pursue this policy in the teeth of opposition from some Central Asian states, especially Kazakhstan and Uzbekistan, which to the very end remained opposed to the creation of national currencies. From Moscow's perspective, however, the breakup of the Russian monetary ruble zone enabled it to break with the traditional model of mutual assistance among the former Soviet republics, to adopt a standard practice of granting financial assistance, and to tighten the terms for issuing interstate credits.

By the middle of 1997, the total debt that the Central Asian states owed Russia amounted to almost 2.9 billion dollars (see Table 7.1). This sum of interstate debts does not include the amounts owned by the Central Asian states for the delivery of Russian natural gas, electricity, and freight services.[1]

Notwithstanding these measures, Russia did not achieve its main goal—total equivalence in economic relations with the Central Asian republics. Moreover, from the end of 1994, one can discern several developments marking the emergence of a new stage in Russia's relations with Central Asia. In the authors' view, the most distinctive characteristic of this stage—which, at this point, is still in progress—is increasing uncertainty and lack of focus. What does this mean in concrete terms?

At first glance, the situation in 1995–97 differed little from the

Table 7.1

Indebtedness of Central Asian States to Russia for Interstate Credits
(millions of dollars)

Country	At the end of 1994	At the end of 1997
Kazakhstan	1,402	1,684
Uzbekistan	422	557
Tajikistan	188	296
Turkmenistan	242	186
Kyrgyzstan	147	150
Total	2,501	2,873

Sources: Unpublished data from the Ministry of Economics and the Ministry of Cooperation of the Russian Federation; *Finansovaia Rossiia,* no. 25 (17 July 1997), p. 7; International Monetary Fund, *Financial Relations among Countries of the Former Soviet Union. February 1994* (Washington, DC, 1994), p. 28.

preceding stage. The states of Central Asia are increasingly reoriented toward economic cooperation and, above all, with the developed centers of world economy. At the same time, in the last two or three years there have been a number of obvious shifts. First, the volume of mutual trade between Russia and some Central Asian countries (as measured in value) has clearly tended to increase. To be sure, this growth has accompanied a continuing decline in the physical volume of trade. The main growth of export-import delivers has been registered by Kazakhstan and, to a lesser degree, by Kyrgyzstan and Turkmenistan (see Table 7.2).

Second, whereas Russian–Central Asian trade remains balanced at the regional level, Kazakhstan enjoyed a favorable balance of trade in 1996 that amounted to more than 500 million dollars. In other words, Russia's imports from Kazakhstan significantly exceed its exports to that country. Accordingly, the growth of export deliveries to Russia became a substantial factor in the stabilization of the Kazakh economy. Precisely the opposite situation has emerged in the relations with Uzbekistan: in 1996 Russian exports to that country exceeded its imports by 432 million dollars.

Third, Russia has continued to remain a creditor for the Central Asian states, although on a significantly more modest scale than earlier (see Table 7.1 above).

Stabilization and, in some cases, a noticeable growth in the value of

Table 7.2

Trade Between Russia and the States of Central Asia

	Exports (millions of dollars)		Imports (millions of dollars)		Russia's share (in percent)			
					Exports		Imports	
Country	1994	1996	1994	1996	1994	1996	1994	1996
Kazakhstan	1,938	2,489	1,996	3,036	64	62	64	75
Uzbekistan	750	1,085	852	653	25	27	38	16
Turkmenistan	112	114	60	146	3	3	2	4
Kyrgyzstan	104	153	98	138	3	4	3	3
Tajikistan	143	152	90	88	5	4	3	2

Sources: V. Zenin, "SNG i Rossiia: soiuz obrechennykh ili obrechennye na soiuz?" *Ekonomika i zhizn'*, no. 21 (June 1997), p. 40; *Statistical Handbook 1996*, p. 394.

Note: The data presented in this table are taken from official Russian statistics and therefore may differ from analogous data compiled by the statistical services of the Central Asian states.

Central Asia's trade with Russia, have led some observers to discern the emergence of integrationist processes in the CIS. Under the pressure of internal (primarily political) circumstances, Russia has expanded its cooperation with the Central Asian republics. To be sure, the creation of a Customs Union (with the participation of Russia, Belarus, Kazakhstan, and Kyrgyzstan) was, to a significant degree, stimulated by objective economic factors. In particular, intervention at the interstate level made it possible to eliminate obstacles to the development of commercial and economic cooperation. However, this inevitably created the impression that the Russian leaders were wavering, attempting to choose between considerations of economic expediency and the desire to increase their role in post-Soviet space—Central Asia included. The result is a climate of uncertainty.

In reality, however, there has not been any substantial increase in cooperation between Russia and its partners in the former Soviet Union. Rather, it is more appropriate to say that, in 1995–96, the economic ties from the Soviet era have fallen to a certain minimal level. Moreover, in 1995–96 there was a further approximation between the prices on trade within the CIS and those prevailing on world markets. The persisting trade-flows fully suit all sides, but the conditions of trade in post-Soviet space satisfy market requirements. In the coming years, one is hardly likely to witness an increase in mutual economic cooperation between Russia and Central Asia: the macroeconomic, structural, and institutional preconditions for this simply do not exist. At most, it will prove possible to sustain the volume of mutual trade at 1996 levels.

One should keep in mind the discrepancy between the economic potential in Russia and that in *all* of the former Soviet republics. Virtually all the members of the CIS, in resolving strategic goals to assert their national statehood or survival, are prepared—at least temporarily—to exchange a pro-integrationist rhetoric for real resources from Russia. Some of these regimes (in Tajikistan, for instance) are prepared to remain dependent on Russian infusions for a long time. Since the end of 1994, under the pressure of domestic lobby groups, one finds a certain resumption of Russia's donor role, although not on so significant a scale as earlier. In some cases, the donorship is realized through interstate credits and in others through an imbalanced trade exchange.

It appears that the economy of Russia will not be able to tolerate an increase in the burden of donorship. Of course, one could reconstruct the indebtedness of the newly independent states, as was done, for example, with respect to Tajikistan and Kyrgyzstan in 1996–97.[2] However, taking into account the midterm economic prospects of Central Asia and Russia itself, this path will only lead to a cul-de-sac.

For certain political circles in Russia, the irritant provoking pro-integrationist rhetoric and policies (including the growth of subventions with virtually no expectation of repayment)—apart from some private and corporative interests—is the mounting assistance given to post-Soviet republics, including Central Asia, by the West. It is no secret that a substantial portion of the contemporary Russian political spectrum is infected with the virus of anti-Westernism. Apart from the fact that this anti-Westernism is often on the level of a crude caricature, it is obvious that Russia itself is in no position to offer the newly independent states, including those in Central Asia, either capital or advanced technology. The model of the transition to a market economy cannot be seriously considered to have proved itself in Russia, much less its transferability to the rest of the post-Soviet space.

Highly developed states can allow themselves some elements of charity, which can also be used as a key to opening up local natural resources for transnational corporations. Under current Russian conditions, such charity is virtually impossible for the national economy. With few exceptions, the Russian quasi-private sector does not have any serious economic interests in Central Asia; nor could it have such interests, which must be backed by real resources for any meaningful attempt at their realization.

As the previous chapters have indicated, the main hopes for the reestablishment of economic growth in Central Asia are associated with the expansion of exports and investments. However, for all the significance that economic ties with Russia bear for Central Asia, further development here will encounter at least two powerful barriers. On the one hand, in 1996, Russia's capacity to pay for Central Asian goods apparently reached its maximum level. On the other hand, Russia does not have at its disposal (nor, for a long time to come, is it likely to have) investment resources, which are so acutely needed for the resumption of growth in the entire post-Soviet space.

In the coming years, moreover, another factor operating to diminish the significance of ties with Russia will be the structural improvements in the economy of the Central Asian states. If this region experiences any substantial growth, it will be mainly in the oil and gas sector. But Russia itself is a major producer of oil and gas; it thus has no need to import these goods from abroad. Therefore, the Central Asian hydrocarbons will have to flow to other markets instead.

At the same time, from a strategic perspective, Russia does have an objective interest in the success of reform in Central Asia and in turning this region into a zone of stabile growth. Apart from the future economic dividends from cooperation with successfully developing countries, this will make it possible, at least partly, to reduce tensions on Russia's southern borders. If in the next five to seven years the Central Asian countries cannot achieve positive growth rates, the contemporary civilized structures in the region will irreversibly disintegrate. As a result, the criminal Afghan-Pakistani economic zone, which exists mainly on the basis of participation in the criminal global trade in drugs and weapons, will shift to areas directly on the border of the Russian Federation. Given that neither the Russian state nor especially its private sector has any substantial resources to invest in Central Asia, it would be Russia's national interests to welcome the arrival of Western capital to the region.[3]

Does this mean that Russia will permanently withdraw from any significant role in the economic growth of Central Asia? Not at all. The dynamic development of Central Asia will open broad opportunities for mutual cooperation with Russian enterprises.

Russia's main economic partner in this region will always be Kazakhstan. In 1996, that country provided two-thirds of all Russian exports and three-quarters of all Russian imports to Central Asia. Given the geographic location, Russia will continue to be ranked as a top-priority economic partner for Kazakhstan.

China

If the intensive cooperation of Central Asian countries and Russia is rooted in a century-old tradition, the establishment of commercial and economic relations with China is an entirely new phenomenon. In terms of its share of exports from the region, in 1994–96 China firmly rose to second place (after Russia) for Kazakhstan, fourth place for Kyrgyzstan, and sixth place for Uzbekistan.

The relations between Central Asia and China have a complex history going back many centuries. In the course of nearly two millennia, Central Asia has found itself within the sphere of Chinese political and economic interests, representing the "most ancient region for the application of power in Chinese foreign policy."[4] The periods of the formation of powerful empires in the history of China were accompanied by an intensification of their activity in Central Asia in acquiring strategically important territories located toward the northwest. The process of forming the Chinese People's Republic in 1949 also culminated in the acquisition of the province of Xinjiang. According to a Kazakhstani specialist on the long-term patterns in Chinese-Central Asian relations, "the Chinese historical tradition links state power with the incorporation of the territories of the southern and northern areas around the Tian-Shan Mountain Range [i.e., the territories of the former Soviet Central Asia—eds.] and with the extension of its influence beyond its borders."[5] If that is so, then it is reasonable to assume that this tradition will continue to constitute a significant factor in Chinese policy today as well.

After the collapse of the USSR, China was regarded as the country perhaps most directly concerned about developments in Central Asia. In December 1991 (i.e., immediately after the dissolution of the Soviet Union and the formation of independent states in Central Asia), a Chinese delegation (headed by that country's minister of trade) made an official visit to Kazakhstan, Kyrgyzstan, Uzbekistan, and Tajikistan. This was, in fact, the first high-ranking foreign delegation to visit these newly independent states. The trip led to the signing of trade agreements and the establishment of constructive relations between China and the Central Asian republics. And since then their economic ties have rapidly expanded. Urumqi (the capital of Xinjiang) and Almaty are now directly linked by rail and air connections.

For the moment, the relations between Beijing and the Central Asian states have been largely business-like and constructive. The heads of Central Asia travel to Beijing, and Chinese leaders are also frequent guests in the capitals of Central Asia. China, if with characteristic caution, has advanced proposals to link the transportation system of Central Asia with its own. Within a few years, it is entirely conceivable that it will build a trans-Asian pipeline to ship oil and natural gas from Kazakhstan and Turkmenistan to China and across Chinese territory to markets in South Korea and Japan. It is presumably in Beijing's interest to support the existing regimes in Central Asia—not only because of a general aversion to instability but also because these regimes are ideologically compatible with the "Chinese model," viz., one that pursues a policy of economic liberalization even while upholding a harsh authoritarian regime. The interest here seems to be mutual. By developing economic ties with the states of Central Asia, China can also help reduce their economic dependence on Russia.

In the context of China's long-term strategic and economic interests in Central Asia, it is essential to examine Beijing's special concern with respect to the volatile political situation in Central Asia, which borders directly with Xinjiang Uygur Autonomous Region (XUAR). Xinjiang is the home of more than one million Kazakhs, several hundred thousand Kyrgyz, and (most important) six to seven million Uygurs. The latter are related to the Uzbeks and have several hundred thousand kinsmen living throughout Central Asia. It is hardly surprising that they should have renewed their desire for unification, which has long been suppressed, and that such aspirations should have found much resonance on both sides of the Chinese border in Central Asia. Needless to say, the prospect of Muslim unrest in western China causes anxiety in Beijing, all the more since it is already plagued by the Tibetan problem.

It would appear that China wants to be assured of the support of Kazakhstan and Kyrgyzstan in the civil strife that has become increasingly serious in the XUAR. The Chinese Uygurs are interested in obtaining the support of their related peoples in Central Asia and Kazakhstan (and, more broadly, the entire Muslim world). For their part, the states of Central Asia and Kazakhstan are interested in ties with China, but cannot close their eyes completely to the common roots and religion that they share with the Uygurs.

Beijing conducts an active assimilationist policy by promoting the resettlement of native Chinese (Han) to the region. During the period since 1949, the proportion of ethnic Chinese has increased from 5 to 38 percent. Nevertheless, the Muslim population (Uygur, Kazakhs, Kyrgyz, Dungans, etc.) still comprises the majority of the population. In contrast to Tibet, Xinjiang can in no sense be regarded as one of China's more backward, undeveloped provinces. The index on per capita GDP shows that XUAR ranks twelfth out of thirty-one regions in China. Beijing is indeed conducting an active policy for the economic development of Xinjiang. One needs only visit the capital of XUAR to be convinced of this. Nevertheless, the Muslim majority of the population in this region is dissatisfied with its current condition; they are deeply convinced that Beijing is pursuing a policy of discrimination against them. Recently, Xinjiang has witnessed a clear upsurge in the separatist movement of Uygurs, which, like many such movements, has made terror one of its weapons in the struggle.

Xinjiang, located in the northwestern part of China, has an area of 1.6 million square kilometers (one-sixth the country's total land area) and a population of 16.7 million inhabitants. This region is now undergoing rapid economic growth. Between 1991 and 1995, its GDP grew at an annual average rate of 12.3 percent—the highest in China's midwestern area.[6]

Together with high rates of growth in the GDP, the character of this region's economy has also changed: from what was recently an agrarian area, it quickly began to acquire a more balanced industrial-agrarian structure. Thus, in the first half of the 1990s, the agrarian share of its GDP decreased from 34.7 to 29.9 percent, whereas the industrial portion increased from 24.8 to 26.2 percent. The industrialization of Xinjiang is manifested in an explosive growth of construction and in an accelerated development of the fuel industry, metallurgy, chemicals and petrochemicals, and electric power. The share of construction in the GDP of this region nearly doubled in the period of 1990–95 (rising from 5.8 to 10.1 percent). One can assume that, to a significant degree, this was due to the creation of new industrial capacities. Above all, this pertains to the fuel industry, which leads in the industrial development of Xinjiang; its share of industrial output in the region increased 11.6 percentage points in 1985–95 (rising from 22.2 of 33.8 percent of industrial output). The growth is also due to the rising investments in the infrastructure of the region. At the same time, although the development of extractive and heavy industry is so striking, Xinjiang nonetheless retains important branches to process the output of the agrarian sector: food processing and light industry (i.e., textiles based on the local cotton production). These two branches, respectively, accounted for 20.9 and 12.4 percent of industrial output in the region.

In 1995, investments in the economy of Xinjiang amounted to 3.97 billion U.S. dollars. Of this sum, 65 percent was concentrated in industry and construction, 30 percent in services, and only 5 percent in agriculture.

Foreign trade and economic cooperation have also undergone a rapid pace of development. At present, Xinjiang has already established trade and economic cooperation with fifty-nine countries, and it now exports more than 200 different categories of goods. In 1996, the total volume of Xinjiang's exports and imports reached 1.4 billion dollars. The main export products included cotton, sugar, cotton yarn, cotton clothing, tomato paste, and various chemical products. The main imports consisted of steel, fertilizers, machinery, and so forth. By the end of 1996, more than 700 foreign-funded enterprises were registered in Xinjiang; direct foreign investment in Xinjiang has amounted to 300 million U.S. dollars. Xinjiang has become increasingly attractive to the international corporative giants; for example, Texaco, Exxon, Mobil, and other large oil corporations are participating in the exploration of the Tarim Basin and have contracted to invest some 250 million U.S. dollars in this undertaking.

Recently, however, doubts have begun to emerge whether the Tarim Basin really has such rich oil reserves. According to the *Financial Times,* the results of exploration there have proven very disappointing.[7] If in the mid-1980s Tarim's reserves were estimated at 482 billion barrels, current estimates have drastically reduced this to just 1.5 billion barrels.[8]

Of the five post-Soviet Central Asian states, Kazakhstan has played the main role in relations with China. Thus, Kazakhstan became the first state in the region to establish full diplomatic relations (at the ambassadorial level) with China.

As far as China is concerned, Kazakhstan is of particular importance as a sovereign state. First, of the contiguous Central Asian republics (Kazakhstan, Kyrgyzstan, and Tajikistan), Kazakhstan has the longest common border (1,700 km), and this constitutes a convenient basis for the development of direct interstate and inter-regional ties. It creates new opportunities for the Chinese to gain access to the territories of the immense Asian region to the north of the Tian Shan Mountain Range and beyond, through the Turan Lowland, to the areas of the Caspian Sea and the Caucasus.

Second, Xinjiang is historically linked to Kazakhstan. Moreover, in this autonomous region, Kazakhs constitute one of the largest ethnic groups. All this leads to the mutual interaction of peoples and their cultures on both sides of the state border.

Third, the vast territory of Kazakhstan (with its economic potential, natural resources, and the industrial base constructed during the Soviet era) as well as its strategic geographical position also serve to increase Beijing's interest in Kazakhstan.

The overarching significance of Kazakhstan is also reflected in trade relations. Altogether, the foreign trade transactions of Xinjiang (total export-import volume) amounted to 1.4 billion dollars. Of that total, 52 percent (730 million dollars) came from trade with the countries of Central Asia. If for China, as a whole, trade with Central Asia (including Kazakhstan) does not play a significant role, such is not the case for its most northwestern region, Xinjiang, where trade with Central Asia constitutes an important factor in its economic development. After Kazakhstan, the second largest trading partner in Central Asia is the neighboring country of Kyrgyzstan. Specifically, in 1996, Kazakhstan accounted for 15.8 percent and Kyrgyzstan for 12.9 percent of Xinjiang's exports. The share of each of the remaining three Central Asian states does not exceed a level of 3 to 5 percent. Still more significant is the role that Kazakhstan plays in imports to Xinjiang; in 1996, it accounted for 43.3 percent of the latter's imports. Kyrgyzstan accounted for another 14.0 percent. The remaining three Central Asian countries provided a substantially lower level of imports.

Both in terms of foreign economic relations and foreign policy, Kazakhstan and Kyrgyzstan represent a kind of tandem. Their economies constitute, in practical terms, a single economic complex. With respect to Xinjiang, these two countries alone accounted for 57.3 percent of imports to this Chinese region. The individual share of other importers (Hong Kong, Russia, Italy, Japan, the United States, Pakistan, Taiwan, and Germany) did not exceed 10 percent of the imports to Xinjiang. From this one can see the significance that Kazakhstan bears for the economic development of western China. The industrialization of Xinjiang, to a substantial degree, is achieved through the delivery of raw materials, cement, steel, trucks, and other heavy industrial products from Kazakhstan. The latter also provides Xinjiang with fertilizers and agricultural machinery. In turn, the Chinese side delivers mainly foodstuffs and consumer goods to Kazakhstan. At the outset of the 1990s, commercial relations between the two partners were realized primarily through barter trade. Recently, the share of barter transactions has significantly decreased, as commercial relations assume a more normal character and an ever greater volume of goods are bought and sold at world prices. In assessing the scale of Kazakhstani and Kyrgyzstani exports to China, one should also bear in mind that a significant part of these goods (for example, trucks) are re-exports from Russia.

Against this background of economic growth in Xinjiang, the situation in Kazakhstan and Kyrgyzstan appears far more dismal. A particularly striking contrast to Xinjiang is the condition of southern Kazakhstan, which has 40 percent of the country's population and currently finds itself in profound economic decline. Here one finds a disintegration of the infrastructure, degradation of the industrial sector, and extremely severe conditions in agriculture. Indeed, the region is experiencing a progressive immiseration of the population, with per capita income here being lower than elsewhere in Kazakhstan. Thus, the dynamically developing Western part of China stands in marked contrast to the degraded, truly impoverished territories of neighboring states: Kyrgyzstan (which is surviving only because of international financial assistance), Tajikistan (with its economic structure in shambles from the civil war), and the poorest regions of Kazakhstan. There is no reason to expect that these areas of Central Asia—which do not have oil—will become attractive objects for serious international investments. In the authors' opinion, these areas face the following alternatives: either continuing decay in all spheres of economic life (with a corresponding depopulation), or a natural tendency toward closer cooperation with the economy of Xinjiang.

The prospects of closer economic ties between Kazakhstan and China are becoming clarified in the light of Beijing's growing, and increasingly transparent, interest in the oil resources of Kazakhstan. According to the *Financial Times,* "China has long looked to closer cooperation with neighboring Central Asian states in oil and gas production to help fuel its rapid growth."[9] The increasing shortfall in oil, compounded by the unjustified hopes on oil production in the Tarim Basin, compels China to accelerate the flow of petroleum imports. The *Financial Times* further reports that "imports are expected to rise to 50 million tons by 2000 (from 22 million last year)."[10] According to the same newspaper, China expects to invest "4.3 billion U.S. dollars to secure a 60 percent stake in Kazakhstan's state-owned Aktiubinsk Oil Company." In addition, the *Financial Times* reports "the China National Petroleum Corporation also plans to spend an additional 3.5 billion dollars on a 3,000 km pipeline linking western Kazakhstan, the site of the Aktiubinsk oil fields, with China's Xinjiang region."[11] Apparently, this shortage of energy resources will affect not only China but also other countries in East Asia. It is therefore realistic to expect that the preferred market for the sale of Kazakhstani oil will become the Asian-Pacific region, and that the oil will be shipped through China. And this will further reinforce the ties between Kazakhstan and China.

The Central Asian region is also of special geopolitical importance for China, for it is the source of a separatist nationalism, Islamic fundamentalism, and pan-Turkish influences. Therefore, China apparently intends to fill this strategic vacuum, which emerged after the collapse of the USSR, and to counteract efforts by Turkey and Iran to extend their influence here. Beijing will thus seek to conduct an active policy toward the Central Asian republics (above all, Kazakhstan). At the present time, China is interested in ensuring stability in domestic and international relations in order to carry out successfully its reforms within the framework of the so-called "four modernization." Hence, it is not interested in reinforcing factors that could upset the relative balance in the countries to its northwest; rather, it will seek all possible measures to ensure their neutralization.[12]

Notes

1. Makhman Gafarlyi, "Dolgi stran SNG rastut," *Nezavisimaia gazeta,* 23 May 1997, p. 3.
2. Ramazon Mirzoev, "Razvivaetsia vzaimovygodnoe sotrudnichestvo," *Nezavisimaia gazeta,* 8 April 1997, p. 3; Makhman Gafarly, "Vyplata dolgov Moskve otlozhena na 15 let," *Nezavisimaia gazeta,* 11 December 1996, p. 3.

3. To be sure, some Russian corporations—above all, the huge gas and oil companies—do have real interests and resources to invest in the Central Asian economy. For details, see O. Reznikova, "Rossiia, Turtsiia i Iran v Tsentral'noi Azii," *Mirovaia ekonomika i mezhdunarodnye otnosheniia*, 1996, no. 1.

4. Klara Khafizova, "Kitaiskaia diplomatiia i kazakhskaia gosudarst-vennost'," *Kazakhstan i mirovoe soobshchestvo*, 1996, no. 4, p. 23.

5. Ibid.

6. The information here (and in the following text) was obtained by one of the authors from the regional planning commission of KhUAR in Urumqi in May 1997.

7. Tony Walker and Robert Corzine, "China To Pay $4.3 Billion for Kazakh Oil Stake," *Financial Times,* 5 June 1997, p. 16.

8. James Dorian, Brett Wigdortz, and Dru Gladney, "Central Asia and Xinjiang, China," Asia-Pacific Issues Paper, Honolulu, May 1997.

9. Walker and Corzine, "China," *Financial Times,* 5 June 1997.

10. Tony Walker, "Sino-Russian Fuel Deal Close," *Financial Times,* 19 June 1997.

11. Walker and Corzine, "China," *Financial Times,* 5 June 1997.

12. See K. Kokarev, "Kitaisko-Kazakhstanskie otnosheniia," in *Kazakhstan: realii i perspektivy nezavisimogo razvitiia* (Moscow, 1995).

Part III

External Dynamics: Foreign Trade

8

Kazakhstan: Foreign Trade Policy

Markhamat Khasanova

Integration of Kazakhstan into the World Economy

Before the Republic of Kazakhstan acquired state sovereignty, it had no experience in conducting foreign trade and hence lacked the conceptions, institutions, and personnel needed to perform this task. Instead, the entire foreign economic activity of the enterprises of Kazakhstan, including foreign trade, was handled by central all-union institutions in Moscow. This did not mean that its foreign economic activity was marginal. On the contrary, because Kazakhstan was as an integral part of the national economic complex of the USSR and because it was endowed with unique, rich mineral resources, it actively participated in the foreign trade of the former Soviet Union. Indeed, Kazakhstan occupied one of the leading places in the USSR in terms of the volume of exports for a number of goods—nonferrous metals, rare and rare-earth metals, ferroalloys, chromite ore, and phosphorous. In the 1980s, more than 180 enterprises were active in producing goods for export. Its array of export goods included about 200 items; the geographical destinations for these goods included eighty countries around the world, with about 60 percent of the total volume of export going to countries in the Council of Mutual Economic Assistance.[1]

The disruption of economic ties that followed the breakup of the USSR triggered a collapse in the trade among the former Soviet republics—which, in 1992, had still accounted for 92.2 percent of Kazakhstan's exports and 85.3 percent of its imports. At the same time, this very same process impelled the republic to turn actively toward world markets. Thus, whereas in 1993 Kazakhstan conducted trade with 62 countries, by 1996 it had increased this number to 134 countries.

Taking into account this starting point, one can conclude that, in a relatively short period of time, Kazakhstan has been remarkably successful in its effort to gain access to world markets. The foreign trade turnover during these years has comprised a significant proportion of the total volume of the GDP, rising from 55 to 75 percent (see Table 8.1).

The main domestic factor in actively helping to establish Kazakhstan's broad network of foreign economic ties is the presence of rich raw material resources that enjoy a high demand on world markets. And these resources are already being exploited, with production exceeding domestic demand. Above all, these include oil, nonferrous metals (copper, zinc, and lead), chrome and its alloys, rolled steel, and products from the oil refining and chemical industries (including fertilizers).

Kazakhstan ranks as one of the leading positions in the world with respect to strategic mineral resources—in terms of the diversity of types, volume of reserves, and quality. If measured by the volume of reserves per capita, the republic is above the world average for oil, coal, iron ore, chromium ore, manganese ore, the most important nonferrous metals, and phosphates. Kazakhstan ranks first in the world in terms of its reserves of tungsten; second for chromite ore and phosphates; fourth for manganese ores, lead, and molybdenum; and seventh for iron ores. The republic is also supplied with significant reserves of nonferrous and rare metals, phosphorites, and other forms of mineral resources.[2]

The most important component of exports is grain. Of the 26 to 29 million tons of grain produced each year in Kazakhstan, the country exported 3 to 4 million tons to other union republics, with a smaller amount—about 0.1 million tons—going to the rest of the world (Hungary, Mongolia, Romania, and Afghanistan). The republic has the opportunity to deliver abroad cotton, raw leather goods, and other products of the agro-industrial complex.

The active involvement of Kazakhstan in world markets, to a large degree, has been due to the discrepancy, in recent years, between do-

Table 8.1

Foreign Trade of the Republic of Kazakhstan

Indicator		1991	1992	1993	1994	1995	1996	1997[a]
Foreign trade as share of volume of GDP (percent)		43.9	81.0	76.5	71.3	77.6	66.7	60.4
Including:	Exports (FOB)	19.0	35.0	31.4	29.6	37.1	31.9	29.4
	Imports (FOB)	24.9	46.0	45.1	41.7	40.5	34.8	31.0
Foreign trade per capital (in dollars)		1,367	488	514	506	778	856	858
Kazakhstan's foreign trade as share of world trade (in percent)[b]			0.07	0.01	0.01		0.13	
Currency exchange (average for given year)		1.8[c]	156.4[c]	2.38	35.76	60.93	67.34	77.5

Source: Data from the National Statistical Agency in the Ministry of Economics and Trade of the Republic of Kazakhstan.
[a]Estimate (Draft of the "Indicative Plan for the Social-economic Development of the Republic of Kazakhstan for 1998).
[b]Data taken from the International Monetary Fund, "International Financial Statistics" (March 1997).
[c]In rubles/U.S. dollars.

mestic and world prices for the basic goods exported from this country. Thus, in 1991, when the average world price for refined copper was 2,518 dollars per ton, Kazakhstan had an export price of 1,849 dollars per ton, with a still lower price (1,000 dollars per ton) for the domestic market. In 1993, when it cost 18 dollars to produce one ton of oil, the export price was 26 dollars (compared to the average world price of 106 dollars). In 1997, the gap between the domestic and foreign prices for oil was still substantial. Whereas production costs ran at 54 dollars per ton, enterprises could expect a world price of 115–125 dollars per ton.

Foreign trade is the most important factor in the republic's efforts to achieve economic stabilization. Exports comprise up to 35 percent of the GDP (a share significantly higher than in the other states of Central Asia and comparable to countries like Malaysia and Iran); they are one means for enabling enterprises to survive and to sustain the current employment level. Export also makes it possible to supply domestic markets with consumer products, fuel and energy, and investment goods. In the future, the foreign trade policy will continue to have a significant influence on the future of economic growth.

One must also realistically assess Kazakhstan's position on foreign markets, which is by no means secure. That is because its main exports consist of raw material goods, which are subject to substantial price fluctuation. Moreover, given the globalization of the economy, the difference between domestic and world prices has been inexorably decreasing. At present, the relative advantages in the production of petroleum and chemical products has been lost, and the same pattern will next overtake nonferrous and ferrous metals. Finally, Kazakhstan accounts for only an insignificant share of world trade—approximately 0.13 percent of the total volume of world trade in 1995 (see Table 8.1).

In general, Kazakhstan does not deal directly with the end-users of its basic export goods. To be sure, there are exceptions: in cases where there are direct production relations with Russian and Central Asian enterprises in the production of oil, natural gas, the ores for ferrous and nonferrous metals, grain, and some other products, quotas and con-tracts are established at the governmental level. But otherwise the re-public cannot participate in world commodity exchanges (because of the shipping costs for large-tonnage freight), and it channels a signifi-cant part of exports (25 to 30 percent) through intermediary companies (from Switzerland, the Netherlands, Germany, and the Baltic states) registered in off-shore zones. In working with such intermediaries, it is virtually impossible to determine the end user of its goods, for the intermediaries treat this information as highly confidential. The export of goods is realized essentially on FOB (free on board) and EXW (ex-warehouse) terms—that is, the good is virtually bought from the warehouses of the producer-seller, or in the best case, is delivered to a ship in a mutually agreed upon port or to the border of the republic.

Moreover, it must be said that trade deals, as a result of the liberalization of foreign trade, are conducted by small firms and scattered among many markets. Moreover, the markets of European countries impose some quantitative limitations on goods from Kazakhstan, such as the export limits on textiles and steel. It appears that this list will increase because of the processes of integration now underway in Europe. Under these circumstances, it is necessary to concentrate efforts on gaining access for raw materials to certain markets by merging firms into larger units and by providing state assistance for them.

In addition to strengthening and expanding the commercial and economic ties with Russia (still the most important partner for Kazakhstan), in the future it will be important to develop direct trade relations with countries in the Pacific Rim as well as the Middle and Near East. To enhance the ties to the Asian-Pacific region, it is necessary to cooperate with the Asian states for the joint use of transportation routes and access points to world markets. In the Asian-Pacific area itself, the most important market is China. Direct business ties are now being actively developed with its western area—the Xingjiang Uygur Autonomous Region; the delivery of goods to this area from Kazakhstan is growing rapidly and represents an estimated 30 to 33 percent of total imports. This trade is promoted further by unorganized petty (or so-called shuttle) trade. A significant proportion of the goods imported by shuttle traders comes from China.

The Development of Trade Turnover and the Foreign Trade Balance

The high volume of foreign trade before 1991 reflected, above all, the high degree to which the republic had been integrated into the single economic complex of the former USSR. But the inefficiency of the old market and cooperative ties, which were mediated by the state, became immediately apparent after the breakup of the Soviet Union and resulted in a sharp contraction in trade among the former Soviet republics (see Table 8.2) But the raw materials produced earlier for industrial plants in Russia and the other Soviet republics had no niche on the domestic market within the republic itself. At the same time, Kazakhstan was still highly dependent on the union republics for goods like motor vehicles, home appliances, raw materials for the food-processing industry, and many other consumer goods. Kazakhstan was also heavily dependent on Russia and the republics of Central Asia for its supply of electricity and natural gas. In addition, the trade turnover between Kazakhstan and the other Soviet republics had, for many years, already been characterized by a surplus of imports over exports—in other words, a negative balance of trade.

The newly independent, sovereign republics did not wish to trade with each other on the terms that had prevailed earlier—that is, at unfavorable prices and for rubles. The deregulation of prices in January 1992, given the acute shortages (especially for consumer goods) inherited from the Soviet system, did not stimulate enterprises to produce "more." There was, in fact, neither the means to produce nor someone able to purchase such goods. The fall in production and galloping inflation were compounded by a severe nonpayments crisis and by a shortage of cash in the general population. As a result, producers were forced to seek buyers in foreign markets, even if they had not had any experience in conducting foreign trade. The desire to earn hard currency, together with other factors (the lack of certification or the means to participate in international exchanges or to deliver heavy-tonnage cargo to ports of destination), often meant that producers had to sell their goods at prices significantly below world levels, or in exchange for consumer goods that were popular on the domestic market. To cite one example, copper was bartered for such things as automobiles and popular candy bars.

In the development of the foreign trade turnover, the last two and a half years have shown a growth in the value of trade (1.5 times in comparable prices) amidst contracting production, even in export-oriented branches, but the country has not reached the level that existed in 1991 (see Table 8.2). The main factors in this growth include the higher prices in foreign-trade deals and the sharp fall of demand on the markets in Kazakhtan and in the CIS. The decline in commodity turnover (compared to 1991 levels) is due to such factors as the contraction in the physical volume of exports in the main goods (except grain), but

Table 8.2

Foreign Trade of Kazakhstan, 1991–97 (in millions of dollars)

Indicator	1991	1992	1993	1994	1995	1996	1997
Trade turnover	22,968	8,241	8,732	8,559	12,992	14,045	13,575
Exports (FOB)	9,947	3,562	3,586	3,553	6,210	6,721	6,609
Exports to CIS	9,167	2,072	2,033	2,120	3,792	3,765	
Exports outside CIS	780	1,490	1,552	1,433	2,418	2,955	
Imports (FOB)	13,021	4,679	5,146	5,006	6,782	7,324	6,966
Imports from CIS	11,111	3,159	3,148	3,015	4,395	4,944	
Imports from outside CIS	1,910	1,520	1,997	1,991	2,387	2,379	
Trade balance	–3,074	–1,117	–1,561	–1,453	–571	–600	–357
Balance with CIS	–1,944	–1,087	–1,114	–895	–602	–1,179	
Balance with non-CIS	–1,130	–30	–446	–558	+31	+575	

Source: Data from the National Statistical Agency in the Ministry of Economics and Trade of the Republic of Kazakhstan.

also the suspension of trade in uncompetitive producer goods that had been delivered to the former Soviet republics (see Table 8.3).

The rapid increase in exports during the last two years is due to the transfer of the main industrial enterprises to foreign firms. More than forty contracts have given foreign companies control over enterprises in ferrous and nonferrous metallurgy, which in fact play a main role in exports. The foreign firms have experience in selling on world markets, and this has played a positive role.

The terms of trade have deteriorated. Although, in the last two years, one can discern a tendency for the rate of growth in export and import prices to achieve a certain equilibrium, import prices have generally tended to grow at a faster pace than the prices on exports.

In the midterm perspective, the growth of exports will come mainly on the basis of oil exports. The two main constraints limiting an expansion of exports include the exhaustion of fixed capital and the inadequate capacities of the transport routes for shipment abroad. If foreign market conditions remain favorable, the volume of exports (according to our estimates) cannot exceed 7 to 8 billion dollars.

A top priority in economic policy is the need to ensure that the income from the export of raw materials is used to increase investments—so as to modernize the production of raw materials for export and to create competitive lines of production in the processing branch. However, for the last three years, the export of goods has not produced more than a total of 3.5 billion dollars. It is essential to stop the diversion of these hard-currency earnings to foreign bank accounts and their use to pay for the import of consumer goods.

In mid-April, the Agency for the Control of Strategic Resources of the Republic of Kazakhstan appealed to the president with an initiative to create a "Budget for the Development of the Republic of Kazakhstan." The proposal was based on research concerning the "Dutch disease," an affliction characteristic of countries rich in natural resources. The authors define this ailment as the negative influence of enormous revenues from developing and exporting mineral resources; this "easy money" increases the value of the national currency on exchange markets. This growth also affects the traditional sectors of the economy that produce goods and services and that, currently or potentially, participate in trade turnover. This syndrome acquired its name after Holland began, in the 1960s, to actively develop its natural gas deposits. Substantial revenues from the extraction of gas flowed into the budget

Table 8.3

Export of the Most Important Types of Goods, 1992–96 (in physical units)

Good	Unit of measurement	1992	1993	1994	1995	1996
Oil and gas condensate	Millions of tons	18.6	12.6	9.6	11.2	14.5
Natural gas	Billions of cu. m.	3.9	3.4	1.6	3.6	2.3
Coal	Millions of tons	44.0	34.6	19.7	12.9	28.7
Ferroalloys	Thousands of tons	726.0	720.0	505.5	578.3	508.2
Rolled steel	Thousands of tons	2,720.0	1,780.0	1,415.6	1,694.1	1,907.9
Copper	Thousands of tons	301.4	273.0	86.4	216.6	261.9
Zinc	Thousands of tons	170.7	166.7	120.6	147.7	149.6
Lead	Thousands of tons	175.8	165.1	48.5	58.4	51.1
Alumina	Thousands of tons	990.0	1,059.0	791.4	758.0	1,125.0
Grain	Thousands of tons	2,898.0	3,586.7	2,677.3	3,876.8	3,943.6

Source: Data from the National Statistical Agency of the Ministry of Economics and Trade, Republic of Kazakhstan.

but, contrary to the expectations of the government, the economic situation in the country worsened. So as not to repeat this unhappy experience, the authors proposed to shield Kazakhstan through two measures: first, protection of the national currency from an excessive strengthening, and second, creation of a Budget for the Development of the Republic of Kazakhstan. Moreover, this Budget of Development (which will accumulate oil and gas revenues from royalties, bonuses, and other assessments, as well as the state's profit from "Kazakhoil," based on projects in the Caspian Sea and other deposits) is to be separated from the regular budget, which is under the control of the government.

In this author's opinion, however, it does not make sense to transfer the incomes from the export of natural resources to a nonbudget fund managed by the Agency for the Control of Strategic Resources, and to do so simply to avoid the "Dutch disease." Even if one believes that the threat of the Dutch disease is real, this fund—even with the best intentions—is hardly likely to reach its goals. If one takes into account the entire practice of creating extra-budgetary funds in the republic (the fund for economic transformation in 1988, the three attempts to create funds to support small entrepreneurship in 1992–97, and others), it is clear that these failed to yield positive results. And one can also expect a diversion of budgetary resources, followed by their pilfering and dispersion.[3]

Several other points should also be kept in mind. First, the "Dutch disease" does not threaten Kazakhstan in the foreseeable future:

- In contrast to countries where the economy is overheated, Kazakhstan has still not achieved full macroeconomic stabilization.
- During the years of reform, the real income of the population has significantly lagged behind the level of prices.
- The country's budget still runs a deficit and is hardly likely to have a surplus in the midterm perspective. Such is the case even if the tax base is significantly expanded and revenues increase: (a) enormous investments (including from the state budget) are needed for economic development; and, (b) the state must pay off its domestic and foreign debts.
- Exports take up 30 to 35 percent of the GDP in Kazakhstan (compared to 68 percent in the Netherlands and 92 percent in Saudi Arabia).[4] Kazakhstan cannot expect the latter kind of ex-

port level in the foreseeable future, given the existing potential and the structural transformation now under way. Thus, in the near term exports will not exceed 7 to 8 billion dollars, rising to about 12 to 15 billion dollars in the years of 2000–05.

- The level of development of export-oriented branches and the corresponding infrastructure requires significant and immediate investments. According to our estimates, just to support the export-oriented branches of production in the fuel and energy complex, in ferrous and nonferrous metallurgy, and in the chemical industry, by the year 2000 approximately 10 to 11 billion dollars in investments will be required.
- The current budget revenues from the export of natural resources now represent modest sums (less than 100 million dollars), and the possible dividends from recycling these funds do not approach the amounts needed to modernize and develop the country's economy (19 to 21 billion dollars, according to our estimates).
- At this stage, Kazakhstan's exports do not even cover the hard-currency needs of state (to service the foreign debts backed by state guarantees) and the National Bank (which, in 1996, compared to a potential demand of 2.4 billion dollars, received 2.2 billion dollars for the hard-currency accounts of enterprises).
- Kazakhstan does not have full national control over the extraction and sale of oil and many other natural resources being produced for export. Therefore, it cannot count on profits and superprofits from the share of property held by foreign firms (given the current legislation on hard currency and foreign investments).
- Despite the fact that the country has significant amounts of natural resources, it does not have an absolute advantage in a single type of resource (including hydrocarbon raw materials).

Second, the creation of an extra-budgetary fund will reduce the current revenues of the state budget. That is because the export-oriented enterprises constitute the only sector of the economy that now shows a growth in production.

Third, given the current lack of control and accountability for spending taxpayers' money, there is no guarantee that the government will use these funds efficiently and effectively. This judgment is completely well justified and based on past experience: it is not deemed necessary for the government to give a full accounting to the taxpayers on how their money has been spent.

Thus, the income from the export of natural resources does not yield any surpluses and indeed is insufficient to cover the demand for investments. The key task is to ensure that these revenues return to the domestic economy and that they increase in the future, since the chief source of revenues for the republic at this point must come from the export of raw materials.

Given the current conditions in Kazakhstan, it is absolutely essential to import modern technologies and equipment for there to be structural changes in material production as well as growth and expansion not only in the processing industry, but especially in the machine-building, food-processing, and light industries. The mounting indebtedness from such imports does not pose a threat to the country so long as all this increases the production of competitive goods. It is essential to develop a conception for investment precisely along these lines: given the limited domestic market in Central Asia and the enormous transportation distances to other outlets, direct foreign investments will hardly be attracted to such modern branches. Rather, for a long time to come, the developed countries will prefer to invest in Southeast Asia and Eastern Europe.

It also bears noting that measures in recent years to achieve a positive balance of trade reflect the competition of opposing goals in macroeconomic policy. From the perspective of preventing large-scale foreign indebtedness, this policy is well grounded. However, if viewed in terms of intensifying investment activity (through the large-scale importation of modern equipment and machinery), this policy has clear negative consequences. Moreover, one must take into account that, even if machinery and equipment represent a low proportion of imports (15 to 16 percent of imports in FOB prices), the total trade balance is nonetheless negative because of the significant volume of unofficial transactions, which consist mainly of imports by private "shuttle traders."

The Shuttle Trade: "Shopper-Tourism"

The volume of shuttle-trader imports represents over half of the imports as reported by the customs statistics for the Republic of Kazakhstan (see Table 8.4).

Table 8.4

Shuttle Trade in Kazakhstan, 1993–97

Indicator		1993	1994	1995	1996	1997[a]
Exports (millions of dollars)	Total	33.1	46.0	289.2	389.3	200.0
	Non-CIS countries	n.a.	n.a.	n.a.	n.a.	n.a.
	CIS	33.1	46.0	289.2	389.3	200.0
Imports (millions of dollars)	Total	466.3	625.4	1,811.6	2,276.8	1,516.0
	Non-CIS countries	367.1	487.5	991.8	1,135.3	
	CIS countries	99.2	137.9	819.8	1,141.3	
Share (in percent)	Of imports reported by customs	52.5	17.6	46.2	53.7	50.3
	Of imports FOB	9.1	12.5	26.7	31.1	46.2

Source: Balance of payments of the National Statistical Agency of the Republic of Kazakhstan.
[a]Provisional estimate by the National Bank of Kazakhstan.

The main cause of this phenomenon is the loss of jobs in industry and agriculture. A further factor is the good income to be derived from shopper-tourism.

According to the data in mid-1996 (compiled from a professional survey of opinion among the shuttle traders and the heads of tourist agencies), this business was especially profitable during the years when there were massive shortages of consumer goods. At that time, retailers could jack up the price on goods by as much as 250 percent of their cost; one needed only 500 to 1,000 dollars in working capital to engage in such transactions. These shopper-tourists traveled mainly to China, but later took advantage of routes to Turkey, India, and Pakistan, and even organized automobile tours to Germany and the United Arab Emirates.

As the domestic consumer market became saturated, however, beginning in 1995 the profit margin from the shuttle trade dropped to 30 to 70 percent. The returns for travel to countries like the United Arab Emirates, Turkey, Poland, and South Korea is about the same; the main exception is China, where the cheap prices on goods mean higher returns. For most traders, the turnover time for business transactions is 1.5 to 2.0 months (compared to 1995, when the turnover time was just 10 to 14 days). Moreover, the basic start-up capital now averages between 2,000 and 4,000 dollars. For example, the start-up capital for deals in the United Arab Emirates is about 2,000 dollars; this includes 520 dollars in travel expenses, another 1,300 to 1,500 dollars for the goods themselves, and another 100 to 200 dollars to cover the costs of airfreight. After the goods have been sold, the total revenue amounts to about 3,000 to 3,500 dollars, with the whole transaction taking 1.5 to 2.0 months. After the shuttle trader has paid all his expenses, on average he is left with 300 to 400 dollars in profit, most of which is spent on current consumption needs. As a result, they can only invest in this business about the same funds, roughly equal to the start-up capital.

The minimum capital required for one shopping-tourist trip to most countries (United Arab Emirates, South Korea, India, Pakistan, Thailand, Turkey, etc.), with the exception of China, is approximately 2,000 dollars. In fact, the majority carry between 2,500 and 4,000 dollars; the rare exception is a big-time shuttle trader with operating capital in the range of 10,000 to 12,000 dollars. However, almost all these traders declare only 2,000 dollars when they cross the border of Kazakhstan, since larger sums are subject to special customs rules and duties. Specifically, anyone carrying goods with a declared value between 2,000 and 6,000 dollars must pay a 15 percent duty; if the total weight is between 70 and 280 kilograms, the customs duty is a flat rate of 2 ECU per kg. In fact, it often turns into systemic bribing: if the value of the goods is plainly greater than the declared sum, the shuttle trader pays the customs officers 30 to 50 dollars for each piece of baggage (which cannot exceed 50 kg).

In recent years, the shuttle trade has shown a tendency toward cooperation and specialization in wholesale transactions. Thus, approximately one-third of the shuttle traders pool their capital and send one or two of their number to escort a container filled with wares. Cities throughout Kazakhstan have witnessed an increase in the number of wholesale goods markets. A significant proportion of the wholesale purchases on such markets are conducted by the citizens of Uzbekistan, Kyrgyzstan, Russia, and other countries.

A survey of shuttle traders who engage in this wholesale business revealed that the majority are not registered for individual entrepreneurial activity. Moreover, many are citizens of the People's Republic of China; others are citizens of Turkey, Iran, India, and other countries. The main destination for their shopping tourism is China.

The owners of these freight containers carry at least 20,000 dollars on a single trip. The return is less than 10 percent of the total value of the imported goods (including transportation costs). The average turnaround time ranges between seven and ten days. The average net profit per container is about 2,700 dollars per month (once accounts have been settled with the retail sellers and various duties and local taxes have been assessed). Each shuttle trader has between two and ten retail sellers.

According to our calculations, approximately 100,000 to 170,000 people are now directly engaged in the shuttle trade. However, that estimate increases several-fold (to somewhere between 700,000 and 1,200,000) if one adds those who participate in this informal trade within the confines of the republic itself. That latter total is about 5 to 8 percent of the entire population; it is 40 percent larger than the total employed in industry or in agriculture. Expressed in another way, this figure is equivalent to the total number of people employed in the following branches: transportation and communications, construction, public health, and organized retail trade. By contrast, the total number of employees in small enterprises is less than 170,000 people.

It is difficult to offer more precise information about the number of shuttle traders because of the inferior quality and inconsistencies in the statistical data. Thus, the State Customs Committee processes only two entries on the customs declarations of travelers: citizenship and purpose of the trip. Since the declaration does not ask for the country destination, one cannot determine the countries involved in such commercial transactions. Moreover, once the government introduced the "green corridor" on 1 November 1996, it ceased to collect systematic information on all those who cross the border.

Thus, the shuttle trade is the largest sphere of small business and has grown to become a special branch of the economy in post-Soviet republics. It is most extensively developed in Kazakhstan and Russia. In the latter case, it is estimated that between 10 and 30 million people (13.5 percent of the population) are engaged in this business.[5]

Another significant factor here is the creative policies on the part of countries that profit from "shopping tourism." Thus, the number and destinations of charter flights have increased substantially; recently, for example, the roster of such flights was expanded to include Italy, Cyprus, the Baltic states, and various other countries. Moreover, these countries have taken steps to create favorable conditions for shuttle traders. The Turkish government, for instance, has carved out "shuttle trade zones" (the Istanbul market of Liapeli and the health resort of Antalya) and introduced a number of special privileges to promote the "suitcase business." The latter include the abolition of the VAT on goods purchased by shuttle traders, the opening of complaint bureaus in areas most frequently visited by traders from Russia and the CIS, the formation of special police units to assist these traders and to guard their hotels, and the allocation of warehouses to store their wares. The government has also decided to reduce substantially the price of aviation fuel for charter flights, to exempt such planes from airport parking fees, and to cut airport service fees by 50 percent. According to various data, the shuttle trade is now bringing Turkey between 8 and 10 billion dollars per year.[6]

Since 1993, shopping tourism has caused a drain of hard currency from Kazakhstan—something on the order of 6.3 billion dollars, or approximately 1.4 billion dollars per annum. By comparison, in 1996 the accounts of enterprises in Kazakhstan showed that they had received 2.2 billion dollars from the export of goods and services.

This shuttle trade has had a contradictory impact on the domestic economy. On the one hand, shopping tourism has reduced unemployment, expanded the supply of cheap goods, increased cargoes in the transportation branch, and created a broad stratum of small entrepreneurs. On the other hand, the uncontrolled deluge of consumer goods from abroad has exacerbated the problems facing domestic producers. Raising customs duties to protect domestic producers will not have much effect since petty private trade is all but impossible to regulate and control. Indeed, stringent measures to limit or liquidate shopping tourism would entail serious social and political consequences:

- By forcing the mass of shuttle traders to abandon their commercial activities, such measures would, in effect, leave them unemployed and ready to join with antigovernment opposition forces.
- It would diminish demand for transportation services and the underlying infrastructure in this branch.
- It would simply replace the domestic shuttle trader with foreigners from countries like Russia, Uzbekistan, Kyrgyzstan, Turkey, Iran, Pakistan, India, and South Korea.
- Hence it would nonetheless fail to achieve the main objective— namely, protect domestic producers from the competition of foreign goods.

The Regional Structure of Foreign Trade

Integration within the framework of the CIS is an important objective in the foreign economic policy of Kazakhstan. Various measures (e.g., abolition of export duties within the "Customs Union" that includes Russia, Belarus, Kazakhstan, and Kyrgyzstan) have improved the trade turnover with Russia, thereby stimulating industrial production in Kazakhstan.

Thus, according to customs statistics, in 1996 the foreign trade turnover with member states of the Customs Union increased 29.6 percent from the previous year, reaching a total volume of 5.5 billion dollars. By comparison, trade with the other members of the CIS decreased by 13.3 percent, falling to a total of 0.94 billion dollars.

At the same time, the plans for integration within the framework of the Central Asian Union (established by Kazakhstan, Uzbekistan, and Kyrgyzstan in 1994) have not led to a significant increase in trade among these three countries. Indeed, volume of trade here has even fallen somewhat, declining from 537 million dollars (1994) to 497 million dollars (1996).

This increase in the monetary value of trade with members of the Customs Union included a decrease in the physical volume of exports (on virtually all the main goods) but also an increase in the physical volume of imports to Kazakhstan. The latter increase included some growth in the import of oil and gas condensate from Russia, automobiles and rolled steel from Russia, trucks from Russia and Belarus, and tires from Belarus. The increase in the value of exports from Kazakhstan was due to the rise in prices on chromite and iron ores, ferroalloys, rolled steel, zinc, lead, copper, and other commodities.

This expansion of trade had several consequences for Kazakhstan. Thus, while the higher export prices increased the profitability of exports, they did not create additional jobs—given the steady decrease in physical volume of trade transactions. Kazakhstan's import orientation derived from the lower prices on such goods and an increase in the physical volume of import.

The main reason why the physical volume of exports dropped during these years was the significant differences in the economic mechanisms at work in individual countries. These differences resulted from the sharp disparities in the rates and character of economic reforms being conducted in the various post-Soviet republics. The former mechanism of mutual deliveries was disrupted, and the transition to some new system has given rise to major difficulties. Moreover, the rate of contraction in exports would have been even greater were Kazakhstan not so dependent on the import of fuel and energy.

At the same time, the last five years have brought a reorientation in the flow of goods to markets outside the CIS. Although the CIS continues to dominate the regional structure of exports (receiving, according to customs data, 45 percent of exports), its share has dropped sharply from the 1991 level of 92.2 percent (see Table 8.5, pages 188–189).

The predominance of CIS countries and, especially Russia, in the regional structure of the foreign trade of Kazakhstan increased during the years 1994–96. This was due to the reorientation of Kazakhstan toward imports from these countries.

At the same time, in the trade with countries outside the CIS, there has been a noticeable increase in the share held by developed countries. This tendency derived mainly from several key factors—the experience of these countries in gaining access to markets and supporting exports, the adoption of programs for technical assistance, and the establishment of commercial offices in Kazakhstan. The main stimuli for this reorientation included the desire to obtain hard currency as well as the opportunity to sell natural resources at world prices, which are still significantly higher than those prevailing in transactions within the CIS.

More than one-third of the trade turnover (an average of 34 percent per year) is held by countries in the European Union. Moreover, exports are approximately 50 percent greater than imports. The active increase in imports, especially from Germany, came during years when these countries provided credits to finance exports to Kazakhstan. The trade turnover was not always equal; in the earliest years, trade was mainly conducted on a barter basis. Thus, in exchange for oil and nonferrous metals (which were sold at low prices), Kazakhstan received obsolescent equipment and consumer goods that consisted mainly of confectionary products.

Obviously, the capacity to purchase equipment and machinery would be significantly greater if Kazakhstan bought these goods with its own hard currency rather than through credits. It bears noting that Kazakhstan's exports to Europe, which accounts for a significant part of the favorable balance of trade, yield the greatest return. Moreover, at present, the trade is conducted mainly on the basis of freely convertible currencies. Hence it is necessary to create conditions favorable for hard currency to come to Kazakhstan and then to channel these resources toward investment in the economy—above all, for the purchase of capital goods and technologies.

In the future, a substantial change in the regional structure of exports will depend on laying a large-diameter pipeline to export oil from Kazakhstan to Western Europe and to other world markets.

Notwithstanding the efforts of the government to expand and intensify integration, in 1997 trade with countries in the CIS, including Russia (Kazakhstan's main trading partner), has tended to decrease. Thus, in the first quarter of 1997, the trade turnover with Russia dropped by nearly 40 percent from the same period a year earlier; this contraction included a substantial reduction in the delivery of Kazakhstani exports like oil and oil products, metallic ores, and almost all categories of ferrous and nonferrous metals. The main dynamic here was the transfer of national control over the raw-material sector to foreign companies, which have assumed control or ownership of enter-

Table 8.5

Regional Structure of Foreign Trade of Kazakhstan, 1992–97 (in percent)

Category	Country	1992	1993	1994	1995	1996	1997[a]
			Exports				
CIS countries	Total	15.9	56.1	58.9	52.9	55.7	44.0
	Russia	3.4	32.1	44.5	42.2	44.5	31.6
	Belarus	1.1	2.5	1.4	1.2	0.7	0.7
	Kyrgyzstan	0.1	1.3	1.8	1.5	1.8	1.2
	Uzbekistan	2.5	3.9	3.6	3.2	3.3	2.9
European Union	Total	15.9	13.6	17.3	20.4	17.9	26.9
	Germany	3.4	0.6	2.2	3.4	2.9	6.1
	Italy	1.1	2.6	1.3	1.2	3.2	5.6
	Netherlands	0.1	1.5	7.6	9.9	5.2	2.7
	Great Britain	2.5	2.9	2.0	2.2	3.7	8.5
	Finland	1.2	0.3	2.0	1.0	1.5	3.1
Other countries	United States	2.8	4.4	2.3	0.9	0.9	1.6
	Japan	1.4	1.1	0.8	0.9	1.4	1.8
	China	6.7	5.1	4.6	5.9	7.4	7.6
	South Korea	0.3	0.7	1.8	1.4	2.8	2.8

(continued)

(Table 8.6 continued)

Category	Country	1992	1993	1994	1995	1996	1997[a]
			Imports				
CIS countries	Total		60.0	61.2	68.7	69.5	53.0
	Russia		21.9	36.1	49.2	55.0	43.8
	Belarus		0.9	1.8	2.1	2.8	1.5
	Kyrgyzstan		1.3	2.6	0.7	2.1	1.3
	Kazakhstan		5.7	7.7	7.0	2.3	1.6
European Union	Total	3.0	3.6	20.6	13.3	13.0	20.9
	Germany	0.4	1.4	8.4	5.4	4.6	8.3
	Italy	0.6	0.6	2.2	0.8	0.9	1.6
	Netherlands	0.0	0.0	0.8	0.8	1.1	1.9
	Great Britain	0.4	0.4	1.9	2.2	1.8	3.3
Other countries	United States	0.1	0.9	3.1	1.9	1.5	4.9
	Japan	0.1	0.1	1.5	0.2	0.4	0.7
	China	4.5	2.0	2.0	1.0	0.8	1.3
	South Korea	0.0	0.1	2.5	1.1	2.0	3.4

Source: Customs data compiled by the National Statistical Agency of the Republic of Kazakhstan.
[a]Data for the first half of 1997.

prises that produce raw materials—the chief exporting branch of the economy. And the short-term interests of these foreign companies do not always coincide with the long-term plans and needs of Kazakhstan. Another factor is the disagreement between Russia and Kazakhstan regarding the payment of the VAT: although the governments of both countries signed a convention on avoiding double taxation, Russia has unilaterally imposed a VAT on exports, which, in the case of Kazakhstan, is a preferential duty (10 percent). By contrast, Kazakhstan does not impose a VAT on the export of its own goods. Hence, goods imported from Russia to Kazakhstan are subjected to a 10 percent VAT, compared to a 20 percent VAT that Kazakhstan levies on domestic goods,

Clearly, a stable growth in the volume of Russia's trade with high-priority partners outside the CIS (above all, members of the European Union) has also contributed to the decline in trade between the CIS and Kazakhstan. In the first quarter of 1997, foreign trade turnover between Russia and the CIS countries dropped by 12.3 percent, while its trade with non-CIS countries rose by 4.0 percent.[7]

Insofar as Kazakhstan unilaterally decided in 1997 to reduce import duties on a broad range of consumer goods (including motor vehicles, furniture, producer goods, and agricultural machinery), a further contraction in Russian exports to Kazakhstan can be expected. That is because Russian goods, given their inferior quality compared to products from non-CIS countries, can hardly expect to retain their market position in Kazakhstan.

At the same time, the shuttle trade imports from Russia have increased significantly. This is due to the fact that Russia has a large distribution network of Western companies producing high-quality goods; other factors include the lack of visas and the fact that travel to Russia is cheaper than to the European countries. Still, in the midterm perspective, this tendency will not survive: the conferral of more favorable terms and an increase in direct charter flights to European countries will encourage shuttle traders to buy their goods directly from the producing country and eliminate Russia's role as intermediary. Moreover, they will be able to choose the goods as they see fit, without being limited to the assortment offered by Russian markets.

Trade with Turkey and Iran has remained at a stable level and, in the future, will likely remain so or even increase somewhat. This is due to their mutual interests in the construction of alternative oil pipelines.

It also bears noting that, at the end of 1996, Turkey ranked fourth in terms of capital investment in Kazakhstan, with 225.5 million dollars in direct foreign investments (6.5 percent of the total). It also ranks first in the number of joint-venture enterprises: of the 995 enterprises operating at the beginning of 1997, Turkey was the partner in 160 of them.[8] Obviously, the close personal relations between the leaders of these two countries have played a significant role here; important too is the fact that the head of state in Kazakhstan is acquainted with the presidents of the leading Turkish firms. Thus, since 1992, a significant number of the largest projects in Kazakhstan have been built by the Turkish company "Fintraco," and most of these contracts have been ordered by the government of Kazakhstan and financed through foreign credits and loans.

Among the countries of East Asia, the share of trade with China has increased, rising from 4 to 7 percent of Kazakhstan's exports in the last four years. If, in the course of 1996, the trade turnover with China amounted to 497.5 million dollars (including exports of 461.5 million dollars and imports of 36.0 million dollars), in the first seven months of 1997 the trade already amounted to 288 million dollars (with exports from Kazakhstan worth 260.5 million dollars). Approximately 90 percent of the exports to China includes goods like raw materials, rolled steel and nonferrous metals; mineral fertilizer makes up the remaining 10 percent. If one takes into account that, according to our estimates, some 50 percent of the goods imported by shuttle traders comes from China, then this amounts to about 0.9 to 1.0 billion dollars in 1996 alone. In other words, the total trade turnover between China and Kazakhstan in 1996 was roughly 1.4 to 1.5 billion dollars—a figure second only to the trade with the Russian Federation (2.1 billion dollars according to customs data).

It is highly probable that the trade turnover between Kazakhstan and China will grow at a dynamic rate and the question remains open: who will be Kazakhstan's top-ranking trade partner—China or Russia? Moreover, during a visit by the Chinese premier, Li Peng, on 24 September, 1997, the two sides signed three agreements: (1) to define the border in one of their three areas of territorial dispute; (2) to establish interstate cooperation in the domain of oil and natural gas; and, (3) to construct oil pipelines from western Kazakhstan to China and Iran, a project that both parties described as being of historic significance. The participation of the Chinese national oil and natural gas company in three oil projects and in the construction of oil pipelines entails a total investment of nearly 9.5 billion dollars.[9]

Trade relations with South Korea have also been growing, chiefly as a result of the latter's direct investments in Kazakhstan. According to data for 1993–96, South Korea ranked only behind the United States in terms of investments, which amounted to 564.1 million dollars—or 16.4 percent of the total volume of direct foreign investments during this period.

In 1997, Kazakhstan also expanded its trade with the countries of East and Southeast Asia. That is because these countries continue to have the highest rates of development. After all, for each individual firm, it is most profitable to invest their resources in the economy of those foreign countries that have the most dynamic growth. Moreover, the legislation of Kazakhstan on hard-currency regulation and foreign capital does not impose strict limitations on the transfer of capital abroad.

Structure of Goods Assortment

Before the republic gained independence in 1991, the republican government had control over an extremely limited range of goods that it could export and import. It was, rather, the central all-union organs that controlled—and exported—Kazakhstan's strategic raw materials, the basis of the republic's export potential. Today, the list of exported and imported goods is extremely complex, encompassing thousands of different goods.

Under the conditions of a transition to an open market economy, the role of foreign economic activity has substantially increased. At present, exports represent one means for enabling producer-enterprises to survive and for jobs to be preserved. The role of imports today is significant in terms of supplying the domestic market with fuel and energy, investment goods (machinery and equipment), and consumer goods. As for fuel and energy as well as investment goods, the shortages result from the irrational distribution of production or even the complete lack of domestic sources. In the case of consumer goods, the republic generally lacks enterprises to produce durable consumer goods as well as the inability of domestic production to compete with imports. The result has been the total decline of the light and food processing industries.

Table 8.6

**Share of Products Exported from the Most Important Branches of
Production** (in percent)

Product	1992	1993	1994	1995	1996	1997[a]
Ferroalloys	68.3	93.0	88.8	74.4	92.5	76.3
Rolled steel	62.0	51.7	61.0	80.7	79.5	97.3
Copper	91.9	86.0	66.9	84.7	98.0	95.4
Oil and gas condensate	72.4	54.8	47.3	54.6	63.1	59.0
Zinc and zinc alloys	73.6	69.9	69.9	87.3	87.8	90.5
Lead	72.4	64.7	35.2	66.0	90.8	
Natural gas	48.2	50.8	35.6	61.0	36.6	
Iron-ore pellets					90.2	
Alumina	94.1	97.1	97.7	74.0	100.0	106.1[b]

Source: Report from the National Statistical Agency to the President of the Republic
of Kazakhstan on the social and economic situation.
[a]Data for January–June 1997.
[b]Includes reserves produced in earlier years as well as re-exports.

The contemporary condition of the country's economy is characterized by a restructuring in the branches of production. The predominant
development of extractive, export-oriented branches (in response to the
influence of the external markets), together with the decline of industrial processing and branches of agriculture, light industry, and the
food-processing branch (because of the contraction of the external and
domestic markets)—all this had resulted in a decrease in production
and jobs. The country's economy shows a growth in imported consumer products; against this background, domestic production has not
proven to be competitive. Because of the stability in the exchange rate
of the tenge and the continuing lack of competitiveness on the part of
domestic goods, a significant part of the purchasing power has been
diverted to foreign goods and therefore "eliminated" so far as domestic
producers are concerned. If the policy of export expansion increases,
this could lead to a negative balance of payments, yet not exert any
positive influence on domestic production and employment.

The bulk of goods produced by the base branches of the economy
are exported abroad (see Table 8.6).

The contemporary structure of foreign trade turnover is a natural
result of the strategy for development for the preceding Soviet period.
Namely, it seeks to compensate for the neglect of advanced technolo-

Table 8.7

Structure of Exports from Kazakhstan to Non-CIS Countries (in percent)

Product	Exports			Imports		
	1991	1994	1996	1991	1994	1996
Machinery, equipment, and means of transportation	1.3	4.2	0.6	21.2	39.7	37.9
Fuel, mineral resources, metals	54.3	73.8	82.4	10.3	5.0	5.6
Chemicals, fertilizer, rubber	16.1	10.9	6.6	5.0	13.7	12.6
Construction materials and components	0.2	0.6	0.0	0.7	1.1	2.1
Raw materials and processed products (nonfood)	25.0	0.6	2.0	7.2	0.9	0.8
Live animals			0.04		0.2	
Raw materials to produce food products	0.9	4.8	1.2	29.2	0.3	0.4
Food products	1.8	1.4	2.2	5.9	16.0	21.3
Industrial consumer goods	0.4	3.2	3.4	20.5	14.4	8.0
Material services (operations)						

Sources: Goskomstat Respubliki Kazakhstan, Statisticheskie sborniki po vneshneekonomicheskim sviazam; calculations by the Institute of Economic Research in the Ministry of Economics and Trade (on the basis of customs data).

gies and the consumer complex by exploiting the natural resources of the republic. Thus, the proportions in foreign trade are as follows: the majority of exports are concentrated in the resource-intensive branches, whereas the imports are in the most efficient spheres of industrial production.

In general, the structure of export goods—especially in trade with countries outside the CIS—shows a predominance of the raw materials (see Table 8.7).

The product mix in foreign trade from the Soviet era could not be rationalized because of the trade policy that Kazakhstan conducted during the first years after it acquired sovereignty. This trade policy had one distinctive feature: it had a whole spectrum of quantitative and tariff restrictions in export regulation but virtually no limitations on imports to protect domestic producers. As a result, the export restrictions served to impede the transfer of resources to efficient lines of production and blocked the formulation of an economic strategy to access foreign markets.[10] At the same time, the wholescale deregulation of imports did not set any limits on competition for domestic producers in the consumer goods and machine-building branches.

Moreover, the list of domestically produced goods was of little significance. Was it possible to establish new lines of production for goods that had not been produced earlier in Kazakhstan and that were now being imported? The experience of developed countries and their integrated unions (for example, the European Union) shows the utility of strict limits on the import of textiles, food products, and so forth. In the case of Kazakhstan, however, the introduction of such restrictions on imports will be problematic because of the republic's desire to gain entry to the World Trade Organization (WTO).

As for the product mix in trade with countries in the CIS, in 1997 one could discern certain changes as a result of shifts in the distribution of foreign trade between countries in the CIS and other countries. Thus, in the first half of 1996, the CIS accounted for 60 percent of the total volume of trade, but this quotient fell to 47 percent in 1997. In other words, according to customs statistics, the trade turnover contracted by 21 percent during this period (9 percent in exports; 33 percent in imports). The sharpest decrease in imports were those emanating from Turkmenistan (fivefold), Belarus (twofold), Kyrgyzstan (29 percent), Russia (28 percent), and Uzbekistan (17 percent).[11]

Kazakhstan has a significant productive base, which can expand the export potential by producing goods with a higher level of processing. In the immediate future, however, it is not feasible to make significant changes in the structure of exports. Nevertheless, if the current levels of production are maintained in the export potential, and if world market conditions remain favorable, the export potential in the near term is estimated to run at the level of 6.5 to 7 billion dollars per year.

To make substantial structural changes in the economy, the republic faces a number of objective barriers:

- Large enterprises in the raw-material complex, at this point, do not have a vested interest in developing the later stages of processing—both because of the presence of the foreign demand for raw materials and because of the enormous capital intensity required to build plants for processing raw materials.
- The creation of new production and branches is possible in the sector for small and middle-sized business, which have greater flexibility and adaptability. However, because of the lack of fi-

nancial resources to purchase capital goods, these enterprises prefer to engage in trade and to survive on the basis of re-exports.
- Under conditions entailing the improvement of the normative legislation (to come into compliance with the rules of international trade and to enter the WTO), the adoption of a selective protectionist policy is quite problematic. That is due to the fact that the republic lacks the corresponding experience and also its own strategy for economic development.

Nevertheless, it is essential to conduct analytical studies of markets for individual goods so as to design a system of tariffs that can ensure maximum investment in new lines of production and defend their sales on the domestic market.

It is also necessary, from the very inception of such new protection, for the government to assist in promoting their products on foreign markets. It should do this by using all the available methods and institutions. That is because the greatest risk lies in the fact that, because these goods have a low level of competitiveness, they will have difficulty finding market outlets.

The Import of Machinery and Equipment as a
Factor in Economic Growth

One of the main factors in economic growth is the modernization of production and use of advanced technology. In recent years, the pool of machinery and equipment has remained virtually unchanged; the majority of enterprises has equipment that is depleted or obsolescent. In the last five to six years, the volume and structure of machinery imports corresponded neither to a policy for modernization nor to the need for a structural revamping of the economy. Amidst a catastrophic decline of production in the machine-building branches and a dearth of domestic sources for most types of capital goods, there has also been a contraction in the share of imports in this sphere. Only in 1997 has there been a certain tendency for the import of capital goods to increase; this was due to the involvement of large-scale foreign investors in the oil industry, the state purchase of agricultural equipment (John Deere harvesters) through foreign loans, and the start-up of infrastructure projects (relocation of the capital to Akmola, the construction of a bridge across the Irtysh River in Semipalatinsk, the development of

Table 8.8

Proportion of Machinery and Equipment in Imports (in percent)

Category	Indicator	1994	1995	1996	1997[a]
Share of machinery and transportation in:	Total volume of imports[b]	28.4	27.4	27.6	37.0
	Total volume of imports (FOB)	20.2	15.1	16.1	20.6
	GDP	8.5	6.1	5.6	7.6
	Foreign investments	57.3	59.0	69.1	
Source of machinery and transportation equipment	Countries in the CIS	46.2	56.0	54.3	46.8
	Countries outside the CIS	53.8	44.0	41.7	53.2

Source: Calculated on the basis of data from customs statistics, balance of payments, and other accounts of the National Statistical Agency of the Ministry of Economics and Trade (Republic of Kazakhstan).

[a]For first half of 1997.
[b]According to customs data.

telecommunications, and so forth)—again, principally on the basis of foreign loans and credits (see Table 8.8).

Whereas earlier imports from CIS countries had dominated (as a result of economic ties based on the unitary economic complex of the USSR) and also increased slightly in 1995–96 (because of the increased trade among members of the Customs Union), the CIS share of trade again decreased in 1997. In this author's opinion, that latest tendency is a natural consequence of the fact that, with Kazakhstan's access to world markets, goods from CIS countries are simply not competitive. Indeed, it was already clear earlier that the products of the machine-building industry (as well as such branches as construction materials) in post-Soviet countries were not really competitive on foreign markets.

As Table 8.8 shows, in 1997 Kazakhstan underwent a fundamental shift toward non-CIS countries to obtain all types of machinery and equipment. The only stable flow of imports from CIS countries was equipment that the enterprises of Kazakhstan can resell (i.e., re-export).

Within the structure of imported machinery, the level of equipment for the machine-building and consumer goods branches is rather low. During 1995 and 1996, the machine-building industry of Kazakhstan accounted for only 2.2 percent of the total value of equipment imports. The country spent 84.1 million dollars for agricultural machinery (compared to an insignificant level in 1991–94); another 194.8 million dollars was spent on automobiles. It bears noting that the decline in agriculture during these years left production in this sector at 43 percent of its output in 1990. Whereas industry has achieved a relative stabilization in the last year, no such turnaround is yet to be discerned in the case of agriculture.[12]

The greatest growth can be expected in the oil-producing sector, where the purchase of machinery and equipment—as a share of direct foreign investment—has increased from 30.2 percent (1995) to 48.3 percent (1996).

As already noted, this year Kazakhstan has increased the importation of machinery and equipment in its extractive and infrastructure sectors (in both absolute and relative terms). Still, it is premature to draw any far-reaching conclusions. Obviously, a gross increase in the import of equipment does not automatically mean economic growth; it is essential that these machinery not be obsolescent, that it be promptly utilized, and that it provide a quick payback (especially if acquired through foreign credits).

The Export of Agricultural Goods

The proportional share of agricultural products—both from animal husbandry and crop cultivation—does not correspond either with the historically developed structure or the potential capacities of the agricultural sector. Indeed, the level of exports reflects the profound crisis that has beset this sector of the Kazakhstani economy. The contradictory and inconsistent character of reforms, which did not fully take into account the level of development and the character of economic relations in the agrarian sector, resulted in a sharp contraction of production in agriculture. As in the case of industry, the export-oriented branches found themselves in the best position; these included the production of grain, cotton, wool, and raw leather, which together account for 70 percent of all agricultural exports. And it was precisely these goods that account for the increase in the absolute volume of agricultural goods and their share in the total volume of exports (which rose from 13.7 percent in 1995 to 16.6 percent in 1996).

The grain market of Kazakhstan has become increasingly oriented toward export. More than 90 percent of these exports currently flow to markets within the CIS. The main importer is the Russian Federation, which buys 60 to 65 percent of Kazakhstan's grain shipments abroad. Significant volumes of grain are also sold to Uzbekistan, Belarus, Kyrgyzstan, and Turkmenistan. A large part of the shipments consists of grain used for foodstuffs (primarily class 3 wheat). By contrast, the grain shipped to destinations outside the CIS consists mainly of grain used for fodder; a steady stream of this grain is shipped to the Baltic states and to Poland. At the same time, the geography of grain shipments is becoming more diversified. Although the volume of grain exports to these other countries is still small, the prospects for growth are substantial, especially for countries in the Near East and Southeast Asia. To be sure, until Kazakhstan has convenient transportation routes to these regions and to ports on the Black Sea, its main partners will continue to be countries in the CIS and in the Baltics.

As noted earlier, the objective opportunities for Kazakhstan to export the products of animal husbandry have been completely neglected. However, it is hardly reasonable to expect that, in the near term, these exports will register a substantial increase. Unfortunately, the state has no coherent policy to promote this branch, which, for centuries, was the very foundation of the national economy and which corresponded most closely to the natural and climatic conditions of Kazakhstan, the vast grain production, and the traditions and skills of the indigenous population. As a result, the country has experienced a catastrophic decrease in the number of livestock and the virtual destruction of this branch of agriculture. To overcome these problems and to restore animal husbandry to its former level, Kazakhstan will require substantial financial resources and plenty of time. The potential markets, in addition to traditional outlets in the CIS (Russia, Turkmenistan, and Uzbekistan), include the countries of Southeast Asia, where economic growth has been accompanied by a significant demand for meat products.

Cotton is a traditional staple of Kazakhstan's agricultural exports, which have increased because of the contraction in domestic demand. The most stable and largest buyers are China and Russia. The latter has, in particular, strengthened its position on the Kazakh cotton market, chiefly because of a desire to find an alternative to cotton production in Uzbekistan. This is a situation that Kazakhstan must, of course, fully exploit. Other destinations of cotton exports include Bulgaria, Hungary, Poland, and Latvia (which have long been active in purchasing cotton from Kazakhstan) as well as some new partners, such as Austria and the Bahamas. The measures taken by Kazakhstan to improve the quality and certification of cotton give grounds to hope that the price for this product will steadily rise.

The market for unprocessed leather is also gradually expanding. In addition to traditional outlets (Turkey and China), some other countries—such as India, Italy, the Czech Republic, and Greece—have also begun to take an interest.

The structure of agricultural exports graphically shows that, as in the case of industry, there is a predominance of raw, unprocessed materials or, at most, commodities that have undergone no more than primary processing (wool, cotton, and leather). Finished agricultural goods comprise less than 15 percent of the total volume of exports from the agricultural sector.

Kazakhstan also has the potential to export wines, cognac, and champagne. The production of these goods is favored by the unique natural conditions in the southern and southeastern parts of the country, by the availability of the requisite machinery and equipment, and by the presence of highly qualified personnel.

Foreign Loans

During its first five years of independence, Kazakhstan advanced from an unsystematic approach to the attracting and handling of foreign loans to a more orderly structure—one where the authority for such transactions is clearly delegated to certain organs in the state administration. That new order was in place by the end of 1996. Previously, the republic did not have a clear set of priorities, a coherent administrative structure, or a clear delegation of functions with respect to attracting, auditing, controlling, and administering foreign loans. One result, first apparent in 1995, was the difficulty in servicing the foreign debt, as the insolvency of borrowers (or their restructuring) forced the government to make good on its guarantees for such loans.

In the course of 1996, the government paid off all current obligations by tapping funds from other budget lines and thereby enabling the country to regain a good credit rating in international lending markets. That enabled the country to float, at the end of 1996, Eurobonds with a value of 200 million dollars and to place these successfully on the European financial markets.

According to data compiled by the National Bank of Kazakhstan, on 1 January 1997 the gross foreign debt of the republic was 3.75 billion dollars. That amounts to 229 dollars per capita, 17.9 percent of the GDP, or 55.9 percent of the volume of exports. In 1996, the cost of servicing the debt represented 10.7 percent of the volume of exports. In the course of 1996, each quarter the debt service costs (whether in terms of percent and absolute payments) exceeded the rate of growth of exports (on average, by a factor of 8.4 times).

As a result of this alarming symptom, virtually the entire profit from the export and sale of strategic raw materials remains in the hands of exporters (i.e., transnational firms). The latter must only pay a tax on their earnings, an insignificant source of revenues for the state budget. According to some data, the majority of firms enjoy additional privileges with respect to income taxes (in return for retiring the debt of enterprises that they purchased). Such a situation gives rise to several problems. Above all, the state has forfeited its power to influence the redistribution of revenues from the sale of the country's basic natural resources; as a result, it lost the means to effect a structural reordering of industry. Aware that the renegotiation of existing contracts was impossible (for fear that this would alarm investors and destabilize the investment climate), the government of Kazakhstan has chosen to stake everything on petrodollars. Namely, it plans to earn revenues from the exploitation of existing and new oil fields and to construct several alternative routes for shipment abroad (once again, with the assistance of foreign investors).

It must said that the current situation with respect to the country's foreign debts is far from being critical. Nevertheless, if one takes into account the emerging economic realities in Kazakhstan, it is essential to attract long-term preferential loans and credits that carry a repayment term of twelve years or more. The aggregate interest rate for current and new loans must not exceed the rate of growth in exports; nor can the increase in foreign debts be greater than the rate of growth in the profits from the export of goods and services.

These restrictions reduce the financing for the economy under conditions of strong dependency on foreign capital. Therefore, it is essential to shift priorities, to attract direct foreign investment and to improve investment climate.

Conclusion

Constantine Michalopolos and David Tarr have given an accurate characterization of the foreign economic activities of an independent Kazakhstan. Its distinctive feature has been to erect a whole spectrum of quantitative and tariff restrictions in export regulations without creating import restrictions to protect domestic producers. Moreover, these export restrictions have impeded the flow of resources into production where Kazakhstan has comparative advantages; they have also retarded the formulation of an economic strategy oriented toward foreign markets.[13] It should also be noted that customs barriers in exports were dismantled just as virtually as all the main enterprises in the core economic sectors were transferred to foreign control and ownership.

This liberalization did stimulate export. The raw materials of Kazakhstan became less costly for foreign buyers, including those in developed countries. Moreover, the profits of exporters rose to new levels. At the same time, this decision brought substantial losses for the budget. According to this author's estimates, the rich natural resources of the republic—which should be sufficient to support 17 million people—in fact yield high incomes for only 3 to 4 percent of the population.

In theory, in the short term these losses should be offset through bonuses and royalties. But in the long-range perspective, one cannot preclude the possibility that the state will have to support exporters of raw materials with special credits. Such will be the case if these producers did not accumulate profits in the better years (and reinvest to diversify these branches), or if the country does not follow Chile's example of creating a fund for copper producers to help them survive years when prices are low.

Therefore, in 1995–96, by the time when the strategic raw material market of Kazakhstan was divided among transnational corporations, foreign trade had been almost completely deregulated. On the positive side, this led to an increase in foreign trade. On the negative side, during the period preceding the liberalization of foreign trade, the country failed to create new domestic production capable of producing competitive goods.

At the present time, in conjunction with entry into the WTO, Kazakhstan faces the task of making further improvements in its foreign trade policy by incorporating the existing normative base of international standards and guarantees. For more than two years, the government has been conducting preparatory work for the country's entry into this organization and expects to become a member in the near future. While the need for this step cannot be questioned. There are nonetheless serious reasons for doubting the need to force the pace of this process.

The participation of developing countries in the WTO guarantees preferential treatment of their exports as well as access to markets in developed countries. However, one should bear in mind that the state loses virtually any capacity to support domestic producers. Hence one should give some consideration to the following: Kazakhstan is not yet threatened with a large-scale export of consumer goods to foreign markets. The transnational corporations, which have divided up the raw-materials market, conduct this trade on the basis of their excellent experience and knowledge of foreign markets. In this author's opinion, the exports of Kazakhstan do not currently need preferential treatment on the part of developed countries. Rather, Kazakhstan is only now in the process of devising a strategy for its own development and has not yet completed its structural transformation; hence it requires, for a limited period of time, a protectionist policy that is both sensible and selective.

The political argument for joining the WTO so quickly is the fact that investors need guarantees on receiving preferential treatment on the markets of developed countries for consumer goods exported from Kazakhstan. The reason is that the domestic market is rather small (17 million people). One would like to believe that investors are lining up to master the market for consumer and industrial goods. Nevertheless, the experience of China and the countries of Southeast Asia show that these states attracted enormous foreign investments during years when they were not members of the Geneva Agreement on Trade and Tariffs (GATT).

The process for approving the memorandum for entering WTO was conducted in a hasty and secret manner. In this writer's opinion, it would not be a bad thing if this memorandum (which, in fact, was prepared with the assistance of specialists from the U.S. Agency for International Development) were published so that commodity producers could be aware of the intentions and obligations of the government with respect to foreign markets.

Notwithstanding the current problems in commercial relations among member states of the Customs Union, it is necessary to maintain this association. First, for a long time to come, there will continue to be an objective need for trade in those spheres that are not competitive on international markets. Second, Kazakhstan needs Russia as its "window on Europe" just as Russia needs Kazakhstan as its "window on Asia." It is therefore essential to find mutually advantageous and mutually acceptable instruments for integration within the framework of the Customs Union.

Participation in the Central Asian Union, in general, bears a political character. The members of this union have not established equal trade policies. In their trade relations, these republics have not abolished tariff regulation, introduced a single order for nontariff regulation, or unified their policies toward third countries. Yet the formation of a "single economic space" among the Central Asian republics presumes a free flow of goods, services, capital, and labor; it should also provide coordinated policies with respect to credits and accounting, budgets, taxation, prices, customs, and hard currency.

A further serious problem concerns the mutual convertibility of currencies. At issue is the inconvertibility of the Uzbek sum, which has remained thus despite repeated assurances of Uzbek leaders to resolve this problem. Whereas Kazakhstan has ratified and implemented an agreement to avoid double taxation, in the case of Uzbekistan there are still problems with respect to the payment of the VAT. One must also note among the countries of Central Asia a continuing reorientation of foreign trade to countries outside the CIS. This is particularly pronounced in the case of Kazakhstan and Kyrgyzstan. All these issues have served to depress trade turnover between Kazakhstan and the other members of the Central Asian Union.

Nevertheless, the Central Asian Union is essential. First, because of the territorial division of labor that developed during the Soviet era, these states will—for a long time to come—retain their mutual dependency on the so-called exchange of critical goods (i.e., electric power, natural gas, grain, and petroleum products). Second, exogenous factors dictate the objective necessity for economic and political integration— for example, the political situation in Afghanistan. Third, integration is necessary so as to use, in a mutually advantageous and coordinated way, the special "transit" geographical location in Eurasia.

Summing up the integrationist processes within the framework of the CIS, it must be noted that the principal means for regulating the relations between Kazakhstan and the CIS states is the bilateral level of agreements and cooperation. The main advantage is the possibility to link, in a single package, agreements involving the most diverse spheres of mutual cooperation—from trade and customs to payment transfers and joint border security.

In fact, however, control over the implementation of these agreements is clearly wanting. It would only be fair to analyze and reconsider all of Kazakhstan's bilateral trade agreements that pertain to processes of integration (the Customs Union and the Central Asian Union) so as to determine the limitations and unfavorable customs duties. This could then lead to the introduction of corresponding measures to protect the interests of the state and the entities engaged in foreign trade activities—in other words, steps to create parity in state policy on such matters.

As for foreign loans, the following should be said: Under conditions where the republic lacks its own financial resources, the main objective must be to attract and utilize direct foreign investment. And such a policy must pursue two goals: (1) structural change in the base industries; and, (2) creation and development of labor-intensive branches that are oriented initially toward the domestic consumer market, but that ultimately penetrate foreign markets as well. In reality, however, foreign investors are striving primarily in Kazakhstan to enter the mining and fuel and energy sectors.

The foreign investors, moreover, are interested chiefly in preserving the raw-material orientation in these branches. There are several reasons for this. First, under current law on foreign investments, foreign economic activity, and hard currency regulations, the export of cheap raw materials (compared with the prices for Russian equivalents) gives the investor considerable profits without any additional capital investment. Second, the successive and final stages of processing are, as a rule, the most energy-intensive phases of production. To develop and expand domestic energy supplies in Kazakhstan, investment is essential; but in this regard Kazakhstan is less competitive: the energy resources in neighboring countries (Uzbekistan, Turkmenistan, and Kyrgyzstan) are in fact abundant and cheaper. Nevertheless, the monopolistic position of the fuel and energy branch in Kazakhstan makes this branch attractive for foreign investments. To be sure, the investors are channeling their capital toward existing enterprises; none is rushing to create new productive capacities. Third, backwardness of the financial (banking and insurance) and productive infrastructures do not provide a stimulus for foreign investors to use their capital to create and develop capacities for the production of end products. Fourth, investment in such production entails certain risks, since such capacities are also being created in neighboring countries. Finally, the investor must also face the fact that the domestic market can generate only a limited demand.

At the same time, the orientation toward the export of raw materials leaves the republic highly vulnerable to price fluctuations.

With respect to the creation of labor-intensive branches on the basis of foreign investments, Kazakhstan is not competitive with neighboring countries—the other republics of Central Asia and the People's Republic of China—in terms of labor costs.

In the midterm perspective, protectionist measures to encourage domestic producers to create new jobs are becoming increasingly imperative. The main focus here should be on small and medium-sized businesses—petty commercial middlemen, farmers and other agricultural producers, and construction firms, but also the so-called shuttle trade.

Notes

1. N.Sh. Dulatov, *Vneshneekonomicheskie sviazi Kazakhstana s zarubezhnymi stranami* (Alma-Ata, 1982), pp. 2–17, 54.

2. "Proekt Gosudarstvennoi natsional'noi programmy razvitiia eksportnogo potentsiala Kazakhstana," in *Indikativnyi plan sotsial'no-ekonomicheskogo razvitiia Respubliki Kazakhstan na 1994 god,* vol. 3 (Almaty: Nauchno-issledovatel'skii institut ekonomiki i rynochnykh otnoshenii pri Ministerstve ekonomiki Respubliki Kazakhstana, 1993), pp. 167–211.

3. M.A. Khasanova, "Pis'ma ot 18 i 20 iiunia 1997 g. Sovetniku ministra ekonomiki i torgovli Respubliki Kazakhstan G-zhe Kantarbaevoi A.K.: 'K voprosu o sozdanii Biudzheta razvitiia Respubliki Kazakhstan' " (Almaty: Institut ekonomicheskikh issledovanii pri Ministerstve ekonomiki i torgovli, 1997), pp. 1–6.

4. M. Ostanov, "Retsept lecheniia 'gollandskoi bolezni'—ne chto inoe kak popytka sozdaniia ocherednogo karmannogo vnebiudzhetnogo fonda," *Panorama,* 1997, no. 20 (23 May).

5. V. Zhuravlev, "Egor Stroev postoit za 'chelnokov'," *Delovoi mir,* 10 December 1996.

6. "Antal'ia prevrashchaetsia v bol'shuiu barakholku (po materialam agentstv ITAR-TASS, DPA, Reuter)," *Karavan,* 7 March 1997.

7. S. Akisheva, "Tovarooborot s Rossiei: prichiny snizheniia," *Al' Pari,* August–September 1997, pp. 45–46.

8. Russia ranks second, with 140 joint-venture enterprises in Kazakhstan. By the end of the first quarter in 1997, however, Russia had overtaken Turkey as the

leading source of joint-venture firms: of 1,029 joint-venture enterprise, 161 were Kazakh-Russian and 159 were Kazakh-Turkish.

9. N. Drozd, "Po mneniiu Nursultana Nazarbaeva, vo vremia vizita kitaiskoi delegatsii byl podpisan 'kontrakt veka'," *Panorama,* 26 September 1997, no. 37.

10. Konstantin Mikalopulos [Constantine Michalopoulos] and Devid G. Tarr [David G. Tarr], *Torgovaia deiatel'nost' i politika v novykh nezavisimykh gosudarstvakh* (Washington, DC: World Bank, 1996), pp. 45–47.

11. Natsional'noe statisticheskoe agentstvo Ministerstva ekonomiki i torgovli Respubliki Kazakhstan, "Sotsial'no-ekonomicheskoe polozhenie Respubliki Kazakhstan. Ianvar'-iiul' 1997 g. (operativnaia informatsiia)" (Almaty, 1997).

12. The deregulation of prices and foreign trade, together with the change in forms of property ownership, had a ruinous impact on agriculture. No developed country in the world subjects its agriculture to the full force of the laws of the market; everywhere else there are special state levers (sometimes quite powerful) to regulate the import of agricultural products and price formation for agricultural commodities.

13. Mikalopulos and Tarr, *Torgovaia deiatel'nost' i politika.*

9

Uzbekistan:
Foreign Economic Activity

Eshref F. Trushin

Initial Conditions

The vast natural resources of Uzbekistan, together with the productive and intellectual potential created during the Soviet era, lay the preconditions for this country's successful integration into the world economy. In terms of the known reserves of such mineral resources as gold, uranium, natural gas, copper, and tungsten, Uzbekistan ranks among the leading countries in the world. Suffice it to say that the republic ranks fifth in the world in the production of uranium and that it produced 60 tons of gold in 1996. Uzbekistan also has significant stretches of irrigated land that support an efficient agriculture and make its main products, above all cotton, competitive on world markets. The presence of a cheap labor force also enhances the country's export potential.

However, Uzbekistan also has the legacy of the Soviet "command economy," including a host of problems. In the words of President I.A. Karimov:

> In the course of many decades the republic carried out decisions and conducted "campaigns," for which the scenario had been written in far-off Moscow. The true interests of Uzbekistan and its specific condi-

tions and potential were simply ignored. The result was a disjointed, one-sided economic structure oriented toward raw materials. The republic was forced to ship not only various kinds of raw materials, fuels and energy sources, equipment and machinery, but also vitally important foodstuffs and consumer goods.

The technological level of enterprises and the quality of output do not correspond to the principles of the modern organization of production or the harsh demands of world competition. Technological equipment in virtually every branch is physically worn out, obsolete, and in dire need of upgrading.[1]

In assessing the foreign economic potential of the republics in the former USSR in 1991 (on a scale of ten), experts from Die Deutsche Bank rated Uzbekistan no higher than a 3 and assigned the republic to the category of countries with a low level of economic development.[2] Given these initial conditions, the foreign economic policy becomes virtually the sole means to modernize the economy.

Organization of the Foreign Economic Sphere

During the years of independence, fundamental changes have occurred in the organization of the foreign economic sphere. Uzbekistan has become a member of the United Nations (UN), the Council on Security and Cooperation in Europe (CSCE), the International Monetary Fund (IMF), the International Bank of Reconstruction and Development (IBRD), the European Bank of Reconstruction and Development (EBRD), and a number of other prominent international organizations. The republic has also established the Ministry of Foreign Economic Relations, the National Bank for Foreign Economic Activities, a customs administration, the National Insurance Company, and corresponding functional subdivisions in ministries, state agencies, and local organs of self-government. Uzbekistan has also created the normative legal basis for the independent access of enterprises to the foreign market and to provide reliable guarantees for the activities of foreign investors.[3] In May 1994, the Uzbek parliament adopted a decree "on foreign investments," which established a number of guarantees: protection from expropriation (except in special cases, for which compensation is provided), the right to repatriate profits, the observance of current legislation for a period of ten years if new laws have an adverse impact on a joint-venture enterprise, exemption from customs duties (for the export of output from joint-venture enterprises as well as the import of equipment needed for a firm's own production), and access to international arbitration.

A number of international insurance companies now operate on the Uzbek market. These include the American International Group, Tokyo Marine Insurance, Multilateral Investment Guarantee Agency, and the specialized programs of several countries (e.g., the Overseas Private Investment Corporation and the Central Asian-American Enterprise Fund for the Development of Small and Medium-Sized Business—both being agencies of the U.S. government). Joint-venture enterprises with more than 30 percent foreign investment enjoy a five-year tax holiday.

Table 9.1 presents data that characterize the foreign trade of Uzbekistan during the period of independence (1992–96). As the data show, during this period the export quota has grown almost uninterruptedly, increasing nearly threefold. The import quota has also grown steadily (with the exception of 1994) and similarly increased by a factor of three. The same can be said about the proportion of foreign trade turnover, which, in 1996, amounted to approximately 40 percent of the GDP. Noteworthy too is the significant export quota on goods from the branches of material production, which amounted to almost 30 percent in 1996. These data demonstrate the enormous influence of foreign trade on the entire economy of the country.

To a significant degree, the value of exports (and hence exports as a proportion of GDP) is determined by the increase in world prices for Uzbekistan's main export goods—cotton fiber, gold, nonferrous metals, and fertilizers.

It is highly revealing that the share of domestic producers in the total volume of commodity turnover for consumer goods amounted to less than 40 percent in 1996, and the majority of investment goods continue to be imported (as was true in the former Soviet Union). The growth in the volume of foreign trade occurred (especially before 1996) amidst a general decline in production and domestic demand. Moreover, the establishment of the country's own production (i.e., for purposes of import replacement) is impeded not only by the lack of the requisite technology, but also by the significant number of institutional, commercial, and price distortions that will be examined herein.

Geographic Structure of Foreign Trade

During the years of independence, the geographic structure of foreign trade has undergone major changes. Thus, in 1994–96, Uzbekistan

Table 9.1

Foreign Trade of Uzbekistan, 1992–96

Indicator	1992	1993	1994	1995	1996
Export quota (percent of GDP)	6	13	14	18	18
"Real" export quota (percent of GDP)[a]	8	19.5	20	25	28
Volume of exports per capita (in dollars)	67	132	131	168	163
Import quota (percent of GDP)	7.2	14.5	13	17	22
Volume of imports per capita (in dollars)	78	149	122	158.5	204
Share of foreign trade turnover in GDP (percent)	13	27	26	35	39
GDP per capita (in dollars)	1,077	1,027	960	936	931
GDP (in billions of dollars)	2.999	22.447	21.508	21.246	21.543
Population (millions)	21.360	21.852	22.400	22.690	23.139
Exports (millions of dollars)	1,424	2,877	2,940	3,806	3,781
Imports (millions of dollars)	1,660	3,255	2,727	3,597	4,711

Source: World Bank, *Ot plana k rynku (otchet o razvitii. 1996)* (Washington, DC, 1996); *Uzbekistan za gody nezavisimosti* (Tashkent, 1996); N. Sirazhiddinov and N. Agaffonov, "Vneshniaia torgovlia Uzbekistana 1991–95," Doklad 96(4), Proekt makroekonomicheskogo analiza i podgotovki kadrov PROON-Tashkent, November 1996; A.A. Adylov, "Opyt vneshnei ekonomicheskoi politiki i osnovnye orientiry razvitiia" (international conference on "The Economic Policy of Uzbekistan after the Acquisition of Independence," in Tashkent, 30–31 January 1997; the World Bank, *States of the Former USSR. Statistical Handbook 1996* (Washington, DC, 1996), 502–36; estimates of the International Monetary Fund.

[a]Calculated as correlation in the value of goods exported to the GDP (material products only; services are not included).

experienced a significant decrease in its trade with the member states of the CIS: their share of exports decreased from 67.6 percent to 22.9 percent, their share of imports dropped from 53.3 to 32.1 percent. Moreover, exports also fell in absolute terms. Conversely, foreign trade turnover with the rest of the world increased sharply, both in absolute and in relative terms (with this share of trade rising from 38.8 to 72.4 percent).[4] In our judgment, this process was due to the following factors:

- Economic decline in the countries of the CIS, accompanied by a catastrophic fall in the purchasing power of the population.
- Deliberate shift of export activity to the countries in the Organization of Economic Cooperation and Development in order to obtain revenues in hard currency.[5]
- Creation of a customs union by four states in the CIS—Russia, Kazakhstan, Belarus, and Kyrgyzstan—that established rather high import tariffs on their territories. This impeded exports to these countries, which, in 1991–96, had accounted for approximately 70 percent of total exports to countries in the former USSR. Thus, in 1994 Uzbekistan had had a favorable balance of trade with these four countries, and in 1995 registered a slight deficit in its trade with Russia and Belarus. But in 1996, after the establishment of the customs union, the negative balance of trade significantly increased, as was also the case in its trade with Kazakhstan.
- A decrease in the share of interstate commercial agreements. In 1996, Uzbekistan signed a treaty with Belarus and, in 1997, with Turkmenistan for the delivery of oil and natural gas condensate. However, this can be regarded as a positive phenomenon; so long as trade is regulated by bilateral agreements, the governments—not the market—will determine the distribution of resources as well as the volume and terms of trade. Nevertheless, given the substantial role of administrative control over foreign economic activities in Uzbekistan, the contraction in such cooperation inevitably leads to a decline in the volume of trade.

It should be said that this tendency is also characteristic for all the countries of the former USSR. Thus, in 1994, the total volume of trade among the fifteen states (measured in U.S. dollars) amounted to just 35

Table 9.2

Principal Trading Partners of Uzbekistan, 1994–96 (in percent)

Country	Share of total imports			Share of total exports		
	1994	1995	1996	1994	1995	1996
Russia	27.8	24.9	21.0	28.7	18.8	11.6
Kazakhstan	5.8	7.5	4.7	11.9	7.7	2.6
Tajikistan	12.0	2.5	0.5	13.2	5.0	1.5
Turkmenistan	3.7	3.4	0.4	3.2	4.8	3.8
Ukraine	1.8	2.1	3.5	6.0	1.4	0.8
Kyrgyzstan	1.0	1.2	0.4	2.5	2.2	1.8
Belarus	0.5	1.7	1.5	1.2	1.0	0.7
Switzerland	12.5	4.0	3.8	7.2	13.7	7.2
Germany	6.9	13.0	12.2	1.0	1.2	2.0
Netherlands	2.0	1.2	1.4	4.9	5.0	0.3
Great Britain	0.7	1.0	2.2	5.6	7.6	8.0
Korea	1.0	14.8	6.9	1.3	4.7	5.8
China	3.4	0.8	0.7	2.5	1.1	2.8
Turkey	2.6	3.0	7.6	1.4	3.5	1.0
United States	3.7	1.1	9.2	0.7	0.4	6.1
Austria	1.1	0.3	0.5	1.3	1.3	0.9
Belgium	0.6	0.1	0.5	0.2	0.0	1.5
Italy	0.9	0.8	0.7	0.9	2.6	2.4
Hungary	3.4	5.0	1.0	0.0	0.1	0.3
United Arab Emirates	0.2	2.4	3.9	0.1	0.3	0.2
France	0.4	0.5	1.2	0.0	0.0	0.8

Source: See Table 9.1.

percent of the level in 1991. There were objective reasons for this. Given the centralized planning of republics in the former Soviet Union, partners generally traded directly with each other.[6]

Table 9.2 provides data on the main trading partners of Uzbekistan in 1994–96. As the table demonstrates, Uzbekistan actively carries on foreign trade with all the countries of Central Asia, Kazakhstan, and Russia. This is due not only to their geographic proximity but also to the traditional complex of mutual ties that survived the dissolution of the Soviet Union. However, these ties are increasingly oriented toward the Organization of Economic Cooperation and Development (OECD). Thus, whereas the Central Asian countries, Kazakhstan, and Russia accounted for more than half of the total trade turnover and exports in 1994, their quotient had fallen to less than a quarter by 1996, whereas that of the countries in the OECD increased.

Goods Structure of Foreign Trade

Changes are also occurring in the goods structure of foreign trade. Thus, there has been a sharp decrease in the imports of energy and fuels (which now represent less than 2 percent of total imports) and cereal grains (due to the significant expansion of domestic production). Indeed, the state has made a significant investment in these branches; in 1996 alone, for example, these branches received approximately 20 percent of all investment. Thus, if in 1991 Uzbekistan produced 4.5 million tons of oil, in 1995 it increased this output to 8 million tons, thereby ending the country's dependence on Russian oil imports.

Nevertheless, the import of foodstuffs has significantly increased, rising from 18.2 percent in 1995 to 30.0 percent in 1996 (compared to 32.6 percent in 1994).[7] These data demonstrate a crisis in agriculture, since Uzbekistan has conditions favorable for agriculture and the processing of its production. There has also been a sharp increase in the import of machinery and equipment (which represented more than a third of all imports); that reflects the state's industrial policy, which is aimed at upgrading and modernizing industry through state investment (with over 70 percent of the imports coming from countries in the OECD). The import of services has also risen sharply; this growth is due primarily to the increase in transportation tariffs on rail cargoes (which rose more than 25 percent in 1996).

A surge in imports, especially for products that could be produced inside the republic itself, has significantly inflated the exchange rate on the national currency, the sum. The net effect is to make imports more attractive for those who have the option of converting money at the official exchange rate.[8]

The exports show a tendency to increase production in manufacturing, primarily through the development of joint-venture enterprises (e.g., "UzDEU-avto," "UzBAT," "UzDEU-elektronika," and others). On the whole, however, the export structure did not change significantly and continues to exhibit a raw-material orientation. Thus, producer goods comprise no more than 3 percent of exports (primarily fertilizer), while light industry accounts for only 2 percent of total exports. The export of energy and fuels—most of which are shipped to the countries of Central Asia—have tended to decrease. It bears noting that the prospects for oil exports to Western Europe are very limited; in part, that is due to the fact that the European Union introduced strict standards, effective 1 October 1996, on the sulphur content of oil products. On the basis of exports to countries outside the CIS (which reflect the existing competitiveness in world markets), the raw-material orientation in exports is particularly striking. Thus cotton accounts for 70 to 80 percent of exports, followed by nonferrous and ferrous metals (4 to 6 percent), fertilizer (2 percent), and services mostly in the form of cargo transhipping (6 to 9 percent). This structure is based on indicators that do not take into account the export of uranium and gold.[9]

Trade Barriers

In general, tight administrative control over export has been reduced, with a gradual shift from export bans and licenses to a system of tariffs. At the present time, export tariffs generally run between 10 and 40 percent, which is significantly higher than those found in the CIS; the main objective of such duties is to raise revenues for the state budget. Moreover, the republic has a centralized system to manage its principal export goods: cotton fiber, nonferrous metals, fertilizer, silk, karakul, goods of light industry, energy and fuel, and electricity. State orders for the main export good (cotton), the fixed set of unprofitable state procurement prices, and the strict licensing of all production—all these factors function to depress an interest in expanding production. In fact, the state procurement prices on cotton represent only a fraction of world prices for cotton (12 to 15 percent) and grain (25 to 30 percent).[10]

Both the high transportation costs on the shipment of goods and the high import duties (10 to 30 percent of the contractual value) stimulated production for the domestic market and formation of monopolies. Contrariwise, these factors did not create the preconditions for making export more attractive.

Measures directed at an expansion of exports by establishing substantial tax advantages can hardly lead to a substantial increase in production for export. Beginning 1 April, 1996, the tax rate on profits from enterprises was reduced in proportion to the share of its total output being exported (see Table 9.3).

However, these advantages are not extended to include raw material exports—cotton fiber, cotton yarn, oil and petroleum products, natural gas, and metals. Moreover, three other factors provide significant disincentives for the export of output:[11]

Table 9.3

Preferential Tax Treatment Based on the Share of Production Exported
(in percent)

Share of export in the total volume of production	Reduction in the tax rate on profits
5–10	20
10–20	30
20–30	40
Over 30	50

Sources: See Table 9.1.

- In general, the rates set for export duties exceed the tax advantages given to the producers of exported goods.
- Strict controls continue to exist for the export of the main part of the country's exports, which are still subject to licensing and quotas.
- The high exchange rate of the sum.

This final point requires elaboration.

Multiple Exchange Rates

Uzbekistan has, in reality, a multiplicity of hard currency exchange rates: (1) the "official rate" established by the Republican Hard Currency Exchange through a complex system of administrative transactions; (2) the "commercial rate," which differs from the official rate because of its surcharge (up to 15 percent) for bank services; and, (3) the exchange rate on the "black" (illegal) market for cash and other monetary instruments, which differ from the official rate by a factor of two or more.

The application of the official, artificially high rate of exchange on the sum can be explained by the following state objectives:

- ensure state purchases of imports, especially investment goods;
- create subsidies for the import of certain consumer goods;
- restrain inflation;
- improve the balance of payments by establishing control over import transactions;

Table 9.4

Rate of Growth in Inflation, Wage Fund, and Exchange Rate (as percent of December in previous year)

Year	Inflation (per consumer price index)	Average growth in wage fund	Growth in the exchange rate of the dollar	
			Republic Hard Currency Bank	Black market
1994	1,217.0	530.0		1,093.0
1995	198.5	299.0	143.2	143.0
1996	183.0	213.7	147.3	225.3

Source: World Bank, *States of the Former USSR. Statistical Handbook. 1996* (Washington, DC, 1996), 502–36.

- stimulate foreign investment by enabling convertibility for earnings from joint-venture enterprises (at the official exchange rate).

It must be noted that many other countries also have multiple exchange rates. However, the experience of countries in Latin America and Asia, as well as the Arab countries has shown that although multiple exchange rates can help countries achieve certain goals in a short period of time, they inevitably cause still greater problems. The attempts to exert an influence on current accounts transactions and to limit budget expenditures by using several exchange rates were undermined by the inability to cope with hidden financial imbalances. As the majority of these countries found, such a strategy is ineffective and a poor substitute for a single, viable exchange rate backed by sound financial and economic policies.[12]

The example of Uzbekistan confirms, just one more time, this conclusion. Indeed, there are serious reasons to doubt whether the goals listed earlier can be achieved through the regulation of hard currency.

Another problem is the lack of equivalency of the sum in cash and noncash forms, a problem created by the limitations of the Central Bank on cash flows. As a result, the price on goods sold for cash are usually two to three times lower than the selling price for noncash monetary instruments.

Table 9.4 shows the rates of growth for inflation, the wage fund, and the exchange rate of the dollar (both at the Republic Hard Currency

Exchange and on the 'black market") as a percent of the last month of the preceding year.

As Table 9.4 shows, this inflation grew faster (1.2 to 1.4 times faster) than the official exchange rate in the Republic Hard Currency Bank. This led to an increase in the real exchange rate of the sum, a factor that, as is well known, does not favor exports. At the same time, the high exchange rate of the sum encourages imports by those who have access to monetary conversion on the hard-currency exchange.[13] The reason for this is transparent: such access ensures a pure profit, based on the gap between the different inflation rates and the fall in the exchange rate at the Republic Hard Currency Exchange. Moreover, the exchange rate of the dollar on the "black market" between January 1995 and December 1996 was, on average, 1.5 times higher than the official exchange rate at the Republic Hard Currency Exchange; at the end of 1996 and in early 1997, this difference had risen to more than twofold. The main point here is that the question of convertibility is handled administratively—through the complex system of the Republic Hard Currency Exchange. Furthermore, this situation does not encourage exporters to exchange directly any remaining hard currency at the official rate; instead, they are driven to look for devious paths to import and sell goods that are in high demand, taking into account the black market exchange rate. And this further aggravates the problem in the balance of trade.

The same table makes clear that the growth in the wage fund for 1995–96 was higher (between 1.5 and 2 times) than the growth in the exchange rate of the dollar at the Republic Hard Currency Exchange. This was due to the fact that wages comprise a significant share of the costs in any production operation, whereas enterprises are obligated to sell 30 percent of their hard-currency earnings (15 percent in the case of exports to the CIS countries) at the higher official exchange rate. Hence the rise in costs most likely cannot cover the earnings in sum after the exchange at the Republic Hard Currency Exchange. This poses a serious problem for the profitability of export branches—notwithstanding all the special advantages accorded to them. What the exporters lose in these transactions is redistributed to importers who have access to the official conversion rate. Moreover, it has been observed that the prices for most imported consumer goods are oriented toward the black market exchange rate, not the official rate. As a result, the consumers do not gain much from this kind of subsidy.

This situation in the sphere of hard-currency regulation also creates a monopolistic position for those who have access to the official market for currency exchanges. This often results in a market monopolization not only for imported but also domestic goods; furthermore, in the latter case, this occurs because of the lack of competition on imported goods.[14] Thus, the administrative regulation of the hard currency course, trade barriers (in particular, high duties and the licensing for exports; state orders; centralized control over export transactions), and the high level of monopoly in many branches all constitute serious obstacles to the economic development in Uzbekistan.

The Need for a Liberalization in Trade Policy

Perhaps the most valuable recommendation on trade policy for any government is that it must reduce its own direct involvement in international trade.[15] In the case of Uzbekistan, this recommendation is of critical importance. Two separate analyses have convincingly demonstrated that, the present system (centralized exports; state orders; licensing and high duties for exports; the requirement that 30 percent of the hard-currency earnings be sold at the artificially high official exchange rate) creates serious disincentives for enterprises to engage in export activities and to raise their competitiveness to world standards. It is, simply put, more profitable to sell their output on a less demanding domestic market than to seek markets abroad.[16]

Given the conditions and scale of the national economy, many such enterprises are monopolies or oligopolies. As a result, they can raise their prices while cutting back on the volume of output. Many concerns are former ministries and blocked a healthy competition, although such competition could have been fostered among subsidiary plants. Given this institutional system, there are objective factors preventing concerns from stimulating strict financial discipline and the stability in monetary convertibility needed for a liberalization in hard-currency policy. At the very least, this system leads to a number of negative consequences:

- A fall in production.
- An increase in the per unit production costs. That is because, under conditions where competition is lacking and there is a shortage of means to purchase and introduce technologies that are

energy-saving and that conserve materials (even as the cost of these factors rise to world levels), any other outcome is impossible. This intensifies the backwardness and provokes demands that domestic industry be protected from imports.

• Acceleration of the inflationary spiral. This results both from the direct consequences of monopolistic price formation and from an indirect factor—higher prices on goods that are not exported. All this usually sets off a chain reaction, leading to higher prices on both exported and imported goods. In the case of exported goods, this inflation is due to the fact that the domestic price increases usually raise the per unit production costs on all goods. The price increases on imported goods results from the higher demand, which will persist until the prices on imports reach their correlation with the prices on domestic substitutes.

This question has been dealt with at length because the level of inflation is an important regulator of economic growth. Research on the relationship between inflation rates and long-term economic growth in eighty-seven countries has shown an annual rate of 8 percent to be the upper limit for a "safe" inflationary tempo. In other words, if this ceiling is exceeded, inflation exerts an extremely significant, negative influence on economic growth. The goal here must be to hold inflation below this ceiling.[17]

Why the Control Over the Foreign Sector?

The emergence of foreign economic activity in Uzbekistan has proceeded amidst a battle between two basic antinomies: liberalization (with the use of generally accepted market instruments of regulation) and strict administrative control. Since both tendencies are rather strong in Uzbekistan, the process of reforming foreign economic activity has unfolded in a contradictory manner. As a result, the country has by no means maximized its opportunities for achieving the highest levels of stable economic growth.

It bears noting that for strict administrative control over foreign economic transactions, certain objective preconditions existed and indeed, at least in part, continue to exert an influence. It is therefore essential to examine these factors so as to understand the survival of certain administrative methods of control and the essentials of a radical liberalization.

After the collapse of the all-union foreign economic organizations and the "iron curtain," it suddenly became possible to reap gigantic profits from foreign trade by merely exploiting the artificial disproportions and gap between domestic and world prices. But the competitive goods consisted mainly of raw materials and semi-processed goods, which are "produced" mainly through sheer natural conditions and actually constitute the wealth of the entire nation. Given the budget deficit, inflation, the fall in the living standard, and similar factors, the state could not surrender its monopoly over foreign trade. Nor did it make economic sense for a multitude of enterprises to establish a qualified foreign trade apparatus of their own.

Moreover, because the former Soviet Union held a substantial share of the market for raw material commodities, any change in the volume of its deliveries to foreign markets was bound to have a considerable impact on world prices. The liberalization of exports for such goods resulted in a spontaneous, massive increase in the flow of raw materials from the former Soviet republics to world markets. The result, already apparent in 1992–93, was a sharp fall in world prices on cotton fiber, gold, nonferrous metals, oil, and other raw material resources.[18]

Naturally, the fall in world prices on the main export goods sharply reduced the country's hard-currency earnings that were desperately needed for macroeconomic stabilization and for the structural transformation to modernize the industrial base of the republic. That is why Uzbekistan, which held a significant share of the world market on cotton (ranking third in the world in terms of production and second in the volume of exports),[19] could not allow a destructive competition among its own exporters. However, this does not necessarily mean that the republic had to establish strict administrative control over this sphere and that certain other forms of regulation were not possible.

The Prospects for Cotton Exports

The foregoing raises the question whether Uzbekistan can exploit its "economic" clout in the cotton market so as to increase prices. One author has questioned whether "Uzbekistan could increase the national income by reducing exports and thereby increasing world prices." Despite the country's role as a cotton exporter, it must not exaggerate its power:

The optimal limitation on exports depends on various elasticities in supply and demand; for example, if world demand is less elastic, a restriction on exports can more likely succeed. However, Uzbekistan does not hold a dominant position on the world cotton market, for there are other suppliers. A restrictive trade policy could extract short-term gains from established buyers, who perhaps would not deem it convenient to change a supplier. But, in the long-term perspective, this would be harmful if the buyers turn to other suppliers.[20]

Moreover, scientific and technical progress has significantly increased the elasticity of demand for cotton. Thus, cotton's share of the world fiber market has declined from 50 percent in 1986 to about 40 percent. As a result, supply has outpaced demand: production for the growing year 1997–98 is planned at 20 million tons, but anticipated consumption will amount to only 19 million tons.[21] In addition, Uzbekistan is hardly the sole cotton producer; were Uzbekistan to reduce its deliveries, the ensuing rise in world prices would only stimulate other countries to increase their own output. A prime contender here is China, which is not a member of the International Consulting Committee on Cotton. Simultaneously, higher cotton prices would also stimulate research on substitutes, further increasing the elasticity of demand on cotton.

In general, the elasticity of world demand for cotton is the key determinant in our export policy. If it is significantly more than a few percentage points, Uzbekistan can obtain larger earnings by reducing cotton prices and increasing demand. That is because this country has substantial opportunities to increase productivity if the appropriate incentives are present. A further stimulus is the relatively low cost of labor, which places Uzbekistan in a more favorable situation compared to other exporting countries.

On the other hand, if elasticity is less than one percentage point, a contraction of cotton exports from Uzbekistan (through a specific program) can generate larger profits than what would be gained through expanded production. The question is how to achieve this contraction. Evidently, it must come through the development of domestic production, above all in the textile branch.

Although the production of textiles by the state productive association "Uzbeklegprom" [Uzbek Light Industry] once accounted for almost the entire textile output in the country, in 1993–96 its gross output decreased from 700 million square meters to about 600 million square meters. The following factors, however, could stimulate an expansion of production in Uzbekistan:

- *An increase in world consumption of textiles.* Indeed, demand grew by 20 percent during the last decade, with per capita consumption rising from 7.1 kg to 7.2 kg.[22]
- *Relocation of textile production closer to the source of raw materials.* The purpose, of course, is to achieve significant savings through reduced transportation costs.[23] The majority of transnational textile companies are already pursuing this policy; examples include the Uzbek-Turkish joint-venture enterprise "Askamtekstil'" (with the participation of the Turkish firm Astop); the Uzbek-Korean joint-venture enterprise "Kabul-Toi-Tepa Tekstil'" involving the South Korean firm Kabool Textiles; the production of cotton yarn by Daewoo Textiles, which has created an enterprise with 100–percent foreign capital; and the Uzbek-Turkish joint-venture enterprise "AsAim-Tekstil'" in Andizhan Oblast. This process is encouraged by the low level of domestic cotton consumption—a total of 180,000 tons, or 14 percent of domestic production.[24]
- *Cheap labor costs.* The textile branch is traditionally labor-intensive. Uzbekistan has favorable conditions for the use of labor resources and therefore is highly competitive in this branch of production.
- *Favorable conditions for foreign investors.* The latter are able to earn large profits because of preferential tax rates and the lower costs of fixed capital, land, and other production factors.

Moving Up the Technological Ladder

In devising a strategy to develop the foreign economic sector, Uzbekistan must take some basic factors into account. The production and export of unprocessed agricultural crops, or the export of untreated mineral resources, do not represent a form of national economic specialization, but rather the desperate exploitation of primary natural resources and persistence of economic backwardness.[25] If Uzbekistan fails to develop and diversify its exports (with an increase in the share of finished goods), it will not be able to achieve stable economic growth. This factor is further accentuated by two key tendencies in world markets:

- The share of agrarian and raw-material goods in the world commodity turnover is decreasing. This tendency will continue in the foreseeable future.[26]
- The prices on raw materials are less stable than those on processed goods.[27]

Hence, in this writer's judgment, Uzbekistan should follow a strategy analogous to that used by the countries of Southeast Asia: namely, it must endeavor to move up the quality ladder. Having modernized and upgraded so as to create competitive branches for processing raw materials, Uzbekistan could then advance to the next rung on the ladder: it could become primarily an exporter of material-intensive and labor-intensive goods, thereby pushing the raw material component to a subsidiary level in its exports. The next step would then be for the country to become an exporter of capital-intensive goods. It will also become an exporter of technology-intensive products—machine tools, conveyer production systems, turbines, motor vehicles, buses, and so forth. Then comes the new stage where exports include R&D-intensive goods in the high-tech sphere. This process of moving up the technological ladder is most graphically apparent in the case of Japan. Lacking its own raw materials, this country began from a stage based mainly on labor- and material-intensive production.[28]

Uzbekistan already possesses the basis for moving up the technological ladder, including phases that are R&D-intensive. For example, the Chkalov Aviation Plant in Tashkent, one of the most advanced enterprises in the republic, has the potential of (1) becoming an exporter of its own goods (primarily by manufacturing the IL-76 aircraft, in various modifications, and by beginning production work on the passenger airline IL-114) and, (2) serving as a "locomotive of progress" for the entire Uzbek high-tech industry. At the present time, however, it must import over 70 percent of the key components for aircraft construction from Russia, not to mention its reliance upon outside sources for scientific research, engineering design, and technical documentation.

In this author's judgment, direct state investment should *not* play the central role in helping the country to climb up the technology ladder. Rather, that should be done by enterprises based on private incentive and foreign investment.

It is also essential to liberalize trade policy in order to create the most favorable environment for a diversification of exports. All the trade barriers are an irritant for exporters. Potential partners are most energetic in identifying new lines of production when they have free access to international markets.[29] As an analysis of enterprises with foreign investment in Uzbekistan has shown, these are generally viable if they are associated with large programs, created on the basis of state property, and endowed with special privileges for taxation and currency exchange. For example, the government entered into a joint-venture enterprise with the American company Newmont Mining, which invested 150 million dollars and plans to produce approximately 5 million ounces of gold in the next seventeen years. The government stuck a similar deal with the British company Lornho, involving a 250 million dollar investment to mine gold from waste and tailings. Similarly, the firm British-American Tobacco invested 230 million dollars in a joint-venture enterprise to produce cigarettes from locally grown tobacco.

In 1996, Uzbekistan established a joint-venture enterprise with the Korean firm Daewoo, with an investment of 658 million dollars, to produce automobiles and small-engined buses. By the year 2000, this enterprise expects to reach a production level of 200,000 vehicles. The prospects for the motor vehicle industry in Uzbekistan, nevertheless, remain rather unclear. The principal reason is economies of size: production costs in this industry decrease as output increases—an important factor in the competitive struggle on the motor vehicle market. According to some studies, the minimum volume of annual output in this branch is about 2 million vehicles for an entire company, and approximately 250,000 to 400,000 vehicles for an individual plant.[30] This is perhaps one reason why Daewoo is so active on the Uzbek market, but for the immediate future this enterprise will fall below the postulated minimum volume of output. Moreover, Korean experts predict that Daewoo sales will drop 10.5 percent in 1998 after import restrictions on imported vehicles are eliminated (in accordance with the plans of the Korean government).[31] Where is the company to find a constant market for the projected volume of vehicle production, especially since countries in the CIS are rather closed (given the four-party Customs Union of Russia, Belarus, Kazakhstan, and Kyrgyzstan) and have their own prospective producers.

The majority of joint-venture enterprises operate in the service sector (chiefly in trade and intermediary roles), with up to 40 percent getting bogged down at the registration phase. But more important is the fact that a significant proportion serve only the domestic market.

Because of the restrictions on money exchange, foreign firms and joint-venture enterprises—unless they have special agreements with the government—have accumulated a large quantity of nonconvertible *sum* (the national currency of Uzbekistan). As a result, such firms are forced to engage in barter to repatriate their profits, and that in turn has elicited new attempts by the government to prohibit and block such barter transactions. And, in any event, those seeking to register a joint-venture enterprise in Uzbekistan must be prepared for a prolonged bureaucratic and hazy procedure, indeed one laced with substantial monetary payments.

Another problem is a virtual monopoly in foreign banking operations: 95 percent of all transactions are now conducted by the National Bank of Uzbekistan. The most active foreign banks in the republic include the Turkish Bank and Americano-Dutch Bank, although there are also offices of the Deutsche Bank, Berliner Bank, and Credit Suisse.

Finally, foreign investors must also overcome certain institutional barriers. That is evident, for example, in the tourist industry. The tourist business is potentially one of the most promising sources of hard currency: Uzbekistan has more than 4,000 historic monuments, the most famous of which are located in the cities of Samarkand, Bukhara, and Khiva and are included in the list of monuments of world culture. Nevertheless, until recently, the tourist branch has generally tended to decline. Thus, whereas more than 1 million tourists visited the country in 1992, that figure had fallen in 1995 to just over 100,000. There are many reasons for this downturn. Apart from the fact that the tourists came increasingly from outside the former USSR (not other areas of the former Soviet Union, as previously had been the case), the state does not permit competition with the national company of "Uzbekturism," which is essentially a Ministry of Tourism. Indeed, to register a firm with foreign capital in the tourist branch, it is first necessary to obtain accreditation from Uzbekturism itself!

Providing Incentives for Foreign Investment

Investment incentives, while helpful, are rarely decisive. More important is the environment—one that makes investors feel confident that they can make a profit and have sufficient security to realize their gains. For that reason, a liberal trade policy is an important instrument for promoting the development of enterprises with foreign investment. It is also essential to dismantle any barriers—for example, the process for registering firms, rules on currency conversion, and market accessibility of imported production factors. The advantages of openness can be intensified if foreign investment is encouraged. Among other things, foreign investors can provide the missing production factors that a branch needs to create new and competitive goods.[32]

The experience of many countries confirms that direct attempts to solicit foreign investment are less effective than the creation of a economic space where the foreign investor feels secure and comfortable. If such an environment exists, the foreign investor has the necessary skills for determining profit opportunities and is more sensitive than state officials to market stimuli (i.e., financial returns and the costs of false decisions).[33] However, the state must not remove itself entirely from this process. On the contrary, the conception of economic "modernization" dictate that the state actively intervene as a guarantor and insurer: "In selected spheres of production, the state supports the development of research and the creation of new lines of industrial production when the risk (technological or economic) is especially high, and when the requisite financial outlays to introduce new technologies and gain new markets are especially large."[34]

All this raises another question: is it necessary to support enterprises with foreign investment through protectionist measures—namely, by establishing high duties on competitive imports? This was done, for example, in the case of "UzDEU-avto" (the Uzbek-Daewoo motor vehicle plant) in the city of Asaka, where the import duty on motor vehicles was set at 40 to 60 percent. Another example is the plant "UzDeu-elektroniks" (Uzbek-Daewoo Electronics): its output is protected by a 30 percent duty on imported household goods. It is essential, in this question, to consider the facts of the specific case. Thus, the buyer of automobiles now finds an adequate supply in the marketplace; as a result, the price of a motor vehicle does not have a critical, negative impact on the standard of living of the general population, while the earnings—given the difficulties of providing a direct state subsidy—are reinvested to create a modern industrial branch and to channel domestic demand from foreign goods. However, it is necessary to devise a detailed reform plan, the purpose of which is to achieve competitiveness in each sphere of production and to specify the times and rates for reducing protective duties (so as to exclude monopolies and the attendant stagnation). It is also necessary to promote the intensive development of domestic suppliers of components for such industrial plants—as indeed was done in Korea itself, where local producers currently provide 30 percent of the components used in the manufacture of motor vehicles.

Is Stable Economic Growth Possible in Isolation from the World?

The growth of exports in the manufacturing sector, as the country moves up the technological ladder, can encounter trade barriers in other countries. Nontariff obstacles could, in the future, become a serious impediment to trade, especially for agricultural commodities, leather, textiles, chemicals, and metals. The new states of the former USSR are still classified as "nonmarket economies" and often devise arbitrary rules on imports.[35] So long as Uzbekistan exports primary raw materials, other countries are not interested in imposing trade barriers, since this will increase their own costs of production and undercut their own competitiveness (especially in countries that lack their own sources of these materials). But the situation can change once industrial goods become a larger share of exports to these countries. In that case, the foreign trade interests of Uzbekistan are best protected by joining the World Trade Organization (WTO), which would force its members to refrain from restrictive measures against Uzbek exports.

At the present time, various agreements have already given Uzbekistan most-favored nation status in more than twenty countries, including the United States, China, England, the Republic of Korea, Turkey, and Israel. Uzbekistan has also obtained this status in the Generalized System of Preferences from Canada and the European Union.

More ominous is the threat of anti-dumping measures, which the United States and European Union have already invoked against Uzbek imports. The WTO affords members a certain degree of protection, although this security is far from perfect. But nonmembers, like Uzbekistan, are in far worse straits, for they simply have no array of countermeasures at their disposal.

Membership in the WTO provides a number of advantages:[36]
- participation in a legal mechanism that regulates 90 percent of the total volume of world trade;

- the right to exercise the most-favored-nation status on markets in the member states;
- the protection of an international legal system against discrimination or other illegal measures by the trading partners in the WTO;
- access to all information regarding the foreign economic policies and intentions of the member states of the WTO.

At the same time, membership in the WTO also imposes certain obligations:

- not to regulate foreign-economic relations by command-administrative means, but to rely upon economic mechanisms (primarily customs duties and, to an insignificant degree, nontariff measures);
- not to raise the level of customs duties, the level of which are set upon entry into the WTO;
- to limit the use of nontariff means of customs regulation;
- not to provide export subsidies;
- to refrain from organizing special bilateral trade, since this violates the interests of third countries;
- to provide, on a regular basis, information about the system of economic management of the economy, foreign economic policy, the condition of foreign trade, and the privileges accorded to other countries.[37]

Participation in the WTO will not only provide a legal shield for Uzbek exports, but also stimulate greater competitiveness and the process of fundamental structural reform. However, substantial administrative regulation of foreign economic activity is not only a barrier for Uzbekistan's entry into the WTO, but also will erase the anticipated gains once it joints this association. Thus, control over access to monetary conversion and the inflated exchange rate make it impossible to compare domestic production costs with those elsewhere in the world; as a result, businesses are simply not in a position to make rational economic decisions. Moreover, the significant share of the centralized exports and imports reduces the role of market mechanisms in guiding business decisions on exports or imports (depending on the preferred price and quality, the terms for delivery, and so forth). Finally, the conditions of trade in Uzbekistan cannot satisfy the expectations of WTO members if the acquisisiton of foreign trade partners depends largely upon administrative decisions by the Uzbek government.

Integration—Yes, But How?

The final question concerns the prospects for economic integration in the CIS and membership in the Customs Union. The member states of the CIS inherited a single energy system, a unified network for transportation and communications, a closely knit economic complex, an integrated grid of oil and natural gas pipelines, the free movement of people and significant migration of the labor force, a single set of technical standards, and nominal internal boundaries. Therefore, the question of reintegration, whatever form it might take, naturally arises, and that is especially true with the formation of the Customs Union by Russia, Kazakhstan, Belarus, and Kyrgyzstan. The formation of the Customs Union has brought changes in the participating countries through five main processes:[38]

1. production specialization in each of the member states;
2. realization of the advantages that a large-scale economy holds over a smaller one;
3. changes in the terms of trade (i.e., the establishment of more advantageous and fair relations between export and import prices);
4. improvement in the efficiency of production as a result of greater competition among firms in all the member states;
5. growth in the rate of industrial development.

However, integration within the framework of the CIS can entail somewhat different results for the participating states. As the experience of integration among third world countries has shown, the liberalization of trade and the creation of a broad economic space, which is protected from outside competition by a trade barrier, can initially stimulate an industrialization to promote import substitution as well as industrial enterprises to sell on the markets of participating states. However, the advantages of such integration flow mainly to the most advanced participants. In itself, the quantitative growth of mutual economic ties in the third world could not overcome differences in their levels of development and alter their status as the least developed. The establishment of a closed economic space, protected by high customs duties and marked by a low level of domestic consumption, inevitably reduced the competitiveness of the goods being produced. That only reinforced backwardness, the inability of locally produced goods to find a niche in world markets, and hence a low ranking in the world economy. In other words, the final result was precisely the opposite of the goals that led to the original economic integration.[39]

This experience is of enormous significance for evaluating the prospects of integration within the framework of the CIS. To a considerable degree, this process depends upon the economic recovery and trade policy of the largest and most industrially advanced participant— Russia, which is also the main investor in Uzbekistan from the CIS. The main point is that the young industry of Uzbekistan may well be devoured by its more powerful partner and that, within the division of labor of the CIS, Uzbekistan's role as raw-material supplier will be intensified.

Can integration into the Customs Union accelerate the rate of our industrial development? This depends upon the investment capacity of the participating countries. Obviously, there is no reason to expect a large influx of investment: the countries of the CIS, at least in the near future, will strive to attract foreign investments to themselves.

However, this does not mean that the incentives for integration in the CIS are totally wanting. Thus, the manufacturing industry of Uzbekistan has especially close ties with partner firms in the CIS and, indeed, still ships the bulk of their exports to destinations in the former USSR. Therefore, measures to create joint-venture firms and industrial groups could provide real support for these branches of industry. Hence, here, one must deal with each enterprise on an individual basis and take into account the particulars of the specific case.

The question of a common transport system is particularly acute for Uzbekistan. That is because the majority of cargo shipments (including transit freight) must traverse Kazakhstan and Russia. Hence any increase in transportation rates and other restrictions by these two countries could create extremely serious problems for the economic development of Uzbekistan.

Notes

1. I.A. Karimov, *Uzbekistan svoi put' obnovleniia i progressa* (Tashkent, 1992).

2. A. Alimov, *Vneshneekonomicheskaia deiatel'nost' Respubliki Uzbekistan: vzgliad v budushchee* (Tashkent, 1992).

3. *Zakonodatel'stvo Respubliki Uzbekistana o vneshneekonomicheskoi deiatel'nosti: sbornik normativnykh aktov* (Tashkent, 1995).

4. N. Sirazhiddinov and N. Agaffonov, "Vneshniaia torgovlia Uzbekistana 1991–95," report 96 (4) to the Project for Macroeconomic Analysis and Preparation of Personnel PROON (Tashkent, November 1996), pp. 5–8, 17–22; A.A. Adylov, "Opyt vneshnei ekonomicheskoi politiki i osnovnye orientiry razvitiia," paper presented to the International Conference on "The Economic Policy of the Republic of Uzbekistan after the Acquisition of Independence" (Tashkent, 30–31 January 1997), pp. 2–5.

5. K. Mikalopulos [C. Michalopoulos] and D. Tarr, "Torgovaia deiatel'nost' i politika v novykh nezavisimykh gosudarstvakh" (Washington, DC: World Bank, 1996), pp. 4–5, 16–17.

6. Ibid.

7. "Piat' let reform: chto sdelano, chto delat'," *Biznes Vestnik Vostoka,* 1997, no. 6: 1.

8. Sirazhiddinov and Agaffonov, "Vneshniaia torgovlia Uzbekistana 1991–95."

9. Ibid.; Adylov, "Opyt vneshnei ekonomicheskoi politiki"; *States of the Former USSR. A Statistical Handbook 1996* (Washington, DC: World Bank, 1996), pp. 502–36.

10. A. Taksanov, "Eksport vmesto importa," *Biznes Vestnik Vostoka,* 1996, no. 42, p. 24.

11. Sirazhiddinov and Agaffonov, "Vneshniaia torgovlia Uzbekistana 1991–95."

12. Mohamed A. El-Erian, "Multiple Exchange Rates: The Experience in Arab Countries," *Finance and Development,* December 1994, pp. 29–31.

13. N. Sirazhiddinov and N. Agaffonov, "Valiutnaia politika Uzbekistana v usloviiakh perekhodnogo perioda," Doklad 96(5) in the "Project for Macroeconomic Analysis and Preparation of Personnel of PROON" (Tashkent, November 1996), pp. 18–20, 23–26.

14. Ibid.

15. Mikalopulos and Tarr, "Torgovaia deiatel'nost'."

16. Sirazhiddinov and Agaffonov, "Valiutnaia politika Uzbekistana"; Idem, "Vneshniaia torgovlia Uzbekistana."

17. M. Sarel, "Nonlinear Effect of Inflationon Economic Growth," IMF Working Paper no. 56 (Washington, DC, 1995).

18. I.A. Karimov, *Uzbekistan na puti uglubleniia ekonomicheskikh reform* (Tashkent, 1995), pp. 96–97.

19. World Bank, *Deiatel'nost' Vsemirnogo banka v Srednei Azii i Azerbaijane* (Washington, DC, 1995).

20. R. Pomfret, "Torgovaia politika dlia perekhodnoi ekonomiki syr'evogo kharaktera," paper presented to an international conference on "The Economic Policy of the Republic of Uzbekistan after the Acquisition of Independence" (Tashkent, 30–31 January 1997), pp. 2–8.

21. "Khlopkovyi buzines: vzgliad iz Tashkenta," *Biznes Vestnik Vostoka,* 1996, no. 41, pp. 1–2.

22. Ibid.

23. A.A. Igolkin and V.V. Motylev, *Mezhdunarodnoe razdelenie truda: modeli, tendentsii, prognozy* (Moscow, 1988).

24. N. Merezhnikova, "Tekstil'noe budushchee Uzbekistana," *Biznes Vestnik Vostoka,* 1996, no. 50, p. 22.

25. B.S. Fomin, *Ekonometricheskie teorii i modeli mezhdu narodnykh eckonomicheskikh otnoshenii* (Moscow, 1970), p. 199.

26. Igolkin and Motylev, *Mezhdunarodnoe razdelenie truda.*

27. Pomfret, "Torgovaia politika."

28. M.A. Portnoi, "Vneshneekonomicheskaia strategiia Rossii i mirovoi opyt," *SShA: ekonomika, politika, ideologiia,* 1996, no. 10, pp. 15–19.

29. Ibid.

30. Young Sae Lee, *A New Trade and Industrial Policy in the Globalization of Korea* (Seoul, 1996), 113.

31. Ibid., 116.

32. Pomfret, "Torgovaia politika."

33. Ibid.

34. V. Hauff and F.W. Scharpf, *Modernisierung der Volkswirtschaft. Technologiepolitik als Strukturpolitik* (Frankfurt/Main, 1975), p. 80.

35. Mikalopulos and Tarr, "Torgovaia deiatel'nost'."

36. Pomfret, "Torgovaia politika."

37. A.B. Terekhov, *Svoboda torgovli (analiz opyta zarubezhnykh stran)* (Moscow, 1991).

38. Fomin, *Ekonometricheskie teorii,* p. 199.

39. L.V. Vinogradova, "Ekonomicheskaia integratsiia v SNG i opyt tret'ego mira," *Mirovaia ekonomika i mezhdunarodnye otnosheniia,* 1995, no. 9.

Part IV

Critical Economic Issues

10

Kazakhstan: The Prospects and Perils of Foreign Investment

Arystan Esentugelov

A Severe Investment Crisis

Ever since Kazakhstan proclaimed independence and embarked on reform, its economy has been in a continuous systemic crisis.[1] Nor has that crisis spared investment. Indeed, the investment crisis has proven to be both intense and broad-based; during the last eight years, the investment sphere has experienced a sharp contraction in volume and deformation in structure. Specifically, in 1991–97, the volume of investments in fixed capital contracted by 90.8 percent; in 1997 alone, amidst signs that the economy was stabilizing and inflation had fallen to manageable levels, capital investments in the economy nonetheless decreased another 6.0 percent. That contraction affected virtually every branch of the national economy; the fuel industry and metallurgy were the sole exceptions. The decrease in investment resulted when the state, faced with severe financial difficulties, suspended the allocation of investment funds that had originally been included in the 1997 budget. That decision effectively scrapped its investment program for 1997. As state budgetary funds constitute only a nugatory (3 percent) of total investments, foreign investments—which grew by 1.5 times in 1997—are plainly of mounting importance.

The 1990s have also witnessed a major deformation in the branch structure of the economy. Although capital did flow into the raw-material branches, trade, and the nonproduction sector, it was sharply curtailed for productive branches like machine-building, light industry, and food processing. These patterns are clearly reflected in the data: whereas the share of investment for the manufacturing sector declined from 9.0 to 5.6 percent, the proportion of investment rose for oil drilling (from 7.8 percent to 20.4 percent), natural gas production (from 1.7 to 2.6 percent), metallurgy (from 5.1 to 10.6 percent), and the nonproductive sphere (from 12.8 to 14.1 percent).

This pervasive and protracted investment crisis was due to two main factors. One was the constant contraction in resources for capital investment, which in turn was due to the endless fall in the efficiency of production and the economic crisis that had already commenced in the Soviet era. By the early 1990s, this caused a massive fall in production and galloping inflation; that, in turn, provoked a rise in unemployment, a fall in personal incomes, and a contraction in the working capital of enterprises. The situation was further aggravated by the new problem of "nonpayments," a scourge that soon enveloped the entire economy of the country.

The galloping inflation and constant fall in the exchange rate of the tenge (the national currency of Kazakhstan, with an exchange rate of 70 to 80 tenge per dollar in 1996–97) led to capital flight and a gradual "dollarization" of the economy. The result was an extremely low level of savings.

The investment crisis in Kazakhstan was further intensified by the steady contraction of investment and downturn in the real sectors of the economy. This was due, in particular, to the high interest rates and the high risk of investing in production. Indeed, during these years, demand and sales contracted, supplies of raw materials fell (with a corresponding rise in prices), and domestically produced goods could not compete with imports.

The Acute Need for Foreign Investment

Obviously, unless Kazakhstan could significantly increase capital investment, it would be unable to find a solution to the economic crisis and return to the path of economic growth.

However, the country's need for investment is immense—both because of the multitude of problems inherited from the earlier period and because of new problems generated by the present system. There are several reasons why only an enormous infusion of capital investment can resolve these problems:

- many branches of the economy and industry have suffered a severe decline and degeneration;
- the manufacturing branches are almost totally degraded;
- given the extensive and rapacious exploitation of natural resources, these have depreciated in value and are on the verge of closing—which, in turn, would deprive many enterprises in the country of their main source of raw materials;
- a powerful blow has been dealt to agriculture, especially its animal husbandry branch, where the number of livestock has fallen precipitously (300 percent in the case of sheep; from 30 to 50 percent for other forms of livestock);
- the machinery and material-technical base of enterprises has reached a level of near-total depletion and obsolescence.

As a result, the economy became resource-intensive, inefficient, and noncompetitive. Moreover, dozens of small and middle-sized towns that depend on one or two enterprises found themselves in severe straits. Such towns, along with many rural areas, are now classified as severely depressed, and some areas also face the threat of acute ecological dangers.

To overcome these complex and extremely serious social-economic problems, it is essential to accelerate the process of fundamental structural reform and technological modernization. In this author's judgment, however, such structural changes require massive investment—of a magnitude that Kazakhstan is most unlikely to obtain. Still, these conditions would appear to dictate attempts to solicit the maximum level of foreign investment. And here Kazakhstan has some advantages—above all, its rich array of energy and natural resources.

From Foreign Investment to Massive Debts

In 1993, foreign capital began flowing into Kazakhstan in substantial amounts, but not merely in the form of "investments." At present, this term includes credits for goods, technical assistance, bonuses from foreign firms to purchase enterprises, monetary contributions of for-

Table 10.1

Data on Foreign Investments Used in Kazakhstan in 1993–96
(in millions of dollars)

| Type of foreign investment | Total for 1993–96 | Amount per year | | | |
		1993	1994	1995	1996
Direct investment	3,448.9	1,131.9	604.4	849.9	863.4
Portfolio investment	267.2	0.0	25.0	37.2	205.0
Loans and credits	3,181.8	558.0	1,134.9	851.9	637.0
Total	6,897.9	1,689.9	1,764.3	1,739.0	1,705.4

Source: Balance of Payments of Kazakhstan 1993–96 (compiled by the National Agency of the Republic of Kazakhstan, 1997).

eign companies that have been in control over Kazakhstani enterprises, the accumulated nonpayments of foreign enterprises, the sums used to create the charter capital of joint-venture enterprises, and so forth. Characteristically, in calculating the flow of foreign investments, official documents from the government and banking institutions differ on the total amount of foreign investments as well as the specific amounts for loans, credits, and foreign debts.

In 1993–94, Kazakhstan attracted foreign capital chiefly in the form of foreign loans and credits, including some on commercial terms that were backed by a state. Such financing came from every possible source: financial institutions (e.g., the International Monetary Fund, the World Bank, The European Bank of Reconstruction and Development, and the Asian Development Bank), industrially developed states, private commercial banks, and so forth. In 1993–96, the IMF provided soft loans of 430 million dollars; the World Bank provided another 950 million dollars. As for individual states, thirty-seven states (including Austria, Great Britain, Germany, Spain, Canada, Pakistan, the United States, the Sultanate of Oman, Turkey, and Switzerland) opened credit lines worth more than 1.5 billion U.S. dollars.

Of all the credits granted, in 1993–96 Kazakhstan accepted credits and loans worth 3.18 billion dollars (see Table 10.1), of which 2.5 billion dollars (46.1 percent of the total) had guaranteed backing from the government of Kazakhstan.

Given the size of Kazakhstan's economy, these loans and credits represented a considerable sum. Unfortunately, however, they were not used for rational, productive purposes; instead, they were diverted to low-priority, nontargeted borrowers who did not even have sufficient collateral and guarantees for repayment. As a result, most of these funds went either to criminal elements or to kinsmen of a few highly placed officials, who then channeled these resources into trade, used them for speculative financial and hard-currency transactions in the fund markets, and squandered them on prestigious homes, buildings, foreign automobiles, and so forth. In the final analysis, credits worth 2.5 billion dollars—backed by government guarantees—have vanished without a trace and now form a large foreign debt for the state.

The flood of foreign loans and credits thus has had no useful effect, come amidst a high level of inflation, and reflects only the principle "if they are giving, take it." The main result has been to leave the state in serious financial straits by imposing a heavy debt burden on the annual budget. If in 1993 the state's foreign debt was about 2 billion U.S. dollars, it has since risen sharply—to 3.3 billion in 1994, 3.1 billion in 1995, 4.0 billion in 1996, and 5.2 billion in 1997. That debt represents a substantial proportion of the GDP: 26.1 percent in 1994, 19 percent in 1995, 18.8 percent in 1996, and 22 percent in 1997.

This extra burden of servicing a foreign debt has naturally had a major impact on the state budget. Budgetary outlays to service this debt has reached a rather large scale, amounting to 190 million dollars in 1993, 150 million in 1994, 466 million in 1995, 360 million in 1996, and 333.7 million in 1997.

According to estimates compiled by the National Bank of Kazakhstan, the costs of servicing the foreign debt will reach its peak level in 1999, when the country will have to pay 600 million dollars. That surge is due to the fact that by then the country will no longer enjoy the special privileges granted earlier by international financial agencies.

In 1995–97, costs of debt service was 14 to 15 percent of its export earnings. By world standards, that appears to be an entirely normal level. However, if one takes into account certain other factors (the extremely difficult economic condition of the country, the unfavorable balance of trade, and the diversion of a substantial proportion of the export earnings to foreign accounts), this burden is actually greater than the 25 to 30 percent level found in Latin America and Southeast Asia.

Kazakhstan had an opportunity to learn from the negative experience of many developing countries in attracting foreign investments (chiefly in the form of loans and credits). Above all, it should have learned how to prevent a small clique of ruling elites from appropriating such resources for their own personal use. The government, however, ignored this opportunity and has thereby aggravated its financial problems during a difficult transition period and systemic economic crisis. All this will most certainly have a profound impact for a long time to come.

Policy Since 1995: Selling Strategic Enterprises to Foreign Firms

From the very beginning of its independence, Kazakhstan could have followed a policy of attracting direct foreign investment by relying upon its rich complex of energy and natural resources. As is well known, such direct foreign investment is plainly superior to loans and credits. They do not, for example, create a national foreign debt (with the attendant costs of servicing this debt) and leave the responsibility for risk on the shoulders of private foreign investors. In addition, direct foreign investment creates new jobs, causes foreign firms to apply their management skills and business experience, and encourages the introduction of advanced technologies and know-how.

In 1993–95, however, private foreign investors were slow to invest their funds in Kazakhstan. This was due partly to the fact that the new republic had a weak system of financial institutions and, in particular, lacked a well-developed legal basis for the protection of private property. Moreover, state law was subject to incessant change, especially with respect to taxation. Another discouraging factor was the high level of corruption among state officials. Yet another impediment is the country's location; its lack of direct access to world markets is naturally a source of concern for foreign investors.

As experience has shown, it has generally been difficult to attract direct foreign investment to countries with a transition economy, especially those in the CIS. First, the available capital resources in the world are rather limited, particularly when compared to the number of countries soliciting investments. Second, since the mid-1980s, there have been substantial changes in the forms and goals of direct foreign investments. Above all, these investments no longer flow to developing countries (as was earlier the case), but to industrially developed countries that, since the 1980s, have given such resources a special role in their strategies for economic development.

Similar circumstances force Kazakhstan to fight aggressively to attract direct foreign investments. In so doing, it must select advantageous forms and terms for different branches of the economy as well as preferential tax treatment and other advantages. In the second half of 1995, the government of Kazakhstan reached some critical decisions on these matters. Indeed, it chose such radical forms and terms to attract direct foreign investment that it has radically altered its economic strategy and the current situation in the country. Namely, it has sold from 60 to 100 percent of the stock or assets of existing industrial enterprises in the core branches of the economy—that is, the enterprises that extract and process the energy and raw material resources of strategic significance for the national economy. These are export-oriented enterprises; they include the oil drilling and refining plants, energy, ferrous and nonferrous metallurgy, and the chemical industry that produce goods of strategic significance and are therefore economically viable and potentially efficient spheres of production. Moreover, these sales were not conducted in an open forum; the terms of such deals have remained a secret not only from society and the press but even from the legislative branches of the government (i.e., the Parliament) and various executive organs of the state.

Thus, the government has already sold off the flagships of industry in Kazakhstan—enterprises that in fact occupy a high ranking in the list of the world's leading producers. These include enterprises like "Balkhashmys," "Kartmetkombinat," "Dzhezkazgantsvetmet," the ferroalloy plants in Aktiubinsk and Aksui, "Iuzhneftegaz," and a number of others. The large energy plants have also been sold off, one after the other. In the course of about a year and half, foreign companies have bought up approximately forty such industrial plants. The enterprises that now find themselves under the control of foreign companies (either as owners and operators) account for more than 70 percent of the country's industrial production and more than 90 percent of its industrial exports. Table 10.2 shows the share of exports of the basic forms of goods being produced at these plants.

These enterprises created the highest incomes for workers and was the main source of hard-currency earnings for the country. It bears noting that, to a very large degree, these enterprises also supported the entire economies of the cities and territories where they operate.

Table 10.2

Share of Total Output Exported in Selected Branches of Industry, 1992–96 (in percent)

Industrial product	1992	1993	1994	1995	1996
Ferrous alloys	68.3	93.0	88.8	74.4	92.2
Rolled steel	62.6	51.7	61.0	80.7	79.5
Copper	91.9	86.0	66.9	84.7	98.0
Oil and natural gas condensate	72.4	54.8	47.3	54.6	63.1
Zinc and zinc alloys	73.6	69.9	69.9	87.3	87.6
Lead	72.4	64.7	35.2	66.0	90.8
Natural gas	48.2	50.8	35.6	61.0	36.6
Iron-ore pellets					90.2
Alumina	94.1	97.1	97.7	74.0	98.8

Source: Calculations by the author.

To be sure, many of these firms found themselves in acute financial difficulties. Namely, they lacked operating capital and investment resources, had large arrears to the state budget, owed debts to suppliers of raw materials and other goods, and for a long time had been unable to pay the wages due their own employees.

All these negative phenomena were due to a variety of factors, such as poor management, the inability of leading personnel to operate under the new market conditions, and the accumulated financial difficulties of individual enterprises. To deal with this situation, the government placed its hopes on private foreign firms. It assumed that they somehow would run these enterprises better, invest in production, retire the debts, and pay wages of their employees on a regular basis.

The Result: Deepening Financial Crisis in Enterprises

At first glance, the government's new policy appears to have been its only option, given the circumstances. However, if one makes even a superficial examination of the activity of industrial enterprises in the raw-materials branch prior to their sale, the results show that this new investment policy has been an enormous mistake.

Certain facts should be made clear at the outset. First, many of the enterprises being sold were still earning a profit. Second, even the enterprises that found themselves in severe financial straits were still maintaining stable operations; indeed, their difficulties stemmed from exogenous causes, not their own failings and mistakes. Namely, their problems were due to the existing tax system, the legacy of the command system in enterprise management, and the general economic problem of nonpayments (which has still not been resolved and indeed is steadily growing worse). Had the government dealt with such problems, these enterprises would not have found themselves in such difficult economic straits and would not have given grounds for their mass sell-off to foreign firms—some of dubious origin and registering their home office in various offshore zones.

During the reform years, problems accumulated in several large enterprises. One example is the flagship of ferrous metallurgy, "Karmetkombinat" (Karaganda metallurgical combine). It was difficult for this enterprise, however profitable its operations, to survive the rapid turnover in directors—five different heads in six years. That is all the more true given the results of investigatory journalism by the television channel NTV and a formal judicial investigation by the Ministry of the Interior of the Russian Federation: pilfering and thieving had long been endemic at Karmetkombinat. And wherever there is such large-scale stealing, no enterprise can fare well. By 1994, the alarming situation at this enterprise and the need for financial restructuring had already become apparent; at that point, it would still have been possible to provide the requisite assistance. Unfortunately, however, the government did nothing more than just replace the director yet again. All this inexorably led to the decision to sell the enterprise to a foreign company—a British company ("Ispat")—and indeed in a secret deal and at bargain basement prices.

A similar scenario unfolded at other enterprises. The story of the long-suffering phosphorous plants of Zhambyl Oblast is particularly instructive: in the course of a single year, this enterprise was successively turned over to the control of three different firms. This led one venerable observer to exclaim: "What self-respecting father would marry off his own daughter against her own will and do it three times in a single year!" Another example is afforded by the mining-enrichment combine in Zhairem. This enterprise, which has rights to a unique deposit of complex metallic and manganese ores, was sold in 1994 for a mere 10 million tenge (and without the preliminary audit of its capital assets) to an obscure Swiss firm called "Nakost AG." At the present time, a combine that once produced 2 million tons of complex metal ores per year has been stripped to the bones. Many more such examples could be adduced.

To be sure, there are some positive examples. Thus, the Sokolovsk-Sarbaisk mining-enrichment combine and the Pavlodar aluminum plant were placed under foreign control, and the condition of both has since improved. But these are the exception, not the rule.

Today, the process of selling strategic enterprises to foreign companies is nearly complete in the oil industry—the final branch of the export-oriented sector of the economy. Ominously, the joint-stock company "Iuzhneftegaz," was sold as quickly and secretly as had been done in the cases of "Aktiubinskneft'," "Embaneft'," and other oil enterprises. At this point, only a single oil enterprise—the joint-stock company "Uzen'munaigaz"—remains to be sold.

This branch shows graphically how enterprises end up in hopeless financial straits. Thus, the condition of "Mangistaumunaigaz" (and the natural gas branch more generally) has deteriorated primarily because of nonpayments. The bulk of indebtedness involves enterprises and the state. As a result, in 1997 unpaid bills for natural gas deliveries from "Mangistaumunaigaz" amounted to 17 percent of its total output. For the branch as a whole, this indicator amounts to 31.4 percent of total output. A significant part of the debts are owed by agriculture. Despite the chronic failure of the latter to pay for fuels and lubricants, each year the government nevertheless forces oil producers to make the requisite deliveries to agricultural enterprises.

The consumers of petroleum products have increasingly shifted to barter transactions to settle their accounts or simply do not pay for their oil deliveries. In 1996, the share of payments made in money ranged from 12.2 to 55.0 percent, with an average of 29.3 percent. In the case of natural gas producers, barter accounted for 30 percent of the gross output by the joint-stock company "Mangistau"; for the branch as a whole, the rate was 35.6 percent. Without question, this creates acute shortages of working capital, delays in paying wages for many months, and a growth of arrears in taxes and bills receivable.

Furthermore, the monetary tax system aggravates the situation. Specifically, the increase in prices year after year, amidst the large-scale and ubiquitous nonpayments, leads to a fictional increase in commodity production and enterprise profits. Although the increase is fictional, it nevertheless jacks up—many times over—the taxes due for a given volume of production. In addition, the plight of enterprises is further

Table 10.3

Dynamics of Inflation, GDP, and Taxes (as percent of 1993)

Indicator	1994	1995	1996
Inflation	54.8	7.0	5.6
GDP	82.2	74.6	75.4
Taxes	1,215.0	3,093.5	3,317.4

Source: Calculations by the author.

undermined by the assessment of huge fines and penalties for tax arrears. For example, in 1996, tax penalties for the joint-stock company "Mangistaumunaigaz" amounted to about 3 billion tenge. Indeed, some producers are penalized twice: they are forced to deliver fuel and lubricants to agriculture and, although the latter does not pay for these goods, the supplier is assessed taxes for the transaction *and* penalties for any arrears on sums that, in fact, were never paid. This suffocating tax burden is characteristic for the entire economy, as Table 10.3 shows.

The data in Table 10.3 demonstrate that, in the last three years, despite a sharp decrease in inflation (with the inflation rate in 1996 running at 5.6 percent of the level in 1993), and despite the continuing fall in production, the volume of taxes has continued to grow. Under such conditions, the only enterprises that could survive were those that somehow evaded paying the taxes.

As if that were not enough, enterprises often find that their hard-currency earnings are confiscated—allegedly for various state needs. As a result, it is hardly possible for enterprises to create and increase their working capital, to pay wages, and to invest in production.

It is also becoming increasingly difficult for enterprises to sell their products. On the one hand, that is because they have failed to gain access to foreign markets; on the other hand, it is also due to miscalculations during the privatization process in general, a problem that is particularly pronounced in the case of the oil industry. Namely, privatization of oil-drilling enterprises was conducted separately from the privatization for refineries, storage facilities, and fueling stations. The effect was to fragment the single technological chain that runs from extraction to refining and then to the sale of the final product. As a result, oil producers became isolated from the market of petroleum products.

As is well known, the leading enterprises in Kazakhstan also shoulder significant responsibilities in the social sphere. For example, the joint-stock company "Mangistaumunaigaz" is the largest enterprise and main taxpayer in Mangistau Oblast; as such, this single enterprise supports local institutions in the social infrastructure.

In short, enterprises are not being ruined by poor management. Rather, their difficulties stem from the failure to solve urgent economic problems at the republic level, by serious blunders in economic policy, and by the tendency to retard, not stimulate, production. All this is leading enterprises to the brink of collapse and bankruptcy. And all this is now compounded by a dubious economic policy of first putting enterprises under foreign control and, later, clandestinely selling off the controlling share of stock or assets. The transfer and sale to foreign companies of enterprises in the export sector—the most promising sector of the economy—is neither economically justifiable nor consistent with national interests and the need for economic security.

Indigenous Management Personnel: Qualified and Abundant

It is simply not true that Kazakhstan lacks the personnel to manage enterprises under the new market conditions. On the contrary, the republic has an ample number of highly qualified and honest people—*if* the government really wanted to use them rationally to run our enterprises. In fact, in the last fifty to sixty years, the country's complex of higher educational institutions has trained a large number of metallurgists, miners, geologists, oil men, energy workers, chemists, machine builders, and many other specialists. Today, many are professionals with lengthy experience in production and in running large enterprises.

The high qualifications and talents of the republic's own miners and metallurgists are beyond doubt. The Kazakhstan school of geology, founded by K.S. Satpaev, is regarded as one of the best—not only in the former Soviet Union, but throughout the world. It was through their efforts that the mineral resources of Kazakhstan were discovered, explored, and brought into production. It was precisely the determination of the oil industry specialists who opened up unique oil fields like "Tengiz." It was the talent of Kazakhstani specialists that created the unique coal reserves of "Bogatyr'," "Sarbai," and "Kounrad," and that conducted the unique explosion at the tract called "Medeu." And it was the metallurgists of Kazakhstan who developed advanced technologies and installations known among specialists as "KIVTset" and "PzhV."

Perhaps, such training and experience alone do not suffice to operate effectively under the new market conditions, and that such specialists also need a knowledge of marketing and must have the ability to react flexibly to current market conditions, to increase the competitiveness of output, to find market outlets, and so forth. But these are skills that our highly qualified specialists *can* master. This is all the more true since many of the export goods enjoy a stable demand and serve a well-known set of market outlets.

Admittedly, many plant directors were appointed from above and, to put it mildly, proved neither mindful of the law nor were professionally competent to manage these enterprises. They squandered foreign loans and credits (backed by state guarantees)—at best on unfocused and ill-advised investments, at worst on the purchase of luxury cars and cottages. All the while, they allowed the arrears—on wages, on raw material deliveries, on equipment for basic production—to mount. In this writer's judgment, the key factor was not the lack of management skills or the inability to run an enterprise. Rather, these facts simply prove that the method used for choosing managerial personnel was mistaken and indeed that state power has become deeply interwoven with criminal elements. The authorities had sufficient opportunities to establish financial control over state enterprises and to expose the misuse of credits backed by state guarantees. No obstacles prevented the government from assessing the activities of the leaders at large export-oriented enterprises, which only numbered a few dozen at most.

In short, the government not only appointed dishonest people to run prestigious enterprises, but failed to establish proper control and to prosecute offenders. All this suggests a pervasive criminalization of the public and economic environments in Kazakhstan.

At the same time, foreign specialists sent to manage metallurgical, petroleum, and chemical enterprises have not demonstrated a superior knowledge of production or achieved any notable success as managers. Such is the case even though they enjoy more favorable conditions than those available for indigenous directors. As indicated earlier, enterprises that are transferred or sold to foreign companies receive the most advantageous conditions. Thus, they bear no obligation to support the immediate social infrastructure; they can reduce the work force without any "headaches"; they can produce for export without worrying about the value-added tax (VAT) and duties; they are free to ship their products to whatever markets they want. And they cannot be forced to sell their products to the agricultural sector and to countries in the CIS—and hence are free from the specter of nonpayments or tax penalties for arrears. There is no reason to assume that domestic managers, if given the same conditions, could not effectively manage metallurgical and petroleum enterprises.

And what does it mean to "run" an enterprise? This is not simply a matter of making investments and paying off debts nor does it just involve the production of goods. Rather, effective managers must be able to achieve a higher end results: improve the quality of goods, reduce production costs, ensure more competitive goods, apply the newest technologies, create and develop new and profitable products, invest capital funds successfully, and so forth.

If measured by this yardstick, enterprises controlled or owned by the foreign firms have not registered any special gains. These enterprises produce the same goods, run their operations as before, and sell on the same foreign markets as they did earlier.

Do Foreign Firms Comply with Their Obligations?

A more weighty argument for selling enterprises to foreign companies is that these firms have assumed important obligations: to invest in production, pay off back wages, and liquidate outstanding debts to the state and other enterprises. To judge from the scanty evidence that sometimes appears in the press, however, the foreign firms are rarely fulfilling these obligations. These reports show that foreign-owned enterprises, like other new owners of privatized enterprises, are neither retiring their debts nor paying off wage arrears.

Even when such enterprises do pay regular wages, it is only because they enjoy enormous special privileges, such as exemption from the VAT, which alone more than covers the costs of whatever obligations they fulfill. Thus, the annual wage fund for enterprises under foreign control or ownership is estimated to run between 18 and 20 billion tenge. But the exemption from VAT alone is worth 29 billion tenge.

As for investment in production, foreign companies have as yet not taken any significant steps. According to data compiled by the National Statistical Agency for 1996, foreign investment totaled only 190 million dollars; in the first six months of 1997, investments amounted to 120 million dollars.

At the same time, the new owners of these enterprises receive financial privileges that domestic directors could only dream about. Indeed, entrepreneurs in Kazakhstan could hardly fantasize about receiving such preferential treatment. Moreover, many foreign firms acquired these enterprises at virtually no cost. Indeed, in some cases the government even agreed to supplement the working capital, as in the deal to sell "Karmetkombinat."

Moreover, these ventures are exempt not only from the VAT but also from export duties and taxation if they do invest in production. They also have ways to avoid paying any taxes whatsoever—for example, by resorting to the loophole of offshore zones and by indulging in elementary machinations with their prices and production costs. They also derive huge profits from the cheap cost of labor; paying their employees only one-tenth of what wages would run at home.

If Kazakhstan's directors had these privileges and access to foreign credits (backed by state guarantees or by using their own production as collateral), they could solve the problems currently besetting their enterprises. Unfortunately, however, the government does not extend to them the same conditions that it does for foreign investors. Therefore, the credits of 2.5 billion dollars extended in 1993–95 (and backed by state guarantees) were not used to support the country's export-oriented enterprises and—to quote President N.A. Nazarbaev—have simply vanished "into the sand." Credits were allocated to commercial firms of dubious origins (and sometimes having only a fictional existence), which did not repay the credits and have thus eluded accountability. Had this not happened, the country would have overcome its economic crisis and now have a far greater chance to overcome its political and social problems.

One cannot possibly argue that in 1996 these foreign-controlled or foreign-owned enterprises increased the volume of production and exports. For example, the National Statistical Agency has clearly demonstrated that the production of electric power—where many foreign firms are involved—has taken a downward trajectory, the growth in 1995 giving way to a decrease in 1996. Significantly, in the branches of electric power and oil production, the fall in production came precisely in enterprises under foreign control or ownership. Examples include plants in the hands of Tractebel (a Belgian company producing thermal power) and Iuzhneftegaz (an oil-extraction enterprise transferred to a Canadian company).

In the case of ferrous metallurgy, in 1996 production dropped in eight of twelve enterprises transferred to foreign companies, despite the fact that these very same enterprises had had smaller rates of decrease or even actual growth in 1995. As a result, there has been a sharp contraction in the production of ferroalloys, coke, steel pipes, white thin sheetmetal, chromite ore, iron-ore pellets, and iron ore—notwithstanding the fact that virtually all the producer enterprises are in foreign hands.

In nonferrous metallurgy, where foreign companies have also come to dominate, the situation is not much better. Thus, compared with the previous year, 1996 showed either a contraction or at least a smaller rate of growth in, for example, five of the eight types of bauxite, aluminum oxide, lead, sponge titanium, and refined gold. The data show a high rate of growth only in the production of copper and silver, along with a small increase in the production of zinc.

As for the increase in exports, 1996 showed only an increase of 8.2 percent, far less than the 74.8 percent attained in 1995, when these enterprises were still mainly in indigenous hands. Nor did 1996 bring any significant structural changes in the export profile.

In short, the policy of transferring enterprises in the strategic raw-materials branches to foreign companies has proven as misguided as the industrial policy that preceded it. In 1992, economic policy amounted to nothing more than the mechanical transformation of producer associations and ministries into concerns. By June 1993, however, the government abandoned this policy and declared that the only feasible solution was to form holding companies, to be created by fiat from above. Many enterprises, which were still efficiently functioning, were amalgamated into artificially formed holding companies, which were headed by people who were either of dubious integrity or who had no inkling of what these enterprises were producing. The result was production chaos; by 1994 the regime embarked on *deholdingizatsiia*—the breakup of these newly formed holding companies.

It was not only this policy that brought the economy to the brink of collapse: its strategy for privatization also played a destructive role. Initially, the regime had merged large enterprises into collectives that had no prospects for survival; these same enterprises were then turned into joint-stock companies, with the government continuing to hold the controlling share of stock. Then came the strategy of mass privatization—through coupons—that violated rudimentary economic principles. Next came the panacea of selling enterprises to foreign companies.

Throughout these years, privatization was shrouded in secrecy, being conducted without public knowledge and without a solid legal foundation. All these activities, conducted in the name of reform, were accompanied by a rapid turnover in enterprise directors, many of whom—as has since come to light—were people of dubious repute or even having ties to organized crime. Many sent huge amounts of capital abroad and no longer live in Kazakhstan.

Long-Term Consequences

Export-oriented production, which is based chiefly on the exploitation of the country's natural resources, became a "large pie" that the government and criminal businesses have carved up to suit their own interests. Indeed, their leaders—as a rule—are now not even citizens of Kazakhstan. This industrial policy will inevitably have negative long-term consequences for the economy. In the most general terms, the sale of enterprises that exploit natural resources of strategic significance and that are export-oriented are causing great harm to the national interests of Kazakhstan and its economic security.

Kazakhstan's economic cooperation with foreign countries has now sharply decreased. That is because if anyone wants to acquire goods from the basic raw-materials industries, they must now deal with foreign, not domestic, companies. Significantly, the government of Kazakhstan has no power to impose its decisions or wishes on these foreign firms. The impact of all this is already being felt. For instance, within the last year, the economic ties with firms in the CIS have sharply deteriorated. In 1996, for example, the overwhelming bulk of metallurgical output was shipped to destinations outside the CIS: 89 percent of the ferroalloys, 92 percent of rolled ferrous metals, 98 percent of the refined copper, and 89 percent of the zinc. The growth in exports to non-CIS countries necessarily means a corresponding decrease in share sent to Russia, Uzbekistan, Turkmenistan, and other former Soviet republics. The latter, however, still supply Kazakhstan with its basic needs for vitally important goods like natural gas, electricity, petroleum products, motor vehicles, tires, and so forth. Earlier, Kazakhstan had paid for such imports with hard currency or through the sale of metals. It is now deprived of this possibility, however, and this has had a negative impact on its balance of payments with the countries in the CIS. In 1996, the debts owed by Kazakhstani firms to enterprises elsewhere in the CIS were four times greater than amounts owed by CIS firms to its own enterprises. More specifically, Kazakhstan's debts to Turkmenistan exceed the latter's by a factor of 3.4 times; the equivalent indicator is 2.0 for Russia and 1.8 for Uzbekistan. This is the main reason for the frequent shut-off of natural gas and electricity as well as the falling volume of production by enterprises in Kazakhstan. An example of the latter is the Pavlodar oil refinery, which in turn caused a sharp increase in the price of petroleum products in this oblast and in neighboring areas as well.

Kazakhstan finds it increasingly difficult not only to deliver metals and other goods of base industries to CIS countries but even to satisfy domestic demand for these goods. That is because the foreign owners ship their output abroad, not to domestic and CIS markets—all the while polluting the environment and exacerbating social and economic problems. This also has ramifications for Kazakhstan's ties to the CIS. Namely, because Kazakhstan no longer provides these goods, Russia has developed its own mineral deposits and erected a protectionist policy to defend its own producers.

As is well known, the former USSR bequeathed many complex social and economic problems and, in a one-sided manner, developed principally the capacities of the raw-material branches. Now, with the collapse of the USSR, Kazakhstan is left alone to face these problems; rather than to address and resolve them, the country can now only watch as these problems proliferate and become increasingly serious. The upshot is that the foreign owners of enterprises are prospering, thanks to the special exemption from customs duties and the VAT on exports—measures that, in effect, divert funds from a meager state budget that are needed to pay wages and pensions to our own citizens. All this is an enormous loss both for the state budget and for the country as a whole. In addition, the state has also forfeited the revenues it earned earlier as dividends from stock holdings. In the final analysis, it is not the foreign companies that assist our country, but just the reverse.

The long-term and strategic import of the losses from selling off basic industries and natural resources is evident from the following: Kazakhstan is no longer able to conduct an effective structural policy with respect to its industrial sector. Obviously, any country that seeks to join the ranks of developed nations must have the capacity to formulate and implement a coherent industrial policy. The industrial policy of any country must seek to achieve an efficient utilization and development of its primary forms of national wealth; in this case, that wealth includes both raw-material resources and a skilled, professional labor force. But these resources are now controlled by foreign companies, which are only interested in obtaining raw or semiprocessed goods, not in producing finished products.

It is indeed arguable that foreign companies, by taking control of the key branches and enterprises, are becoming the economic masters of Kazakhstan. Naturally, they will direct production and sales not to serve the needs of Kazakhstan nor at a tempo and in ways that contradict their own interests. Moreover, as masters of the national economy, they will have a major impact on the country's foreign economic policy, in effect undermining the economic integrity and political sovereignty of Kazakhstan. The property owners, not managers or workers, will determine the profile and power of a country; this is a basic law of economics and politics, and will inexorably make itself felt. That is why the people of Kazakhstan are alarmed that the country's most valuable, strategically important property is now in the hands of foreign companies, leaving its own citizens virtually empty-handed.

The question as to who shall own natural resources and raw materials (not to mention the enterprises that process these goods) is a central question of national interest and economic security for any country that has large reserves. Such countries must prepare a serious raw-material program to develop these resources—as is the case in 135 countries around the world.

Such countries have learned how to protect their interests and economic security when it is necessary to admit foreign companies to develop and exploit their natural resources. At the present time, this is true mainly with respect to oil fields. Countries throughout the world have developed reliable mechanisms to combat swindling and fraud by investors and to interdict selfish attempts to extract minerals at unjustifiably high rates.

As already noted, the sale of enterprises to foreign companies—in direct violation of the Law on the Privatization of State Property—has been conducted in great secrecy, without disclosure of the exact terms of the transactions. As a result, neither the general public, nor legislative organs, nor high-ranking officials know the terms of such deals. This serves to raise doubts about the mutual utility of such contracts, and to raise suspicions of illicit, criminal machinations. Such doubts are redoubled by the scandals that have recently surrounded certain contracts.

The people did not empower authorities to sell national property to foreigners. After all, those in power were not elected on a campaign program that proclaimed their intention to sell the natural resources and the enterprises that exploit them. Not a single law empowered authorities to embark on this course; that includes the Law on Privatization. One must bear in mind that, apart from the plants producing copper, aluminum, zinc, lead, and so forth, authorities are also selling some extremely valuable rare and rare-earth metals. These metals are in short supply and of great value; a kilogram of such metals is worth several times more than a ton of the basic raw materials.

A market economy has no pity, no selflessness, no friendships, only economic interests, maximum profit, and an urge to seize resources and markets and to eliminate competitors. For the sake of such interests, people are capable of everything: the rapacious exploitation of natural resources, seizure of the richest deposits, cutbacks in the production of certain goods, and reductions in the work force—if the law allows this. But Kazakhstan does not have laws to regulate such impulses. Hence production by "dirty" branches will undoubtedly be pushed to the limit, aggravating the difficult ecological situation that already prevails in the republic.

It is quite simple to sell off enterprises in strategic branches. But this is not necessarily the right decision; rather, it merely demonstrates an inability or unwillingness to address the key economic problems. And such divestiture only generates a multitude of other and still more serious problems.

In general, many believe that solving problems in the economy (nonpayment, investment, and so forth) depends on completing the privatization process. That is a profoundly mistaken view, for privatization is not a panacea for all that ails the economy. It cannot, for example, solve the problem of nonpayment. Apparently, it is assumed that, once all enterprises are privately owned, the state will bear no responsibility for them. However, whether the enterprises belong to the state or private owners, the state nonetheless bears ultimate responsibility for economic and social conditions in the country.

It is frequently said that it makes no difference "as to who owns the enterprises, since the taxes will be paid all the same." But it *does* make a difference. First, are the taxes paid in full? At this point, state revenues are declining, as in the case of the VAT on export goods. But even if the taxes were paid, that would still not justify the sale to foreign companies. If these enterprises had remained in domestic hands, ownership would have changed, but within the boundaries of the country, and the enormous hard-currency earnings from exports would return to Kazakhstan and provide a source of investment and development in other branches of the economy. In 1996 alone, the hard-currency earnings from exports amounted to 6.72 billion dollars. Now, however, these earnings will go almost entirely to destinations outside the country, with the profits simply remaining abroad. Kazakhstan is thereby deprived of these investment opportunities. This wreaks direct harm on the economic security of the country. Earlier, we could regard strategically based branches as high-priority areas, as levers for growth, since their development would also stimulate growth in other branches as well. That is no longer the case.

German economist, L. Hoffmann, has observed that Kazakhstan has rich natural resources and, therefore, high current receipts for the budget, and that this allows the country to make expenditures that can later be recovered through hard-currency earnings from the export of natural resources.[2] But in fact the budget will no longer receive revenues from such exports. Apparently, Hoffmann believes that Kazakhstan, like other countries, still controls its natural wealth. His assertion that it is advancing "along our own Kazakh path" is bizarre: the world has never known such a large-scale and headlong transfer of state industrial enterprises to the control and later to the ownership of foreign companies.

Although the foregoing does not imply that most citizens of Kazakhstan oppose the infusion of foreign investments, certain facts must nevertheless be kept in mind. First, every country has branches—mainly those deemed strategically vital—that are off-limits to foreign companies. Other countries simply do not put such branches up for sale but, even as far back as the 1950s, insist on keeping control over these strategic national assets. Significantly, the Russian Federation is preparing a law to prohibit foreign investment in strategic spheres and to limit its scale in a number of other spheres. The People's Republic of China has a list of specific spheres in which foreign investors may operate. Second, a country must select the most advantageous forms of foreign investment. These include production sharing, the creation of joint-venture enterprises, the floating and purchase of stock, leasing, and the acquisition and construction of new enterprises in manufacturing. For example, no one is opposed to the construction of electric power stations in Aktiubinsk Oblast or to deals with Chevron for production sharing (based on the joint-venture enterprise "Tengizshevroil"), or to the sale of the tobacco factory in Almaty. One could welcome the foreign domination in the manufacturing industry of Kazakhstan and open the doors to a foreign presence in all the basic branches but on condition that the Kazakhstani side retain dominance (i.e., hold the majority share of stock) so as to protect the economic security of the country.

Certainly it would be preferable, from the perspective of Kazakhstan, if foreign investors were to develop new deposits, construct new enterprises, and create additional jobs. For the time being, however, they are engaged only in the purchase of existing enterprises, something that not only fails to create additional jobs but actually leads to reductions in the labor force, with no regard for the employment of those who have lost their jobs. All this is creating enormous tensions on the labor market.

It would not be surprising if Kazakhstan soon goes abroad for more loans and, in three or four years, is mired in a deep pit of debt, where the coexistence of poverty and wealth become a characteristic feature for many years to come. This process is being accelerated by a faster rate in the sale of the oil industry. And the authorities will later attribute the failures to some new complications, mistakes, and miscalculations—preferring to engage more in hindsight than in foresight.

Notes

1. The data in this chapter are based on research by the author at the Institute of Economic Studies in the Ministry of Economics and Trade of the Repulic of Kazakhstan.

2. L. Khofman [Hoffmann], "Vozmozhnosti i granitsy gosudarstvennoi zadolzhennosti v Kazakhstane," *Al'Pari* (Institut ekonomicheskikh issledovanii pri Ministerstve ekonomiki i torgovli Respubliki Kazakhstana), 1997, no. 1.

11

Uzbekistan: Problems of Development and Reform in the Agrarian Sector

Eskender Trushin

Agriculture is the largest sector of the economy in Uzbekistan. Measured in terms of GDP, employment, and export potential, it is the leading sector and forms the basis of the entire national economy. The development in agriculture determines the well-being of 40 percent of the labor force, the condition for half of the industry and other sectors, the bulk of exports, and the resolution of key social and economic problems (see Table 11.1).

The agrarian sector occupies over 71 percent of the land and about 86 percent of the available water resources of Uzbekistan. It is based on irrigated land cultivation; such irrigated land, which encompasses 9.5 percent of the republic's territory and 15 percent of its arable land, produces 97 percent of all agricultural output. The republic's water management system is closely tied to the agrarian sector and forms a complex engineering system; it includes a broad network of irrigation canals (some 171,000 km in length) and 53 reservoirs with a total capacity exceeding 16 billion cubic meters. Thus, the rate of economic growth and stability in Uzbekistan depend on implementing a complex of measures to transform the agrarian sector.

Table 11.1

Basic Macroeconomic Indicators for the Development of Agriculture in Uzbekistan, 1990–96

Indicator	1990	1991	1992	1993	1994	1995	1996
Share of rural population (percent)	59.4	59.9	60.2	60.7	61.2	61.4	62.2
Agricultural workers (percent of total workforce)	39.2	41.8	43.4	44.5	44.2	41.2	40.8
Value added of agricultural output (percent of GDP)	33.2	37.2	35.2	27.8	34.4	28.1	22.5
Share of fixed capital of agriculture in total fixed capital (percent)[a]	33.6	34.0	24.6	28.5	36.4	26.2	25.2
Share of agricultural output in total exports (percent)[b]					52.6	60.4	58.7
Share of cotton fiber in total exports (percent)					49.2	58.2	52.5
Share of food products in total imports (percent)					32.6	18.2	52.5
Share of grain in total imports (percent)					16.8	8.5	17.0
Rate of growth in gross agricultural output (percent)[c]	6.3	–1.1	–6.4	+1.3	–7.3	+2.2	–7.3
Rate of growth in gross agricultural output (1990=100%)	100.0	98.9	92.6	93.8	87.0	88.9	82.4
Gross agricultural output per capita in constant prices[d]	549.5	533.4	487.5	482.5	437.4	439.7	398.0
Rate of growth in gross agricultural output per capita (1990=100%)	100.0	97.1	88.7	87.8	79.6	80.0	72.4

Source: Calculations by the author.

[a]Excluding land and water.
[b]Excluding gold and uranium.
[c]In constant prices.
[d]Thousands of national currency.

Agriculture: Donor in the National Economy

The agrarian sector in Uzbekistan donates financial resources to the other sectors of the economy. The main point is that the state prices for agricultural goods are significantly below those on world markets. At the same time, the prices on certain production factors used in agriculture are either at or above world prices. This price structure does not reflect the true alternative costs of agricultural enterprises and causes substantial distortions in the distribution of resources.

The government subsidizes the price for certain resources needed by agricultural enterprises, the goal being to provide some compensation for the losses incurred by selling their products at low state prices. In general, these subsidies include the free use of water, special rates for the land tax, and privileged rates for the use of electricity. However, these subsidies do not provide full compensation for those losses.

Although the lack of hard data makes it impossible to calculate precisely the scale of these subsidies, some rough estimates are nonetheless possible. The magnitude of the subsidies are determined by comparing domestic prices for agricultural commodities with world or export prices, or with the maximum domestic price for the alternative use of a given commodity.

As the author's calculations have shown, the subsidy of productive resources used in Uzbek agriculture amounted to about 608 million dollars in 1995. This figure follows from the difference in the special low rates set for agricultural use of electricity (a rate advantage of 250 million dollars) and the exemption of the agrarian sector from paying for the use and maintenance of the national irrigation system (510 million dollars, including amortization). From this subsidy one must also subtract 152 million dollars to account for the fact that the domestic prices that the agricultural producers must pay for diesel fuel, gasoline, and mineral fertilizers are somewhat above the world level. The net subsidy is thus 608 million dollars.

This calculation of the net flow of finances from agriculture took into account the main agricultural crops of Uzbekistan—cotton, wheat, rice, and potatoes. The scale of lost funds from agriculture was derived by comparing domestic prices for these commodities with those for exports and on world markets, or with the prices paid when these commodities are imported to Uzbekistan.

According to the author's calculations, the hidden tax imposed on agriculture in Uzbekistan amounted to 1,223 million dollars in 1995, of which approximately 940 million dollars fell on cotton growers. According to other estimates,[1] the direct and indirect revenues obtained by the state budget from the goods regulated by state procurement prices (cotton and grain) amounted to 1,098 million dollars.

For lack of data, transportation costs—which play a role both in the import of certain production resources for agriculture and in the export of agricultural commodities—cannot be included in this estimate of financial flows in agriculture. A calculation that takes transportation into account would make it possible to avoid either exaggerating or underestimating the flow of financial resources out of the agricultural sector.

Thus, if the incoming flow through subsidies amounted to 608 million dollars, and if the outward flow of means from agriculture was between 1,098 and 1,223 million dollars, the net result for agriculture ran between 499 to 615 million dollars. This represents between 2.3 and 2.9 percent of the GDP of Uzbekistan, or 8 to 10 percent of the GDP produced by the agricultural sector.

The main loser in this situation is obviously the agrarian sector, which directly provides revenues for the state budget. Therefore, the reform of prices in the agrarian sector must also consider the government's ability to find alternative revenues for the state budget. Nevertheless, further price reform in the agrarian sector is absolutely essential: only that can enable agricultural enterprises to increase their productivity and volume of output. At the present time, when large-scale expansion of the irrigated land area is impossible, it is necessary to create strong economic incentives for agricultural producers to increase productivity and hence financial means for the rest of the national economy. However, they will be able to do this over the long term only if certain financial resources have first been returned to the agrarian sector.

The Extensive Path of Development in the Agrarian Sector

The large-scale development of irrigation systems was, for a long time, the basis of agricultural development in the republic. Whereas the total land area under irrigation increased in Central Asia from 3.25 million hectares in 1913 to 7.0 million hectares in 1990, the proportional increase in Uzbekistan was far greater, rising from 1.49 million hectares to 4.25 million hectares during the same period. Between 1960 and 1990, the area of irrigated land in Uzbekistan increased by 2 million hectares, coming to represent about 60 percent of all the irrigated land area in Central Asia.

Uzbekistan does potentially have much more land suitable for irrigation—another 12 million hectares (27 percent of the entire land area of the republic). However, by the late 1980s the water resources of the Syr-Daria and Amur-Daria river basins were fully utilized, and work to divert water from the Siberian rivers and other sources was abandoned. That led to a sharp contraction in efforts to expand land areas under irrigation.

Until 1990, the use of water resources in Uzbekistan was based on the principle of extensive agriculture. Namely, the main goal for water management organs was, at all costs, to expand the area under irrigation, to construct new canals and reservoirs, and so forth. Therefore, only a small proportion of canals had taken measures to prevent evaporation and seepage: 39 percent of the canals between agricultural enterprises, 14 percent of those within enterprises. The percentage of irrigated land with advanced technology and equipment to provide for agricultural crops was also low.

The proportional share of water consumption per hectare of irrigated land (brutto) in 1991–95 remained at the level of 12,000 cubic meters (compared to 8,000 cubic meters per hectare in the United States). Thanks to the efforts of the Ministry of Water Management, which lowered the limits on water delivery, there was some tendency for this usage level to decrease. The efficient use of irrigation water tended to increase, especially after 1985, when the massive development of new irrigated lands had come to an end. However, since the beginning of the 1980s, the effective utilization of irrigated lands has tended to decrease at the rate of 1.6 percent per annum; in the last decade, the effective use of land has been lower than it was in 1970.

The main part of the growth in crop production in Uzbekistan in 1971–95 has been achieved mainly through the use of more productive resources, not through more efficient utilization. These resources can, for purposes of analysis, be divided into land and water. Thus, in the case of water use, an increase in consumption (an extensive factor) obtained approximately a 60 percent increase in output during this period; more efficient usage (an intensive factor) accounted for the remaining 40 percent. In the case of land use, the expansion in the area under cultivation (an extensive factor) yielded 98 percent of the increase in output, while higher productivity (an intensive factor) accounted for only 2 percent of the greater output.

The dominance of extensive agriculture is due to two factors: (a) the significant reserves for extensive growth, given the adequate amount of land and water resources; and, (b) the lack of sufficient technical and organizational conditions (e.g., a system of incentives and efficient forms of enterprise organization) needed for a radical improvement in the efficiency of agriculture. It must be conceded that a predominantly extensive path of agricultural development was, under the historical conditions prevailing in Uzbekistan, the cheapest approach and yielded significant economic results.

The Price of the Extensive Path

That extensive path, however, also entailed serious negative consequences. Thus, the expansion of irrigation caused serious ecological problems and undermined the republic's resource base. The most dramatic problem has been the desiccation of the Aral Sea. Since 1965, the sea level has decreased from 52.5 meters to 37.0 meters, a fall of 15.5 meters; the coastline advanced 80 km and more; the sea lost approximately two-thirds of its entire volume; more than 4 million hectares of sea bottom and river deltas were exposed; the delta areas, once covered by thick vegetation, are now covered by salt. As the water level continues to drop, the sea is now divided into two sections and, if the desiccation continues, will eventually devolve into a string of isolated salt lakes.

The climate in this region has changed, as dust storms sweep across the areas around the Aral and the water of downstream rivers becomes less and less suitable for human consumption. The ecology and social-economic life of people within several hundred kilometers of the Aral Sea are in a state of crisis, leaving the local population on the verge of ecological and demographic catastrophe. In the judgment of the presidents of the five Central Asian countries, "the growing shortage of water and its deteriorating quality have caused a degradation of soil quality and vegetation, changes in the flora and fauna, a decline in the fishing industry, and a decrease in the efficiency of irrigated agriculture. An intensification of the ecological situation is having a direct and indirect negative influence on the living condition and health of the 35 million inhabitants of the Aral Sea basin; it is also disrupting their economic activities. All this, in the final analysis, is leading to an intensification of migration processes in this region."[2]

The key to the ecological problems of Uzbekistan, amidst an extensive development of agriculture, has been the concentration upon a cotton monoculture. In 1986, the land sown to cotton constituted 60.6 percent of the arable land in the republic; among enterprises growing cotton, this quotient was 73.4 percent. That level of specialization is found nowhere else in the world. The obsession with cotton-growing impeded the use of crop rotation (the basis for soil conservation) and animal husbandry (which, in turn, leads to a shortage of organic fertilizers).

This has resulted in the large-scale and unbalanced application of mineral fertilizers and pesticides, which have undermined natural biological processes and degraded soil quality. Because of the low efficiency of chemical compounds, more than 30 percent of the phosphorous-potash and more than 50 percent of the nitrogen fertilizers cannot be absorbed by the plants and form a runoff that pollutes the soil, rivers, and underground water.

The previous method for expanding agricultural production was simply to increase the area of land under irrigation. Agricultural output ceased to increase in the mid-1980s and then experienced a decline in the 1990s (see Table 11.2). Although the expansion of cultivated land proceeded successfully, agricultural technology did not show significant progress; as a result, productivity remained virtually unchanged. Despite the numerous foreign and domestic inventions to raise the productivity of agriculture, producers lacked sufficient economic incentives to stimulate the application of these discoveries. Although the state budget allocated enormous funds for agricultural research, the latter had limited real impact on production.

The irrigated lands in Uzbekistan have shown a tendency to degrade because for a long time investments were mainly targeted for the development of new irrigated land, not the improvement of those already under cultivation. According to data from the State Nature Committee of Uzbekistan, in the last fifteen to twenty years the humus content has decreased by more than 30 percent. That agency further disclosed that salinated land had increased by 850,000 hectares and now represented more than 50 percent of the irrigated land area; of this salinated land, 40 percent had salination rated as severe or moderately severe.[3]

Table 11.2

Gross Output and Productivity for the Main Crops of Uzbekistan, 1990–96

Indicator	Crop	1990	1991	1992	1993	1994	1995	1996
Gross output	Grain (total)	1,899	1,908	2,257	2,142	2,466	3,215	2,953
(thousands of tons)	wheat	552	610	964	876	1,362	2,347	2,435
	rice	503	515	539	545	498	328	396
	Raw cotton	5,058	4,646	4,128	4,235	3,938	3,934	3,350
	Cotton fiber	1,593	1,443	1,274	1,321	1,259	1,208	1,072
	Potatoes	336	351	365	472	567	440	514
	Vegetables	2,843	3,348	3,494	3,039	2,975	2,725	2,484
Average yield	Grain (total)	1.88	1.73	1.86	1.67	1.62	1.92	2.01
(tons per hectare)	wheat	1.28	1.18	1.55	1.26	1.54	2.00	2.10
	rice	3.42	3.22	2.95	3.01	2.97	1.95	2.46
	Raw cotton	2.76	2.64	2.48	2.50	2.56	2.64	2.26
	Cotton fiber	0.87	0.84	0.75	0.78	0.82	0.84	0.72
	Potatoes	8.0	8.7	8.3	9.7	10.13	9.2	10.1
	Vegetables	19.20	18.8	18.1	18.8	18.0	17.6	17.5

Source: Calculations by the author.

Although Uzbekistan, upon acquiring independence, took measures to develop 20,000 to 25,000 new irrigated hectares each year, it obviously cannot continue to follow that extensive approach in the foreseeable future. The main goal in agriculture must be to increase efficiency.

Management of Water Resources

Problems involving water exist at the level of the individual state (including Uzbekistan) and also at a regional level (involving all the states of Central Asia). The demand for water here continues to increase because of the population growth, development of industry and agriculture, and ecological needs. At the same time, the water resources of the Syr-Daria and Amu-Daria river basins, for all practical purposes, have already been allocated to satisfy the needs of the various Central Asian states; it would be exceedingly difficult, if not completely impossible, to satisfy an increased demand for water. Hence the use of water resources here must shift (and is already doing so) from an incessant increase in the volume of water diverted for use (i.e., so as to increase supply) to a redistribution of demand (by improvements in the utilization of the existing water supply).

Central Asia has three main water problems. The first is to allocate and rank the demand on water from the natural ecological system of the region. The second problem involves measures taken by states in the region to distribute water to satisfy the social and economic demands of the population. The third problem concerns the rational use and conservation of water resources both within each state and in the region as a whole.

Within the framework of the former USSR, Moscow decided how water installations situated on the territories of two or more republics were to be used. The location of water management installations in Central Asia was often done without regard to republic borders; hence vitally important installations for providing water to one state were often located on the territory of another. The former Soviet Union did not promulgate any guidelines to regulate interrepublic disputes over water usage (the sole exception being the principle that the population has first claims to water for economic and drinking needs). Once the republics of Central Asia became sovereign, it was essential to regulate the interstate use of water, while taking into account international experience in this sphere.

In 1992, the five states of Central Asia (Kazakhstan, Kyrgyzstan, Tajikistan, Turkmenistan, and Uzbekistan) created an Inter-State Coordinating Commission on Water Management. Its executive organ consists of two agencies to oversee the Amu-Daria and Syr-Daria river basins; these are to control water diversion from all rivers and canals that affect the interests of more than a single state. Moreover, these states agreed to preserve the structure and principles of water division that prevailed prior to the breakup of the USSR; Uzbekistan, accordingly, receives 50 percent of the river water resources in the region. Nevertheless, these old principles confront a new system of property ownership in Central Asia that reflects the new political realities, as each state asserts its claims to the water crossing its territory.

Although the quotas for water division have thus far proven satisfactory for all parties, a growth in demand for water will make it difficult to maintain the existing principles for the allocation of regional water supplies. Above all, the upstream states will be able to make prior claims and do so without regard to the needs of downstream states. There is also a growing tendency to think that, given the property claims of each state, the commision also has a legal right to exact fees for water usage from the downstream states.

At the interstate level, Uzbekistan faces several threats with respect to the use of water:

- The Islamic republic of Afghanistan, should the civil war come to a halt, has the potential to divert 6 to 15 billion cubic meters from the Amu-Daria River each year (from the total of 78 billion cubic meters that, on average, flow through this river); such a development would substantially complicate the task of providing water for four oblasts in Uzbekistan, Turkmenistan, and the Aral Sea.
- The Islamic republic of Iran, which has an enormous land area and needs irrigation, could reach an agreement with Afghanistan to divert water from the Amu-Daria River on mutually beneficial terms.
- Turkmenistan has an enormous area of desert and could divert a huge volume of water from the Amu-Daria. Moreover, Turkmenistan has the water supply installations of two major canals that provide Uzbekistan with 15 percent of the water used on its irrigated land.
- Tajikistan has increasing water diversion from the Zarafshan

River and is, simultaneously, polluting its water with discharges from industrial plants, thereby reducing the water supply for two oblasts in Uzbekistan.

- The mountainous republics of Tajikistan and Kyrgyzstan have an interest in producing and exporting cheap hydroelectric power. They therefore would have the capacity to divert water from their reservoirs (approximately in equal volumes year round) in order to ensure that the hydroelectric power stations keep operating. In other words, they are interested in using the water reservoirs for purposes of generating hydroelectric power. Uzbekistan, by contrast, is interested in a schedule oriented toward irrigation needs (i.e., one where water is stored up in the winter and released downstream in the summer to irrigate fields of crops). With the collapse of the USSR, the conflict of interests in the use of water reservoirs—whether as sources of hydroelectric power and water for irrigation systems—underlay fundamental contradictions in the economic interests of the states of Central Asia.

These problems and the potential threats are too serious to ignore. The time has come to prepare for a reduction of water consumption in Uzbekistan in the event that the conditions for the regional distribution of water resources change for the worse.

As for the water consumption in Uzbekistan, 86 percent is used for agriculture, 10 percent for industry, and 4 percent for public utilities. The population and industry have the top priority to water usage; their share of water consumption, moreover, will increase as a result of population growth and industrial development. Therefore, if one considers the potential threat that the water supply will decrease at the interstate level, and if one takes into account the interest of the future development of industry, the most promising sphere for eliminating the unproductive loss of water is in the sphere of irrigated agriculture.

The opportunities for water conservation involve both the irrigation network and the fields themselves. According to estimates by Uzbek scholars,[4] the water loss in the irrigation network can be ascribed partly to organizational factors (33 percent), but chiefly to technical factors (67 percent). While it is quite costly to reduce the losses from technical factors, it is far less expensive to cut back on the losses caused by organizational factors.

The subjective human factor can play a major role in water conservation, with the application of a broad range of measures: (1) water retention in the soil by deep, timely fall ploughing; (2) cultivation of the soil during the vegetation period; (3) leaving remnants of vegetation in the fields; (4) improvement in the soil's capacity for water retention; (5) accumulation of snow melts and rainwater in ponds; and, (6) reduction in evaporation and absorption by the subsoil through the use of mulch, direct watering between rows, and so on.

These inexpensive methods for the more efficient use of water are well known and have been applied in Uzbekistan during times when water was in short supply. However, to ensure that such measures be applied systematically, it is necessary to provide strong economic incentives and to make those working in agriculture and in water-management organizations accountable. At the present time, however, irrigated agriculture in Uzbekistan lacks an economic system to ensure a rigorous application of water conservation.

Thus, agricultural enterprises have not paid for water in direct proportion to their level of consumption. The water control agencies and the network between agricultural producers (collective farms, state farms, private farms) are supported by state funds, which actually represent the financial resources obtained by setting procurement prices on agricultural commodities (cotton, grain, etc.) at an artificially low level. That kind of economic system, clearly, provides no incentives for water conservation.

In 1989–92, several districts in Uzbekistan conducted experiments to assess fees on water usage (based on two main indicators: volume of water consumption and land area under irrigation). However, because of inadequate support and poor implementation, the experiment was not successful. Nonetheless, according to some evidence, the levy on water consumption had some positive effects on water conservation.

Effective in 1997, the republic assessed a water usage fee on all agricultural enterprises (except private plots) in the amount of 0.015 sum per cubic meter of water (approximately 0.025 cents per cubic meter). This fee is set administratively; it reflects neither the cost of water itself nor the cost of maintaining the water management system. This assessment goes directly into the state budget; hence the water control organs are supported not by those who use the water but by the state budget. In other words, water management is still isolated from economic realities.

Over the course of many decades, there have been numerous proposals to assess fees for the agricultural use of water. These discussions have now generated a consensus among economists that such a fee should be assessed; the only unresolved issues concern the mechanism for assessing such fees. Still, this idea must overcome three main obstacles:

- attempts by the government to impose fees without radical measures to excoriate price disproportions in the agrarian sector;
- lack of interest among agricultural producers in changes in the existing water relations, behavior that can be attributed to fears of greater demands on labor and tighter controls over the use of water;
- difficulties in equipping the points of water distribution with modern instruments to measure the volume of water consumption and also problems in preparing the documentation and personnel for such an undertaking.

The laws of the free market cannot set the fees for water usage, since the system of water management is a natural monopoly. Such a monopoly is necessary where the functions of generating, accumulating, delivering, and allocating water resources can most cheaply and efficiently be conducted through a single system that exploits both surface and subterranean water supplies. Hence the state must set the rates on water use. In the case of agriculture in Uzbekistan, it would be most expedient to establish three types of fees for water usage, based on the methods of assessment and functions being performed: (1) payment for the right to use water; (2) payment for water management services, (i.e., for the delivery of water); and, (3) payment for the quality of water delivered.

The organs of water management at the district level should be self-financing, with enterprises paying for the water and associated services. The bulk of the fees is to pay for water consumption; these funds should be used to maintain and develop the water management system. Fees for the right to use water and for water quality should go to the central state budget or to regional funds to develop water control. Heavy fines should be imposed on any enterprises in agriculture and water management that violate the prescribed order for water delivery.

The Alternative: Grain or Cotton

The Soviet Union laid the main emphasis on regional specialization. In the case of Uzbekistan, this meant responsibility for providing the entire Soviet Union with cotton. The enormous dependence on cotton growing, with the violation of recommendations on cotton and lucern crop rotation, led to soil depletion, inadequate attention to foodstuffs, and hence a strong dependency on imported food products. Thus, in the case of cereals alone, Uzbekistan had to import 70 percent of what was consumed.

Uzbekistan naturally wants to bolster its political and economic independence. It must also take into account the volatility of world grain markets and potential contraction of output at various points in the future. As a result, the government has made self-sufficiency in grain production an important part of its plans to ensure a secure food supply. It has therefore made plans for a gradual reduction in the area sown to cotton (in favor of cereals), and to compensate for the lost income by raising the level of productivity in cotton-growing.

Hence, since 1990, the government has taken measures to increase the area sown to grain by cutting back on the cultivation of cotton and forage. Specifically, in 1990–96, it reduced the areas sown to cotton (from 44 to 35 percent) and forage (from 25 to 13 percent), while increasing the arable land used to raise cereals (from 24 to 41 percent). In 1996, the republic was cultivating cotton on 1.48 million hectares and cereals on 1.75 million hectares. As a result, gross output of cereal grew by 1.6 times; that increase enabled domestic producers to satisfy approximately half of the total demand for cereals.

The strategy of self-sufficiency in grain production, if judged from a short-term perspective, was successful. However, this policy will eventually lead to long-term problems. First, it will be increasingly difficult to sustain cereal production after privatization and the reduction in state procurement orders. Second, this policy brings a loss of hard-currency earnings, since the contraction in cotton-growing has not been offset by an increase in productivity. For the moment, the republic has been "saved" by the significant rise in world prices on cotton fiber in recent years. Third, the cutback in forage crops has caused a decline in animal husbandry; the government has therefore decided to increase the production of forage crops in 1997 and to reduce the irrigated land used for cereals (by 200,000 hectares).

Moreover, the average yield for wheat remains rather low—about 2 tons per hectare (compared to 6 to 8 tons per hectare in developed countries). Hence, at this point one cannot speak about the economic utility of cereal production. In 1995, for example, each hectare of cotton produced an average yield of 0.84 tons; given the price on world markets (1,779.20 dollars per ton), the gross earning was 1,494.40 dollars. By contrast, each hectare of wheat produced an average of 2 tons; since the price of imported wheat in Uzbekistan was 163.70 dollars, the cereal cultivation yielded 327.40 dollars per hectare. In other words, under these conditions, cotton cultivation produces a gross income that is 4.5 times greater than that from cereal production. Similarly, according to the World Bank, in 1994 the gross margin in Uzbekistan (i.e., the difference between gross earning and material costs) for cotton was 1.2 to 3.0 times greater than that of wheat cultivation. This means that each hectare of land used to produce cotton produces 1.2 to 3.0 times more added value than each hectare sown to wheat. In short, the cultivation of wheat in lieu of cotton is in the same degree more costly.[5]

In general, although domestic social concerns may justify development of the grain sector, it is essential to achieve self-sufficiency in cereals at lower costs and through a more efficient use of national resources. A preliminary analysis shows that Uzbekistan has significant opportunities to do this: a correct geographic distribution of cereal cultivation among different areas in order to maintain (or increase) the gross output of grain while reducing the area sown for this crop; improvement in the productivity of grain cultivation; reduction in the loss of grain during storage, shipment, and processing; optimization of grain reserves; and so forth.

Greater Efficiency in the Agrarian Sector: Reserves and Prospects

An increase in cotton yields can offset the tendency for hard currency earnings to shrink because of the reduction in area sown to cotton. What, however, are the possibilities for increasing the productivity of cotton growing in Uzbekistan?

Ever since the beginning of the 1980s, the efficiency of the agrarian sector has declined—a process driven by several long-term factors. With the economic crisis triggered by the breakup of the USSR, the efficiency of agriculture declined still further. During 1991–96, agricultural production fell 17.6 percent from the level of 1990.

Moreover, for years the yield of cotton—the main crop—has not tended to rise. During the last twenty-five years, for example, cotton productivity has not increased beyond 2.7 to 2.9 tons per hectare, and one-quarter of the land showed a yield below 2.0 tons per hectare. In general, the cotton yield has tended to fall, as the average yields (tons per hectare) show:

Years	Tons per hectare
1971–75	2.85
1976–80	2.94
1981–85	2.67
1986–90	2.57
1991–92	2.56
1993–94	2.53
1995–96	2.45

Nevertheless, the Uzbekistan republic has real opportunities to increase the productivity of cotton growing, especially since yields are now at a relatively low level—indeed, below that in developing and developed countries with a similar climate. Still, the expenditure of production resources is significant and, in many cases, far from rational.

The relatively low soil productivity here is attributable to basic technological factors: (1) the salination of the soil because drainage is inadequate or altogether lacking; (2) compacting of the soil by heavy machinery; (3) formation of a subsoil "heel" by continuously ploughing at the same depth; (4) water and wind erosion; (5) infestation of weeds, plant disease, and pests; (6) lack of crop rotation, which leads to soil exhaustion; (7) inadequate development of animal husbandry, which means a shortage of organic fertilizers; (8) low levels and imbalances in the mineral nutrition for plants; (9) deficiencies in the irrigation and land-reclamation system, including the technology for watering crops; and, (10) low quality of the water used for irrigation.[6]

The fall in soil productivity is generally due to the fact that the requisite steps are not taken on the scale necessary or at the time required. This even includes measures that have long since been commonplace in scientific research, not to mention the development of new methods. However, the ultimate cause is the lack of sufficient economic stimuli to increase yields, to conserve land and water, and to enhance the receptivity of the agrarian sector to scientific and technical progress.

The land resources offer an unfavorable picture. In 1995, the arable land area fell from 0.21 hectares in 1990 to 0.18 hectares per capita, with the land area per rural inhabitant falling to 1.9 hectares. The soil also declined in fertility. If such tendencies persist, this will inevitably exacerbate problems in the food supply.

However, it is not necessary to expend greater material resources to increase productivity in agriculture. As the author's estimates indicate, Uzbekistan has "organizational reserves" that can be tapped to make the use of production resources more efficient and that require neither enormous exertions nor substantial investment. According to the author's estimates, it is possible to increase the productivity of agricultural crops by an average of 30 to 50 percent.

Thus, peasant farmers are familiar with ways to increase soil productivity and have personal experience in using soil and water resources more intensively. However, the current situation does not encourage peasants to apply methods that they have known for a long time: such efforts would have virtually no impact on their material condition and would only entail additional labor inputs on their part. As a result, they only apply—indeed, to a limited degree—these reserves in drought years, when virtually their entire harvest and income is at risk.

The result is an "organizational loss of water": losses due to an inefficient use of water because producers have no incentive to limit consumption. In Uzbekistan, the resulting waste is estimated at 17 percent; this could, however, be reduced to 2 to 6 percent. According to the author's calculations, the reduction of organizational losses could provide another 5.7 billion cubic meters of water per annum (i.e., enough to cultivate another 530,000 hectares of land). Were this area added to the existing 4.2 million hectares, Uzbekistan could increase agricultural production and that part of the GDP produced by the agroindustrial complex by 13 percent.

However, large outlays of investment are not always required for increasing the productivity of the soil: it is also possible to achieve improvements by adopting measures with low capital intensity. For example, higher productivity could be gained from better cultivation of plants, deeper ploughing of the soil, and also timely and adequate application of land-conservation, agro-technical, and agro-chemical measures required for production. That figure could be further raised by reducing the losses during storage, transportation, and processing. Altogether, these measures could bring a proportionate increase (20 to 30 percent) in the GDP of the republic.

The actual experience of agrarian reforms confirms the validity of these estimates. Thus, during two years after the agrarian reform of 1925, the family farms—on the same land as used by the large landowners, and without any additional material resources—began to produce 1.5 to 2.0 times more cotton and to pay off bank loans prematurely.[7]

In China, the mere replacement of large-scale agriculture by family household units brought a 28 percent increase in the volume of production. In 1978–84, the volume of agricultural production grew at 7.7 percent per annum; altogether, China increased its agricultural output by 56 percent. Approximately half of this increase—28 percent—was achieved without significant material expenditures.[8]

Thus, having exhausted the predominantly extensive path of agricultural development, Uzbekistan must shift to an intensive approach. For this purpose, the republic has significantly unrealized potential in irrigated land. According to the estimates of specialists, the potential yield of basic crops—given the natural and climatic conditions of Uzbekistan—is 6 to 10 times greater than current productivity. It is possible to realize this potential by gradually, consistently applying—in the optimal scale and proportion—measures to increase efficiency in the agrarian sector. However, that requires a new system of incentives for adopting modern technologies and developing new ones; only then can Uzbekistan capitalize on its relative advantages. Agriculture needs a labor force that is creative, free, responsible, and imbued with a strong sense of personal interest in the results. For that, however, it is essential to transform the social-economic relations that currently prevail in the agro-industrial complex.

Problems in the Processing Industry of the Agro-Industrial Complex

An important sphere—second to agriculture itself—is the processing, storage, and shipping of agricultural commodities. However, over 70 percent of the labor force, and 73 percent of the fixed capital of the agro-industrial complex, are concentrated in agriculture; only 16 percent of the labor resources and 15 percent of the fixed capital are in the processing industry and other branches of the tertiary sphere. In the last twenty to thirty years, the republic has expanded the capacity of the cotton gin, fruit and vegetable, wine-making, meat and dairy, food, flour and groats, and fishing industries.

Prior to the time when Uzbekistan acquired independence, the main objective was to ensure that the former USSR be self-sufficient in the supply of cotton. The result was a one-sided development of the agro-industrial complex: it was primarily oriented toward the production and primary processing of raw cotton into cotton fiber. At present, only 11 percent of the cotton fiber is subjected to further processing, the balance being shipped abroad for processing. In the immediate future, the government plans to increase the proportion of domestically processed cotton fiber from 11 to 28–30 percent.

The cotton gin industry now consists of 130 plants, along with a network of procurement points to procure and store the raw cotton. This branch is closely tied to the textile, oil fat, and chemical branches of industry. It is also undergoing constant upgrading; the capacity of cotton plants has developed and expanded at a higher rate than the increase in the production of raw cotton. As a result, cotton plants are now capable of receiving and processing about 7 million tons of raw cotton, even though raw cotton production has recently run at just 3 to 4 million tons.

In the first years after the dissolution of the USSR, the branch for processing agricultural commodities suffered a sharp deterioration because of the disruption of economic ties with the former Soviet republics. The latter had, traditionally, been the main suppliers of equipment and machinery and some raw materials for the agricultural sector. For example, over 90 percent of the mill and mixed feed industrial capacity was engaged in the processing of imported cereals (coming mainly from Russia, Ukraine, and Kazakhstan). Similarly, confectionary plants relied mainly on Ukrainian sugar; the wine-making branch depended heavily on imported spirits. The republic's only glass container plant (in Kuvasai) could satisfy just one-third of the demand for beer and nonalcoholic glasses, jars, and bottles for the wine-making branches. Virtually the entire equipment in this branch (which urgently needs to be replaced) was imported from the other republics of the former USSR; Uzbekistan simply does not have the capacity to produce machinery for the food-processing and light industry branches. However, during the first years of independence, the government of Uzbekistan did adopt measures to increase sharply its own production of grain and its products, grain alcohol, and also sugar.

Because of the high population density (where the average family consists of 5.5 persons, ranging from 4.5 in the city to 6.2 in the village), development of labor-intensive branches like processing and light industry, as well as the service sector, is regarded as an important way to provide jobs for the population. The placement of small industrial enterprises in rural areas (to process vegetables, fruits, grain, and other agricultural products) and the development of branches in the productive infrastructure (packing, storing, shipping, and refrigeration services) will help to reduce the surplus labor force in rural areas and increase the general efficiency of the agrarian sector in Uzbekistan.

The principal problem in the processing sphere has been—and remains—the discrepancy between the capacity for processing and the potential raw-material base. Thus, the republic processes only 10–12 percent of its vegetables and 5–6 percent of its fruits and grapes, even as it imports foreign juices, jams, and drinks like Coca-Cola. The processing industry needs to upgrade its entire complex of equipment in order to mechanize and automate production. In recent years, however, this branch has received only 2 percent of the total investment in the republic. There are two other key problems: (1) restoring Uzbekistan's role in providing fruits and vegetables for the CIS and (2) the relocation of processing plants closer to the sources of raw materials (in order to cut transportation costs). At present, small processing plants and branches in rural areas account for no more than 10 percent of the total volume of processed goods.

The processing enterprises have a negative reputation, and for years have paid for raw vegetables and fruits at monopolistically low prices. The quality of these commodities was determined arbitrarily: as an auxiliary lever of power, the processing enterprise had authority over the control and weighing service for receiving the raw materials. Predictably, that service acted in their master's interest, setting a low value on the quality of the raw fruits and vegetables. The result was an unequal relationship between agricultural producers and processors.

A reasonable solution here would be for all these parties to take into account their mutual interests. When agricultural producers own a significant (and possibly controlling) block of shares in processing and sales enterprises and therefore determine the distribution of a significant part of the profit from the final sale, they will be interested in supplying raw materials in the quantity and quality required. Currently, however, the privatization of processing enterprises has divided almost all the stock among the enterprise employees, state organs, and buyers from the general population.

State Agrarian Policy

The government believes that the successful implementation of economic reform, to a large degree, depends on the development of agriculture as the very foundation of the republic. As President I.A. Karimov has written:

> In the entire chain of economic reforms, the chief principle significance is attached to the task of transforming the agrarian sector. This is because of the dominance of rural inhabitants in the population structure, because of the agro-industrial character of the economy, and because of the role that agriculture can play in resolving vitally important problems. It is precisely the agrarian culture that now holds significant reserves. By tapping these resources, one can not only improve the supply of food for people and raw materials for industry, but also ensure the prosperity of the rural populace. The village is the most important source of national income; it produces the main [export] item for earning hard currency. But, most important, the village is that unit in the economy that can enable the entire republic to achieve prosperity and well-being. If the peasant is well off, the entire republic will be rich. It must be admitted that today we live at the expense of the village.[9]

The problem of agricultural development is thus the critical component in the entire strategy for this country's transition to a market economy. The course of the whole economic transformation will depend on how thoroughly the agrarian sector is restructured, how far the reforms go in the village, and whether the broad mass of rural inhabitants accept the very idea of the reforms.

Therefore, the first stage of agrarian reforms devoted much attention to institutional change. The government began to convert state farms *(sovkhozy)* into collective farms *(kolkhozy)* and other forms of cooperative agricultural enterprises. The number of state farms thus fell from 1,066 (1992) to just 16 (1995), in the process creating 530 collective farms, 324 cooperatives, and more than 100 joint-stock companies. In 1996, the so-called "nonstate sector" produced 98 percent of the gross output in agriculture.

In 1990–96, the president and government of Uzbekistan adopted a host of laws, decrees, and resolutions on a number of significant changes. Thus, with respect to landowning and land utilization, land remains state property but is made available for a fee. In 1994, the government introduced a tax on the use of land in urban areas (either as a land tax or rental fee, depending on the location); in 1995, it established a land tax for rural agricultural enterprises.

The new legislation does permit private ownership of nonagricultural land and the sale (through auctions and competitive bidding) of land plots for firms engaging in sales and service; such plots may be bought by individuals or juridical entities; such owners may be either Uzbek or foreign. The land can be assigned for long-term or short-term leases, as well as life-long, inheritable use. This set of laws also provides for auctions to sell land to urban inhabitants (likewise for life-long and inheritable use); such plots may run up to 0.04 hectares for the construction of individual houses and 0.06 hectares for household garden plots. However, the state reserves the right to confiscate land allocated for household plots or peasant farms if this land is subjected to irrational utilization. If, however, the land is used rationally, the state can increase the allotment from 0.25 to 0.35 hectares of irrigated land and from 0.5 to 1.0 hectares of unirrigated land.

The average size of household garden plots increased from 0.08 hectares in 1989 to 0.17 hectares in 1995. As a result, the share of total agricultural output from these plots has increased from 25 percent in 1986–90 to 48–50 percent in 1994–95. The number of such plots has also grown, rising from 2.3 million in 1990 to 2.9 million in 1995. Altogether, more than 500,000 hectares of irrigated land has been allocated for use as household plots.

The state has also created a legal framework to develop individual farms. Thus, land is available for such farms on a life-long, inheritable basis (with a minimum term of ten years). By 1996, the number of peasant farms had increased to 19,500; these occupied up to 295,000 hectares (representing 7.5 percent of the sown land area of the republic). Such farms employ 107,000 people and occupy an average of 15 hectares of land.[10]

The state also allocated credits for livestock enterprises and peasant farms (with property serving as collateral). There are also plans to allocate additional land to peasant farms and to transfer small garden plots and vineyards to private ownership. In 1994–95, the government privatized 12,700 hectares of garden plots and 6,100 hectares of vineyards; each raion opened a network of stores to sell fertilizers, spare parts, fuel and lubricants, and other goods needed by the nonstate agricultural producers. It also established stations to provide service and maintenance and to perform various forms of agricultural work. Joint-stock companies have also been established to engage in animal husbandry. In addition, the state also created a single Ministry of Agriculture and Water Management. Its task is to improve the administrative structure in these two spheres and to ensure that they work in a closely coordinated fashion.

The government, moreover, has laid plans to ensure the rational use and conservation of water. These include several measures: (1) the assessment of fees for special water use, for polluting, or for otherwise damaging water installations; (2) tax, credit, and other privileges for enterprises and citizens that adopt water-conservation technologies and take steps to protect and economize on the water supply. In 1994–96, the government introduced fines for agricultural producers who do not make rational use of water. Moreover, the government has identified the top-priority objectives in agricultural reform. Namely, it proposes to reorganize collective enterprises into joint-stock companies, create a market infrastructure, and increase the efficiency of agricultural production. As for unprofitable agricultural enterprises, the state has written off the debts on bank loans. It has also deferred the repayment of interest by agricultural producers that have a low level of profitability.

At the same time, the government is systematically reducing the share of state procurement orders for agricultural commodities. Earlier, it abolished the procurement of milk, meat, and poultry; at present, it has retained procurement only for cotton and cereals. In the case of these commodities, however, the state is reducing its procurement orders and raising the purchase price. For any cotton and cereals that it buys beyond the procurement order, it pays free market prices.

The government is also planning to develop a network of insurance and leasing companies in agriculture. These firms, which can include the participation of foreign investors, will lease to peasant farmers the machinery and equipment to process agricultural commodities.

The Shortcomings in Agrarian Reform

Notwithstanding all these measures and plans, implementation is incomplete and slow, and therefore the reform is not yielding the desired result.

The rudiments of the old system are still intact, as the government continues to intervene in all aspects of agricultural production. For example, the government holds total power over the allocation of land; it also determines the volume of production for the main crops as well as share to which it has a direct claim. Moreover, it sets the procurement price for cotton and cereals as well as prices for the main production resources. Finally, save for peasant bazaars, the state retains its monopoly over the processing and distribution of cotton and cereals as well as supplying the main resources for foodstuffs.

As a result, the peasant—who, in a market economy, is the primary agent in the system of decision making—remains passive and inert. Hence, on three-fourths of the irrigated land used to grow cotton and grain, the republic is deprived of the peasants' knowledge and experience as well as their entrepreneurial skills. Agricultural producers still do not have sufficient incentives to increase the yield from cotton and cereals.

There are three main reasons for this: disproportions between costs and prices, insufficient earnings from domestic and foreign trade, and institutional disproportions.

1. *Cost and Price Disproportions*. This combination of price disproportions and inefficient subsidies ultimately means a discrepancy between production costs and commodity prices in agriculture.

During the attempts to make the peasant master of the land, the government has constantly ignored the principle that agriculture must be capable of recouping costs and being self-financing. The procurement of most agricultural commodities was done at prices that not only failed to enable the necessary capital accumulation but also made it impossible to pay a normal wage. The regular increases in state procurement prices for raw cotton and other agricultural commodities did not establish parity with the prices on industrial goods. At the end of the 1980s the government decided to shift state and collective farms to self-financing and to base pricing on this condition. However, the deregulation of prices in 1991 created disproportions in prices for urban and rural goods that were even greater than before. The price disparity had a negative impact on agricultural production—whatever the form of property involved. In 1991–95, the prices on agricultural goods rose more than 4,400 times, whereas the prices on industrial material-technical resources and services increased 13,300 times. In other words, the price disparity in 1995 was 0.33. That disparity varied substantially according to the industrial branch: 0.29 for cotton, 0.26 for fruits and vegetables, 0.39 for silk, 0.65 for milk, and so forth.[11] As a result, many agricultural producers began to operate at a loss. The average profitability of agricultural producers (assessed in terms of the ratio of profit to costs) was 2.3 percent in 1995 and 4.1 percent in 1996; such returns do not enable these enterprises to finance investment on their own.

State control over prices has been eliminated for the majority of agricultural goods. However, the state still sets and controls the prices for cotton and grain (at the level of the agricultural enterprise). The Ministry of Finance sets the prices for cotton (whether in raw form or as fiber) and cereals, as well as certain services and other machinery and technical resources used in agriculture. The price of wheat is set at all levels—from production to processing and to retail trade in flour and bread.

There is also an unofficial control for most agricultural goods sold to industrial processors. This is because of the monopsonistic power exercised by processing enterprises; it is reinforced by state ownership of the controlling share of stock and by the oversight powers of local authorities.

The domestic prices of most agricultural goods are substantially below those on world markets. However, the prices of many products have tended to move closer to those on world markets.

Despite government guarantees to pay 90 percent of the fixed price for cotton deliveries, it in fact delays payment for six to seven months. Given the effects of inflation, this means a reduction in the real income of agricultural producers. This practice of delayed payment is the main reason why more and more agricultural products are being sold at bazaars and on the streets. Producers are simply seeking to circumvent the formal state system for the sale of commodities and thereby obtain, through barter, producer goods and whatever else they need.

2. *Insufficient access to the earnings from foreign and domestic trade.* The foreign trade policy of Uzbekistan aims to achieve a gradual liberalization and to lower the barriers to foreign trade. In general, the state had reduced its stringent administrative control over exports; it has steadily introduced export duties in lieu of bans and licenses. However, most of the remaining regulations do not stimulate exports and favor state enterprises and foreign investors.

There are three main types of trade barriers: (1) the requirement of licenses for cotton exports; (2) export duties for most agricultural commodities, which, since mid-1996, have been set at 30–40 percent of the contract value of exports—a rate higher than the average in the CIS; and, (3) the requirement that 30 percent of the hard-currency earnings be sold at the official exchange rate for the sum. Thus, to export cotton, one must first obtain a license from the Ministry of Foreign Economic Relations; the export of wheat, wheat products, and dairy goods are categorically banned.

In addition, producers must also overcome unofficial trade barriers, such as the centralized control over cotton and silk exports. Another obstacle is the state trade monopoly, which is based on trade associations and industrial processing enterprises; these are essentially monopsonists with respect to the sale of agricultural commodities. Moreover, although these are nominally independent, in fact the state holds a significant share of the stock in such enterprises.

State enterprises are thus the main channel for selling most agricultural products. Apart from cotton and wheat, this applies as well to ambari, fruits, milk, wool, and many types of vegetables and wine. As earlier, the state continues to dominate the sale of most agricultural commodities.

The monopsony of industrial processing enterprises, the low procurement prices for agricultural raw materials, and the delays in the payment for agricultural goods—all this leads to a diversion of goods from industrial processing to sales in bazaars and on the street.

The volume of state orders for cotton and grain are established in the aggregate and calculated together. Therefore, the shortfall in the production of one crop is compensated through a surplus in the other.

3. *Institutional disproportions.* This refers to the insufficient property rights over resources and products as well as inefficient forms for the organization of enterprises and for the distribution of profit.

The beginning of agrarian reform in Uzbekistan was not without distortions in the sphere of institutional transformation. From the end of the 1980s, the republic established two forms of leasing: (a) "free" leasing, whereby a collective leases land and other means of production from the state and operates on equal terms with collective and state farms, and, (b) leasing agreements with collective and state farms, whereby the labor collectives lease land and resources, but functions as a subdivision of the collective or state farm.

Along with the conversion of state farms to the nonstate sector in 1993 (primarily in the form of collective farms), the government intended to create peasant farms within the framework of collective farms. In that way, such peasant households could also use the infra-structure of the collective farm. Of 20,000 peasant farms, about half have thus been created as a subunit of the collective farm and depend completely on the latter's administration. As a result, such farmers lack real independence; they are subject to a system of collective-farm leas-ing, whereby they are not only saddled with a production program but must also pay rent and taxes from their earnings. The so-called "peas-ant farm lessees" must also sell their crops to the collective farm at the latter's own prices (which are lower than the state procurement prices), thereby forfeiting virtually their entire profit. The collective farms also make illegal demands that the peasant farms produce part of their crops to fulfill the state procurement order. Such a system of "peasant farms" render the peasants completely dependent on the administration of the collective farm.

The republic's law "on land" and the resolution of the Cabinet of Ministers "on additional measures to implement economic reforms in agriculture" have established rules that land is state property, that it is placed under the control of collective enterprises, and that peasant farms can receive land only for a specified term and on the condition that they pay a land tax (through the collective enterprise). Peasant farms are not given credits directly, but only on the basis of a guaran-tee from the collective farm.

Peasant farms are created essentially at the expense of the collective farm, but the latter's obligations with respect to the state procurement are not proportionately reduced. That is why collective farms feel com-pelled to regard peasant farms as a source of the commodities needed to fulfill the procurement order.

Although existing law asserts that the head of a collective farm, cooperative, or peasant farm has the right to manage his funds at his own discretion, it also requires that the land be used in a rational manner—that is, in accordance with its specialization. If this mandate is not observed, the peasant farmer's right to use the land can be revoked and the chairman of the collective enterprise dismissed from his position. In practical terms, a plan is still lacking for the production of cotton as well as for grain and other agricultural commodities.

Local government organs appoint the heads of collective agricul-tural enterprises, industrial processing plants, and trade enterprises.

The peasant farmers are also dependent on the collective farms and the state for access to material and technical resources. Although the state has a policy of creating various small suppliers for material and technical resources to serve small producers, thus far implementation has been of little significance. In most cases, the collective farms and state trading associations are the sole means for peasant farmers to gain access to the market. This discourages the creation of private business services; it is difficult for private farmers to establish trading cooperatives.

The allocation, confiscation, and reassignment of land does not follow any precisely defined rules. Implementation of land reform is essentially assigned to local state authorities and collective farms. In many cases, however, their desire to dominate local markets make them unsympathetic toward state policy on agrarian reform.[12]

For the present, peasants are generally inclined to remain within the framework of the collective farm. There are several reasons for this:

(a) The fall in the standard of living and the weakening of the social net for peasants. As is well known, a collective enterprise affords mutual assistance and therefore makes it easier to ensure a subsistence minimum and survival. This factor is especially compelling when incentives for highly productive labor and salaries are weak.

(b) The need for constant dealings with various authorities. In reality, independent farmers are forced to have direct, systematic and, often unpleasant, contact with the personnel in the state service infrastructure (e.g., electric power and water) and the tax inspectorate.

(c) The peasants' ignorance of basic economics. To this must be added objective factors, such as the extremely high cost of productive capital, compounded by the lack of full state support under conditions of inflation and higher financial risks.

Peasant farms should be created as an alternative to the collective farm. They should be independent and directly subordinate to local authorities, with the right to use land on equal terms with the collective farms. The denial of equal rights for peasant farms is apparent in the very law "on peasant farms," which essentially proposes to allocate them marginally productive land from state reserves. Moreover, when members of a collective farm dissolve that unit to form peasant farms, in most cases they do not receive a share of the fixed capital resources.

As a result, these conditions do not favor the development of peasant farms. The latter are potentially the most progressive forms of agricultural organization, but for now are the weakest type operating in Uzbekistan. Thus, despite the large number of such farms and despite the fact that they occupy 7.5 percent of the arable land, they produce only 3 to 6 percent of all crops. The bulk of peasant farms engage in animal husbandry, although here too they represent a small share of total output (10 to 12 percent). Peasant farms are disadvantaged in comparison with other forms of organization; they suffer from bureaucratic controls, experience difficulties in obtaining credits (especially long-term credits), lack the means to acquire capital, and do not have sufficient knowledge and experience to manage their farms as a business. Not surprisingly, 1,646 peasant farms failed in 1993–95 (including more than 800 in 1995 alone).

The cultivation of household plots is based on manual labor, for the population lacks virtually any form of mechanization. Moreover, the land assigned for use as such plots by no means has the best soil; the livestock is also of a low quality. Realization of the full potential of such plots is impeded by a host of other factors as well—for example, the poor supply of machinery, inadequate transportation, underdeveloped trade services, water shortages, and the weakness of the banking system.

Although the state has approved, in principle, the idea of pluralism in the types of property for agricultural enterprises (in order to overcome the alienation of the worker), the agrarian reforms have been implemented slowly and have not as yet yielded the anticipated results. Only in 1996 did the state begin to conduct experiments in devising a complex of normative documents to reform the collective farms and to transform them into private joint-stock companies or into cooperatives.

Conclusions

1. Agriculture, the largest sector in Uzbekistan and the foundation and financial donor for the national economy, has developed primarily in an extensive manner. However, the full utilization of water resources in the Aral Sea basin impose natural limits to the economic growth on the basis of an expansion in the area of irrigated land. The extensive line of development is now exhausted. Therefore, in the long-term perspective, the inevitable and rational strategy for development in the agrarian sector is to increase productivity through more efficient use of the land, water, labor, capital, and technology. The republic has significant potential in its agro-industrial complex.

2. Economic growth in Uzbekistan is possible only if the significant reserves for more efficient agriculture are realized. The natural historical reduction in the significance of the agrarian sector, along with its share of the GDP and work force, can occur only if it undergoes a systematic and rapid development and if it raises its productivity. The strategy of an artificial solution, whereby the share of the agrarian sector in GDP and employment is reduced but the old technology of production is maintained (with a corresponding low level of productivity and depressed standard of living in rural areas), can lead to stagnation in the entire economy, not just to economic growth.

The agrarian sector represents an enormous source for economic growth. It is the supplier of food products, raw materials, labor, and financial resources for industry and other sectors of the economy. However, the opportunities for a simultaneous, balanced development of agriculture and industry will not depend upon the forced extraction of resources from a stagnating agrarian sector but will mean a natural channeling of resources from a developing agrarian sector (with the assistance of bilateral market ties in the production and distribution of goods). All this will ensure rapid, stable growth throughout in the entire economy.

3. The main obstacles to shifting the agrarian sector of Uzbekistan to the intensive path of development and achieving a radical increase in efficiency consist of the following factors: (a) unreceptivity to scientific-technical progress; (b) backwardness of economic relations; and (c) lack of necessary incentives for agricultural enterprises. It is therefore essential to make fundamental reforms in the existing order of agrarian relations and to create a system of incentives for development in the agro-industrial complex.

It must be admitted that, in just six years since becoming independent, Uzbekistan has advanced a considerable distance in this direction. One must not forget that precisely this evolutionary approach to reform and the presence of a viable agriculture saved Uzbekistan from a massive decline of production and ensured social stability.

At the same time, the agrarian reforms—which have been implemented at a slow pace and incompletely—have not yielded the expected results and are essentially still in the initial stages. Under the existing system of economic relations, agricultural producers are passive; as yet, they do not have a sufficient interest in expanding the yield of the basic agricultural crops. The main causes include the pricing, institutional, and commercial disproportions. It is therefore necessary to continue the structural reforms—above all, in the prices, institutions, and trade policy of the agro-industrial complex.

4. The main thrust of *price reform* in agriculture is twofold: (a) eliminate inefficient subsidies by establishing scientifically grounded payments for the use of land and water resources; and, (b) establish parity between the incomes of agriculture and industry.

It is necessary to shift from a general price regulation of grain to targeted subsidies of consumers. This will shift the burden for social protection to the budget and shield the productive sector from distortions. Even if the existing controls on grain prices are justified by social priorities, this argument obviously does not justify the price controls on cotton.

5. The main thrust of *institutional reform* in agriculture is to create a flexible structure based on the new model of private utilization of state-owned land. Above all, it also means the transition to the family form of organization for agriculture enterprises, with a vertical cooperative (joint-stock) organization of agricultural services and industrial enterprises for the primary processing of agricultural commodities.

The solution does not lie in creating private ownership of land and allowing the sale and purchase of agricultural land. Rather, the main task is to create a new model for the lease of land that remains state property. For this purpose, it is necessary to eliminate all the uncertainties of the lessee with respect to actions by the state, and to make leasing as attractive as possible (by conferring the character and advantages of the classic model of privately owned land).

The main features of the new model for leasing state-owned land should consist of the following: (a) leasing of land should not include any time limitations and should be liable to unlimited renewal by the lessee (i.e., it should last as long as the lessee is capable of paying the fair leasing fees set by the state, as long as all the state rules and the contract are observed, and as long as the lessee wishes to retain the lease); (b) the state, as the proprietor of the land, has the right to expel the lessee only with preliminary warning and full compensation for all the improvements that the lessee has made in the land; (c) the leasing fee can be increased in the future, but it should not include the value of any improvements in the land made by the lessee. Moreover, the bulk of the leasing fee should be used by the state in the interests of the land users, for example, to improve the fertility of the soil; (d) the lessee should wield the rights necessary for an agricultural producer (e.g., the right to exchange one plot of land for another); and, (e) the lessee must be given the legal right to dispose of most output in whatever fashion he chooses.

These steps will eliminate the uncertainties that have such a pernicious influence on stimulating productivity in land use and will also make investment in the long-term improvement of land more attractive.

In order of descending efficiency, the main forms of agricultural enterprise consist of the following: (1) family farms, with a vertical cooperative organization of agricultural services; (2) horizontal associations of family farms, in the form of joint-stock companies, where the share of each family is precisely determined in the charter fund and in the profits earned by the collective enterprise; (3) horizonal associations of family farms in collective enterprises with indivisible shares of the charter fund (i.e., the current collective-state farms). The essence of reform in agriculture producers is to make the transition from the third to the first or to the first and second forms.

In creating joint-stock companies in agriculture, one must bear in mind that the usual model for a joint-stock company has certain shortcomings. Namely, the allocation of profits due to each shareholder is determined not by the quantity, quality, and intensity of work performed, but by the shares of stock. Differences in the qualification and intensity of work is expressed only in the wages, while profits are distributed without regard to the labor and efforts of the individual. This system clearly does not provide a proper stimulus for intensive labor by the shareholders.

In the case of agriculture, the author proposes a new model for the joint-stock company, one where the profits are distributed not according to a juridical principle (based on the ownership of shares), but according to an economic principle. The latter takes into consideration all the factors of production according to a unified scheme. Namely, expenditures to replace depleted productive factors should be part of the production costs; expenditures for an expanded replacement of the production factors, as well as income from ownership of these factors (land, capital, and labor force) are paid from the profits. Moreover, the owner of labor (human capital) should receive not only wages (which is only a replacement for the "depletion" of this production factor) but should also draw an income from the profits, just as the owners of the capital and land do.[13]

It is also necessary to consider individual conditions and the willingness of agricultural producers to adopt new technologies, construct installations, and conduct other measures to increase the productivity of the agrarian sector. These require steps to optimize the combination of leasing, amortization, tax, and credit privileges.

Notes

1. V.A. Dukhovnyi and M.A. Pinkhasov, "Problemy platy za vodokhoziaistvennye uslugi i rekomendatsii po ee vnedreniiu v usloviiakh Uzbekistana," *Tezisy doklada v Ministerstve sel'skogo i vodnogo khoziaistva Uzbekistana* (April 1997).
2. "Nukusskaia Deklaratsiia gosudarstv Tsentral'noi Azii i mezhdunarodnykh organizatsii po problemam ustoichivosti razvitiia basseina Aral'skogo moria" *(Nukus,* 20 Sept. 1995).
3. Goskomprirorda Uzbekistan, "Okhrana okruzhaiushchei Sredy i ispol'zovanie prirodnykh resursov Uzbekistana" (Tashkent, 1993).
4. V.K. Tian and R.M. Gorbachev, "Izuchit' fakticheskuiu velichinu KPD [koeffitsient produktivnogo deistviia] tipichnykh orositel'nykh sistem, ustanovit' effektivnost' sushchestvuiushchikh sposobov povysheniia KPD i ikh priemlemost' v usloviiakh ekspluatatsii (otchet o nauchno-issledovatel'skoi rabote, tema 5.03.HI) (Tashkent, 1978).
5. "Marketing i tsenovaia politika Respubliki Uzbekistan" Otchet po issledovaniiam Konsul'tativnoi gruppy po voprosam agrarnoi i prodovol'stvennoi politiki (FAPU TACIS) (Tashkent, 1996).
6. R.Kh. Khusanov, R.M. Gorbachev, E.F. Trushin, and S.Ch. Dzhalalov, "Raschetnoe obosnovanie ekonomicheski optimal'noi vodopotrebnosti skorospelykh, srednespelykh i tonkovoloknistykh sortov khlopchatnika po prirodno-klimaticheskim zonam Uzbekistana (Otchet o nauchno-issledovatel'skoi rabote, tema 5.03HI) (Tashkent, 1991).
7. A.M. Davydov, *Agrarnye preobrazovaniia i formirovanie sotsialisticheskogo zemlepol'zovaniia v Uzbekistane* (Tashkent, 1965).
8. "Institutional Requirements to Support Policies and Investments in Transition Economies," Materials of a National Seminar on Sustainable Agricultural Development in Uzbekistan held by the EDI of the World Bank (Tashkent, 26 February–3 March 1996), 5–6; Justin Yifu Lin, "Rural Reforms and Agricultural Growth in China," *American Economic Review,* (March 1992): 46; D. Gale Johnson, *The People's Republic of China, 1978–1990* (San Francisco, 1990).
9. I.A. Karimov, *Uzbekistan—sobstvennaia model' perekhoda na rynochnye otnosheniia* (Tashkent, 1993), 89.
10. R.Kh. Khusanov, *Agrarnaia reforma: teoriia, praktika, problemy* (Tashkent, 1994).
11. "Marketing i tsenovaia politika Respubliki Uzbekistan" (Otchet po issledovaniiam Konsul'tativnoi gruppy po voprosam agrarnoi i prodovol'stvennoi politiki (FAPU TACIS) (Tashkent, 1996).
12. Ibid.
13. E.F. Trushin, *Reformirovanie zemel'no-vodnykh otnoshenii kak uslovie ekonomicheskogo rosta (na primere Respubliki Uzbekistan)* (Avtoreferat doktorskoi dissertatsii), (Tashkent, 1996).

About the Editors and Contributors

Arystan Esentugelov is an advisor for the Parliament of Kazakhstan.

Umirserik Kasenov is vice-president of Kainar University and director of the Center of Strategic and International Studies (Kazakhstan).

Markhamat Khasanova is department head at the Institute of Economics and Market Relations (Kazakhstan).

Boris Rumer is a fellow at the Davis Center for Russian Studies at Harvard University.

Eshref F. Trushin is a senior research associate at the Institute of Macroeconomics and Social Research (Uzbekistan).

Eskender Trushin is department head at the Institute of Macroeconomics and Social Research (Uzbekistan).

Stanislav Zhukov is a senior research associate at the Institute of World Economy and International Relations (IMEMO), Russian Academy of Sciences.

Index